THE FORTNIGHTLY REVIEWS

THE FORTNIGHTLY REVIEWS

POETRY NOTES 2012-2014

By Peter Riley

ODD VOLUMES

OF

THE FORTNIGHTLY REVIEW

LES BROUZILS 2015

ODD VOLUME 6 | 2015

ISBN 978-0692373057

The Fortnightly Review

Château du Ligny

2 rue Georges Clemenceau

85260 Les Brouzils, France.

info@fortnightlyreview.co.uk

These essays were first published in The Fortnightly Review's New Series

online at fortnightlyreview.co.uk.

PREFACE

These pieces were all written as book reviews for the website *The Fortnightly Review* at the rate of one every four or five weeks between March 2012 and January 2014, preceded by 'An Attempted Credo', which was my way of introducing myself to the site. Two other articles, groups of short reviews, are not republished here. There has been some minimal revision, in the attempt to remove some of the most glaring errors of fact or judgement. Some new footnotes have been added, indicated by *(2014)* at the end of the note, mostly for the sake of updating and in a few cases to accommodate second thoughts or elaborations. I have also cut from some articles one or two brief appended reviews which I thought inadequate. For the most part they are exactly as first published for better or worse.

Questions have been asked as to why I am doing this. At first it was mainly through a wish to satisfy myself as to what was actually taking place in the work of poets I have been aware of for some time but whose work remained evasive and clouded by commentary based on ideology and adulation. My essay on Barry MacSweeney in the festschrift *Reading Barry MacSweeney*[1] was the first of these, which I think of as my "Some brilliant things here but we don't have to take all of this" pieces, of which there were a few others in review form before I was invited to contribute reviews regularly to *The Fortnightly Review*. Since then it has become rather more of a campaign to insist that a certain kind of mind, one not easily retentive of specialised or pseudo-scientific matter, one not loaded with authoritative reasons *why* poetry should be thus or thus (reasons theoretical, moral, political, populist, etcetera), should be admitted without hindrance to even the most difficult and highly-wrought poetry, and if the poetry does not cede that welcome there is something wrong. But also to insist through that inclination that poetry which presents no barrier whatsoever to the reader needs to offer a richer reward than self-endorsing satisfaction. Since I have been involved in contemporary poetry in Britain the concept of appropriate poetical subject-matter has shrunk and shrunk. At one time it comprised, sometimes disastrously, a total comprehension of the human world; now it thrives at large mainly on ironic everyday social perceptions or polemical support for singular causes. Poetry is no longer admitted as a value in itself. The shrunken version was always around and always successful; we used to call it *vers de société*. But the large vision wrecked itself in adversarial ravings and the lapse into sheer inhumanity[2] and poetry had little recourse but to rescue itself by a return to lyrical virtuosity, which was a return to poetry itself, or by attaching itself to going causes. My job is to sort through these scattered and diminutive products in search of what is worth the trouble, which I increasingly interpret as that which offers some kind of hope beyond the page. I think "uplift" is quite a good word for it.

Denis Boyles, editor of *The Fortnightly Review*, has been a valuable accomplice, by inviting me to contribute in the first place and encouraging me to continue.

Peter Riley

---

1   Edited by Paul Bachelor,Bloodaxe Books 2013

2   This is sometimes called "the crisis of Modernism". See my review of John Goodby, *The Poetry of Dylan Thomas*, in *Poetry Wales* vol. 49 no.4, 2014.

CONTENTS

AN ATTEMPTED CREDO

With poetry you are, basically, on your own. Obviously it is not a social art and doesn't bring people together the way theatre or music do, but the solitude of poetry goes deeper than that, and concerns the reader as much as the poet. When it comes to the actual confrontation, you and the poem, there are finally no alternatives to your own mental resources and life experience in order to cope with it.

There is of course an entire culture out there, with attached industries, eager to tell you that you are not alone in poetry and to make your choices for you. There are critics, prizes, festivals, courses, reading tours, many kinds of institutional endorsement, etc. always ready to guide you firmly to "the best" (since the Trade Descriptions Act seems not to apply, the word "best" is used a great deal). This is the big public arena of poetry (actually quite small) and its message is that poetry is one happy thriving world. Art and commerce are united in this paradigm: what is most popular (within certain limits of respectability and caste) is clearly the highest quality, and what is rejected is what doesn't sell because it's weird and "nobody wants it". It is outwardly a very simple structure. In fact, of course, the popularity is largely created by the publicity, so that the value of the guidance offered is questionable, and when you look at the poetry elevated by these routines it turns out to be extremely varied in both nature and quality.

It is not surprising that many readers depend on these mechanisms in the quest for the real thing, since there has been such a violent splintering of the poetical function, which now comprises such diverse activities under the one heading that nobody really knows what poetry is any more. Plenty are willing to say what poetry does – invariably something very good for you – but there is no definition. Something called "poetry" may be verse or prose or not a linguistic entity at all, and may include anything from a few purple letters upside-down in the middle of the page, to people on trapezes wearing lettered underwear, and even more disturbing performances.

Guidance out of this chaos is by means of categories and sub-categories, which lead you by the hand into cults and enclaves (read "markets") which ask your allegiance: ecopoetry, political (or "revolutionary") poetry, "linguistically innovative" poetry, performance poetry, women's poetry, queer poetry (currently the preferred term), poetry of particular ethnic groups and regions, "survivors' poetry", "concrete" poetry, "dub" poetry and many more, including unnamed cartels. Obviously you would patronise most of these markets through considerations or inclinations which are not primarily poetical, so that poetry itself is to some extent sidelined, or poetry's solitude is avoided by a collective engagement. Can a poem be good for solely ecological or political reasons, or because it violates normal linguistic usage? Some of the camps are exclusive and aggressive; the militant political poet for instance may well believe that if you are not with us you are against us, so if you are a "landscape poet" you are probably an enemy, not only of political poetry but also of mankind.

This galloping cell division is an elaboration of the big split in the early years of the 20th Century between advanced and reactionary poetry from which the term "Modernist" derives. Poetical Modernism is held by an influential critical tradition to be dead, except that it continues and thrives everywhere, and the argument continues. But when you look into the details of the history it is not such a straightforward map. Ezra Pound, for instance, respected and was on good terms with a number of poets whom current "Poundians" would probably despise or ignore, such as Laurence Binyon, whose version of Dante he particularly admired. (Unfortunately by the time Pound wrote an essay on Binyon, 1934, he was sinking into the ranting nonsense which occupied him for the rest of his life). I came across a similar instance when I was researching the career of the poet Nicholas Moore, who did important editing in the early 1940s and was thought of as a radical poet influenced by European Modernism. Among the young bloods he included in his collections Andrew Young appeared regularly, a Scottish vicar who wrote an entirely traditional poetry in which Moore recognised a virtue of sheer craft, and to whom he always remained faithful. The question raised in the current context is whether there is a poetical quality as such, which transcends categories, and whether the term "craft" covers it.

Can you not then treat poetry as one vast department store, and pick and mix, guided by a sense of "craft" or something else? Indeed you can, and I think probably you should, rather than throw in your lot with a singular option. The most culturally threatening aspect of the situation is that most of these camps claim a central position, viewed from which all others are peripheral or negative. Not only do we then have a state of permanent internecine warfare, but we no longer know what "the truth" is. All we have is versions or opinions. Poetry as an art of the totality is lost, except from within particular air-raid shelters.

The only answer I know to this is to insist on poetry as a personal art by which the solitude of the poetical experience makes possible a meeting of minds untainted by prejudicial issues, because the persona confronted in the poem is a recognisable reality, recognisably involved with the world, no matter how idiosyncratically. A thread of language passes from writer to reader, and any bit of bar-room chat can supply that (so many admired poems are no more than that) but the speech of the poet is enlaced with the world, and the poet is masked and sculpted. Then narrowness is avoided because what you face is simultaneously both open and closed, transmissive and inert, and through this paradox the real is sighted, and once you have the real in view the world starts to come into focus. To push poetical writing to the limits of the sayable is surely a perfectly valid way of attaining this condition, though not the only one. What, after all, do we ask of this privileged activity but that it furnish some grounds for hope in the condition of the world, for which we need to recognise the possible varieties of experience, and which can only stand on this scale of recognition?

DENISE RILEY AND THE
FORCE OF BEREAVEMENT

In February *The London Review of Books* published a set of 20 short poems by Denise Riley called *A Part Song*[1]. This occasioned some excitement among the cognoscenti, since she had not published a new poem since about 2000 and was thought to have abandoned the activity. Her following has been specially strong among adherents of radical politics and "linguistically innovative" poetry, encouraged by her writings on language and philosophy, though she has been far from easily categorisable. She has been a feminist who criticised feminists for tunnel vision, and a poet who rejected the poetry scenes for their careerism and cultural hysteria. The new sequence is concerned with the death of her adult son in 2008 and maintains this focus in quite normative terms and in a poised and even formal manner, and does not yield readily to expectations either of ideological fodder or literary experiment. At the same time an essay deriving from the same occasion, *Time Lived, Without Its Flow*, which is clearly a companion piece to the poetry, appeared as a small book[2].

The prose book is a careful and circumspect description of a state of "arrested time", a separation from the normal temporal flow, which occupied her experience of bereavement for three years, and which is analysed as a maternal response to the loss of a child, of whatever age. Partly in the form of a diary, it largely avoids technical language and faces the "impossible" task of making this experience known mainly through a discourse of simile —again and again it is "as if..." It is a paradoxical condition, experienced within disbelief, for it is a separation from the normal flow of time while that flow is witnessed busily continuing all around. It is a redoubled solitude, a suspended disbelief, a felt separation from all time-bound processes including language itself, and writing, the very structures of which press forward towards a future which is excluded from the bereaved mother's comprehension. She avoids any psychological or biochemical discourse of trauma, and makes no attempt to represent the condition in reduced or suspended language (such as sounding like Gertrude Stein) but, being determined to "keep it simple", remains strictly bound to her personal experience as something sharable and explainable. What is offered to the reader is the recognition of states of experience which, though not rare, seem not to have been written about[3] but are "common enough, and capable of being discussed". Indeed, although there is no political aspect to her account, such states are perhaps increasingly common in current conditions of widespread technological danger, not to mention the apparently increasing popularity of governance by massacre, which she doesn't refer to at all. "We might reconsider," she says, "the possibility of a literature of consolation."

So we have in this small book a complete picture of a human condition brought about by (but perhaps not unique to) a form of bereavement, elegantly and appealingly written, leaving us in no doubt as to its reality and terms of manifestation — you'd think that were enough, but there is also the poetry, *A Part Song*. There are many links across the two works, and the prose is sometimes a useful clarifier, but what I find most engaging about the poetry is its demonstration of its own necessity beyond what prose can perform. Reading the two texts together it becomes obvious that poetry is an extra, a thing not demanded by any rational sense of completion, or any desire for a satisfying depiction or representation of the world or any part of it. Poetry moves the whole thing to somewhere different, a kind of theatre, in which the condition becomes dramatic and fictive, and, whatever its subject, has a duty to be attractive or even entertaining. Instead of calm, connected discussion there are wild monologues, invocations, one-sided dialogues, imaginings and imagings, and there are songs. In poems of four to fourteen lines, some of them sonnet-like, the poet rails against the death imposed upon her, addresses the dead son, remembers, forgets, contemplates suicide, demands that he return home... All this is focused on the one condition of loss but in a range of poetical voices rich in irony and mock elegy, including subsumed quotations from well-known texts ("She do the bereaved in different voices") as easily as from sentimental bereavement poems unknown to all but the bereaved. But the intensity also opens into calm realisations reaching beyond the occasion. Number 4:

> Each child gets cannibalised by its years.
>
> It was a man who died, and in him died
>
> The large-eyed boy, then the teen peacock
>
> In the unremarked placid self-devouring
>
> That makes up being alive. But all at once
>
> Those natural overlaps got cut, then shuffled
>
> Tight in a block, their layers patted square.

Contrariwise, there are passages of address to the dead in a rough-spoken staged language, sitting in fact on the edge of comedy, wobbling to left and right. This from number 7—

> O my dead son you daft bugger
>
> This is one glum mum. Come home I tell you
>
> And end this tasteless melodrama – quit
>
> Playing dead at all, by now it's well beyond

> A joke, but your humour never got cruel
>
> Like this. Give over, you indifferent lad,
>
> Take pity on your two bruised sisters....

Always there is a certain detachment, sometimes self-mocking, which operates as a refusal of all the given, easy and evasive modes of lamentation[4] and an admission of the absurdity of these attempts to cancel the irrevocable fact. The poetical line normally has a classical feel to it, which will occasionally break out into pentameters, and in one sardonic poem rhyming octosyllabic couplets, just as there is a delving into the literary past for images of after-life and survival which are not believed-in but, as it were, entertained provisionally from within this cocoon of suspended time which also suspends modernity – Penelope and Hades, Orpheus returning from the underworld (explicated fully in *Time lived...*) — or simply notions of survival and resurrection which are entertained only in the fiction of the poem, or are tried in case they offer comfort.

And in the sequence of pieces all these stylistic and fictive elements gather into a narrative, which is a quest for the song which will unite the two voices, hers and her dead son's, and release the singers back to reality. A part song is a song for multiple voices as well as a song of apartness or part of a song. Each small poem is an attempt at this song, following the initial dismissal of the possibility. The goal is sighted strongly in the very short poem 18 as a song which if achieved will cancel death and at the same time restore modernity—

> It's all a resurrection song.
>
> Would it ever be got right
>
> The dead could rush home
>
> Keen to press their chinos.

But this is clearly too apocalyptic to end the sequence. The introduction of sea imagery over half way through (we know from *Time Lived...* that her son's ashes were poured into the sea) leads through modes of demand and renunciation to the song itself, which finally emerges as poem 20, the final Shakespearean underwater song at which the voice is passed back, and the dead boy sings the answer to all this suspension and yearning—

> *My sisters and my mother*
> *Weep dark tears for me*
> *I drift as lightest ashes*
> *Under a southern sea*
>
> *O let me be, my mother*
> *In no unquiet grave*
> *My bone-dust is faint coral*
> *Under the fretful wave.*

There is no mysticism here, and neither is there any messing around with the pseudo-sciences of 'poetics', neither antiquarianism nor psychologising. It is the poetical sublime enunciating pure fact.

1   *London Review of Books,* Vol. 34 no.4, 9th February 2012, currently only viewable in printed form, but the author can be heard reading the work on the LRB website.

2   Capsule Editions, London 2012. 78pp paperback.

3   Towards the end of *Time lived...*, as a factor of emerging from isolation, she seeks and locates her subject in only a handful of poems, by Henry King, Emily Dickinson, Wordsworth and Fanny Howe, plus short excerpts from Don DeLillo and Merleau-Ponty.

4   Denise Riley insists that neither the state of mind she describes nor any of the writing about it is "mourning" and neither is it elegy or lament. I'm inclined to think that it is a form of lament, if only because I recognise formulations with which I'm familiar through my knowledge of traditional funeral laments in the Balkan regions, where direct address to the dead is common or even obligatory, and will readily involve accusations of unkindness to the family in the act of dying.

POETRY PRIZE CULTURE AND THE ABERDEEN ANGUS.

In January the poet John Burnside won the T.S. Eliot Prize with his book *Black Cat Bone*[1]. Three months earlier he won the Forward Prize with the same book. These are the two most prestigious and financially rewarding poetry prizes in the country. Burnside has now gained twelve literary prizes (of which four for books of prose) since his first collection won the Scottish Arts Council Book Award in 1988. That's not counting short-listing. But short-listing for prizes like these does count: it is added to the honours list and furthers all aspects of the career. The total of Burnside's awards including these is nineteen. This is what poetry prizes are like in U.K. – they tend to come in convoys.

Burnside writes a strong, impressionistic poetry centred on the declaration of personal experience and attitude, often cloaked in a sombre, nebulous kind of symbolical tissue. The poems are rich in linguistic resource and rhythmically and phonetically alert; he could be said to be expert at what he chooses to do. So it would be good to be able to say that Burnside deserves all his prizes. The trouble is that I don't think anybody does.

It's a question of disproportion – not of whether some poets are better than others (of course they are) but of whether a very small number of poets (less than a dozen) are really about a thousand times better than all the rest, and so should pick up all the prizes, for such is the structure that prize culture creates. And anyway the word "better" is not used: the elected poets are invariably "best". The back cover of *Rain* by Don Paterson,[2] another multiple prize-winner, bears a blurb by Colm Tóibín claiming him as "One of the greatest poets now writing anywhere". What in that case could possibly make you think twice about buying it, except perhaps doubt as to whether Mr Tóibín has in fact read the works of all the living poets in the world? It is a culture of the superlative exclusively.

Suppose we picture the reward status of your average success-ful poet late in his/her career, who has had several books published by specialist mid-scale publishers such as Carcanet or Bloodaxe, with a reliable if not vast following of readers, invited from time to time to give readings in UK and occasionally abroad, moderately in demand from anthology and magazine editors, interviewed once or twice a year, perhaps sometimes asked to judge a minor poetry competition... Such a poet does not expect to gain any income worth mentioning from poetry in his/her entire life, nor to gain any academic or cultural appointments as a direct result of the poetry, nor necessarily to gain access to cultural journalism because of it. Such a poet has nothing to complain about — this is simply how poets, including probably most of our worthiest, normally go through their careers these days, and by comparison the increment of the big prize-winners in financial terms alone is incalculable. A multiple of 1,000 is a conservative guess. But as suggested, the rewards are not only financial: for most of them the big prize is an opening to an entirely different career from that of the vast majority of successful poets. Since socialistic credentials are very common among them perhaps they would not like to be called members of an élite but the word might be quite difficult to avoid. Indeed, the resemblances between the reward structures in poetry and those in operation generally in the west, especially among the "financial community", have not gone unnoticed.

Inevitably the big prize structure has met with a lot of resentment, and therefore attack, including accusations of favouritism, monopoly and narrowness. Most of this is undoubtedly sour grapes, though some of it is ideological, but there is always a ready answer enshrined in the word "best", which is a mighty fortress against all accusations. You can't complain about narrowness or exclusivity or anything. It is all down to the simple fact that these are the *best*. And when you're busy identifying and promoting the *best* there is no other priority. If most of the winners are published by the same handful of larger-scale publishers, well that's because those publishers have been shown to publish the *best* and as long as they continue to there's really nothing we can do about it. (P.S. We decide).

What is happening is of course that success creates success, prizes create prizes. To be published as a young poet by Faber and Faber is in itself like winning your first prize, and with luck the rest of them will follow, especially if the judges are themselves published by Faber or one of the other favoured houses. Another theory is that some of the people involved in judging poetry competitions couldn't tell a good poem from a decayed kipper and they know it, so they reckon if it's already won several prizes somebody must like it. In any event, the word "simply" joined to "the best" sweeps aside all possible objection in one powerful marketing slogan (which has been in use in this context for at least half a century; I remember Seamus Heaney being offered as "simply the best" in the late 1960s.) The "simply" is very important. As well as rendering it unnecessary actually to say anything about the poetry, this innocent word offers to relieve the poor worried purchaser who doesn't know what to do about all these poets, of all personal choice and responsibility, the whole fraught matter reduced to a kind of brand loyalty. "You know you're getting the best." While poetry remains economically insignificant (Andrew Crozier compared it to hill farming[3]), the award structure openly mimics large-scale commercialism. Like the festivals it is a promotional machine which creates a star system in order to market a few products as exceptional. Compared with fiction all poetry sales are peanuts: only some dozen poets, at the most, reach sales figures beyond a few thousand; after that there is an immense plunge into the hundreds which is where poetry belongs. The upper thousands are of course the big prize winners.

It is not true that the prize-winners all write the same kind of poetry and that it is all conventional and belongs within one concept of the canon. But neither is it true that there is no favoured concept of poetical writing. There is one and it can be defined, though no one poet will show all its traits. We can turn again to John Burnside's winning book *Black Cat Bone* to recognise how the poems are, as it were, integrally set up for prize-winning and success in general in the "big" poetry world, which is not to imply any cynicism on his part.

Here the first-person singular is very prominent as mediator between the poem's material and the reader. All poems, of course, are mediated through the author, but the "I" figure of Burnside is something you are constantly aware of, directly or fictively, normally seeking to elicit sympathy. Everything passes through this self-figure on its way to the reader; the poetry is basically subjective and the process at work is, typically, one of internalisation. Equally significant are certain technical habits such as an insistent metaphorism, sometimes remote but generally (at its worst) clever or arty ("the Sanskrit of rain" ... "the rollright in the mind"... "the Hundertwasser sky"..."the tinnitus of longing"...)[4] ; and the preference for fully discursive and explanatory sentences unfolding a situation or position. Such features as these would to some define him as "mainstream", a term I normally try to avoid because the implication of conformism is largely unjustified. One "mainstream" trait which he only indulges occasionally in blatant form is the device of initial obliquity, teasing the reader with an almost riddle-like opening which is later solved, as when he begins a poem, "It never lasts / but for a while at least / I forget ... ? and watch..." — "It" turns out to be snow. It's possible too that a kind of gloomy pessimism he is prone to adds to his appeal, a tone reminiscent of earlier Eliot, and a good dose of nature mysticism reminiscent of Ted Hughes — nature red in tooth and claw, terrestrial space coldly isolating and threatening. There is also a toying with religious imagery without commitment to belief; he is happy to use biblical and doctrinal terms (soul, God) within metaphors and similes but not in open statement. To opponents of this kind of writing the indulgence in a hinted mystery of natural process, with magical or fantasy auras, never openly divulged as belief but part of the figurative decor attached to the authorial self, is highly diagnostic of "mainstream" allegiance, typically flirting with the transcendental without espousing it. But if the avant-gardists were to accuse him of attempting to deploy his own psychology as a poetical and critical tool, that would be the pot calling the kettle black.

His success must also owe something to negative aspects: the avoidance of idiolect or dialect, as of disrupted syntax, neologisms, references beyond the cultural sphere, and avoidance indeed of any serious degree of abstract thought: it is all immediate and sensory. But there are some common "winning" traits he doesn't indulge in, such as heavy end-rhyming, argumentation, or flashy displays of street-wise contemporaneity (quite the reverse in fact: gloomy wanderings in snowy waste lands and mediaeval forests). However much all these characteristics may seem to key him into the circuits of success, they remain held in the consistency of his writing and in the accumulative sense of the book's mission. He says, at his most winning, "I live in a separate country, white as snow / on rooftops and stained glass" and is, I suppose, perfectly entitled to.

There is some exception to the evidence of a favoured manner for prize-winners in the recent and unexpected awarding of prestigious prizes to poets such as R.F. Langley (Forward Poem of the Year 2011) and Michael Haslam (Cholmondeley Award 2011), [5] which may indicate not so much cracks in the barriers of exclusivity, as a more general realisation that the Modernist vs. traditionalist dichotomy which has haunted British poetry since the times of the Anglo-American Modernist monsters, is wearing thin.

There are hundreds of poetry prizes each year but the big prizes are in their own class. They are financed from above, through investment or legacy (two poets, Alice Oswald and John Kinsella, withdrew from the Eliot Prize shortlist this year on ethical grounds, because it was sponsored by the investment firm Aurum Funds who manage hedge funds). Poets do not enter themselves personally nor pay a fee — their publishers submit them. Many of the lesser prizes are either business ventures aiming to make a small profit, or quasi-philanthropic exercises done for the vanity or prestige of the person in charge. It is unusual for a poet's career to begin with small prizes and work its way up towards the top; mostly those who are going to reach the top begin there, or at least in the upper-middle ground. A great deal of happiness and self congratulation from both contestants and officers seems to characterise these awards, and there is a sense of significance attached to them which is rarely justified in a poet's subsequent career, for all the talk of "prestige". Most of them by far are never heard from again. (This is partly true too of the special first book award which is part of the Forward Prize package). A fellow-poet who wishes to remain anonymous has sent me this report on the atmosphere of the award ceremony at one of the middling-rich prizes, which he won—

> "...there existed an atmosphere of a school prize giving at which good honest effort had been rewarded by the staff and the prefects, who smilingly stood by

and handed us our badges and record tokens... and perorated with skull-numbingly dull readings, at great length, of their own poetry which showed how it was done by the professionals."

This brings us to the big questions about all these guarantors of success: what are the social and intellectual implications? If in writing poetry you are involved in "the society of the poem", what do you want that society to be? To the accusers the poetry hierarchies erect a simulacrum of some near-eastern state in which a band of hereditary potentates live in immense luxury in a fortified palace and everyone else endures grinding poverty in the fields. Such an accusation is certainly unfair in view of the absolute levels of reward, working life-styles and commitments of almost all the "best" poets this system produces. Socialism and democracy, ecology and gay rights are very strong among them, and indeed a significant number of them are of working-class origin, including the two most successful poets in the land, Simon Armitage (Millennium Poet 1999) and Carol Ann Duffy (currently Poet Laureate). And it is integral to their work.

What remains is the underlying assumption of the whole structure of poetry prize-giving — that however much we and our poetry may protest and campaign, however much the cultural sphere may be at odds with the administration, it is itself settled and satisfactory and in perfect working order. Merit will inevitably be recognised and rewarded, thus encouraging the progress of the art. It is all clear and continual. Awkward questions about the unrecognised are mute, as they are about the former unrecognised such as Gerard Manley Hopkins or Emily Dickinson... No, no, there may have been aberrations in the past but fundamentally we know what is happening, we know what is important, nothing escapes us, we find it and we give it the prize. But it does escape, of course, it must. And while some of what escapes is no doubt raving lunacy, hippie smoke-dreams or revolutionary idiocy, some of it is not. Some of it belongs to entirely separate and unacknowledged categories of poetry (such as rap and dub); some of it is simply different, or even more simply similar but unnoticed. The judging criteria, being tied to a system of familiarity and recurrence, are inevitably subjective and self-propagating. What chance is there of objectivity in an art where there is no common agreement as to what constitutes its qualities?

If at a county show you are one of the judges in the section for Aberdeen Angus cattle, you will have a comprehensive list of points which must be fulfilled. There is the carriage of the creature's head, with even teeth and broad muzzle. It should have a long body and strong legs with the joints well set. The back should be straight with a slight dip at one end. It should be well and evenly muscled with not too much fat. Viewed from behind the rump should be rounded, the legs straight and the hooves correctly positioned. When it walks its hind hoofs should enter the marks of its front hoofs without overstepping or understepping. If it is a cow its udder should not be pendulous and the teats should be of the right size and placement. If it is a bull the testicles should be large and the sheaf firmly attached and not pendulous. But all these distinctions should be weighed against the proportions of the whole animal and the aim is to assure that both it and its progeny should fulfil their commercial function. If all these boxes are ticked, you have your winner. Surely some version of this schemata could be devised for judging poetry competitions, rather than, as one suspects, relying on pronouncements of the order of "It sent shivers up and down my spine". I leave it to others to work out what these definitive points of excellence may be for poet or poem, which will by means of a truly objective procedure end all the bickering about merit and favour. The alternative is to admit that we don't know and never shall, and the best procedure is to relish finding our own paths through it all. Meanwhile I look forward to seeing our "best" poets walking around with enormous rosettes attached to their chests.

1   Chatto, 2011

2   Faber, 2009

3   In his essay "Resting on Laurels" (2000) reprinted in *An Andrew Crozier Reader*, Carcanet 2012.

4   Some of these metaphors are to me so clever as to be worthy of the avant-garde, i.e., completely impenetrable. The Rollright Stones are a group of three neolithic monuments in Oxfordshire, and what they mean when they are "of the mind" is anybody's guess.

5   Candour forces me to add to this list my own acceptance of a Cholmondeley Award in 2012. This does not, however, make me a "big prize winner". *(2014)*

PETER HUGHES AND OYSTERCATCHER PRESS

The latest issues from Oystercatcher Press[1] have arrived. They are *Cloud Breaking Sun* by John James and *When blue light falls 3*[2] by Carol Watts. Oystercatcher is a small press run by the poet Peter Hughes, and his particular way of finding audacity and liberality complementary impresses itself on both his poetry and the press he runs. He has a regular column headed "small press" on the Poetry Book Society's website[3] in which he says such things as–

> Of course, some poems pulsate and wriggle more than others. They force vocabulary from disparate discourses into the same pen, juxtapose contradictory tones and undermine expectations. Some readers respond enthusiastically when these kinds of challenges are cranked up. Some readers get very irritated and have to go for a lie down in a darkened room.[4]

So his position is clear as an exponent of the innovative or radical end of the poetry scale. But what he says bears no burden of militant endeavour – the characteristically wry tone denies it. There is no campaign afoot here, no pioneer corps slash and burn, and consequently no programmed narrowness. It is more like a cultivated inclination which becomes a conviction, with a lot of leeway allowing widely different approaches. That at any rate is how the press is run. Its very name contributes to this sense of civilian endeavour. Some small poetry presses have for a long time paraded their negativity and virulent oppositionality by choosing names as off-putting as possible. There was one called Strange Faeces in the 1970s, and if you search for it I'm sure you'd find one called Unspeakably Awful Poetry or Rubbish Productions. Indeed so-called rubbish theory is taken seriously by those poets who see the purpose of their art as essentially destructive. Peter Hughes lives on the top of a cliff on the Norfolk coast and oystercatchers must be a common sight there. The fact that it is a rather comical-looking and a noisy bird is certainly relevant. It is possible to maintain distinctly radical beliefs, political and cultural, without classifying the contemplation of sea hill or plain as "pastoral" betrayal.

OYSTERCATCHER WAS STARTED in 2008 and to date has published 49 titles, all 20 to 30 pages long, in a standard A5 stapled format, most of them with an attractive front cover featuring a painting by Peter Hughes, though never attributed. It is by such economies of production, and a "special arrangement", I believe, with a printer related to the concept of "print on demand", that the series has been so prolific and that an editorial freedom is possible, unthreatened by sales figures.

What is demonstrated by Oystercatcher is the great range possible within a broad concept of the continuity of modernism, which means in effect that whatever the ambience of the poetry there is a strongly verbal textuality. Whatever it is concerned with, however it approaches the world, it takes no words for granted, but turns them on their sides and holds them against the light until the balance of intent and accident is clear. And this is indeed what so many of the brighter things are doing these days, not just the young ones. Oystercatcher's catchment zone goes from hoary old sages like myself and John James, to bundles of youthful energy such as Emily Critchley (*Who handles one over the backlash*, 2008) and Sophie Robinson (*The Lotion*, 2010) – these are both works I value for keeping their heads aligned towards a purpose through wild thickets of linguistic disruption. It is particularly felicitous when the press catches a work which is an integral whole of the right length and one of the most remarkable of these has been *The Son* by Carrie Etter (2009), a kind of drama concerning a lost son, very moving and in a tone and manner unlike anything else of hers I've seen.

Sets of very small poems feel particularly at home in the Oystercatcher environment, like whitebait perhaps. *the deer path to my door* by the senior Scottish poet Gerry Loose (2009) consists of two-line poems focused on environmental detail in his own backyard with as little authorial mediation as possible, producing things like

> autumn behind the apple tree I'm almost not
> here the barn owl's screeching

or as little as

> old jam
> feed the slugs

A very different use of the small poem structure is *Py* by Anna Mendelssohn (2009), a collection of 27 six-line acrostics on (mostly) the word "poetry", somewhere at the far side of surrealism and completely dotty.

> *paloma polperro*
> Olmec mesh
> Empfindlichkeit
> Trabazone

Rainbow trout

Yippee

You can't say it doesn't end on a positive note.

A lot of my favourite poets are in the Oystercatcher list, and I'm reduced to jabbering names rather than attempting any further description: Kelvin Corcoran (of whom more later), Michael Haslam, Maurice Scully, John Welch, Nigel Wheale – not to mention attractive books by people I've never heard of. One of these that I'm not going to let slip by is *The Reluctant Vegetarian* by Richard Moorhead (2009) which is a set of outwardly playful and humorous imagistic redefinitions of various fruit and veg, uncovering words you'd never expect to find hidden behind such commonplace things, and liable to become serious when least expected. Thought is released in the sequence of images, without discourse:

blueberry

n (1) owl pellet

swollen with

fairy bile; (2) goose

tumour stitched

with burdock; (3) jar

of seal eyes, lustrous

when wet; (4) a mesa's

moonless indigo;

(5) blue Cambodian

skulls in a punnet;

v (6) to ash

the darkened skin

with chalk; adj (7)

the tight baby eye

of a teenage heart;

adv (8) how innocence stirs

in the mouth first;

adj (9) the taste

of a bitten tongue or

a wrecked planet.

THE TWO NEW arrivals are quite different from each other, but either might occasion a rush for the couch in the darkened room on the part of the unaccustomed or uninclined, for different reasons.

John James is a senior poet of importance and I shall leave to a later opportunity any comprehensive coverage of his work. Although he never uses punctuation, his verses are set in normal spoken syntax and speak directly of his own experience, with outbursts of delight or rage now and then. It is most obviously a gathering of the threads of a life, holding on to those channels of memory which bore fruit, and it is a chronicle of recompense. For the most part it is spoken gently to himself, so that nothing is, or needs to be, identified or explained as to an outsider. The fondly remembered "Barry" for instance, may be the artist Barry Flanagan in one poem and the poet Barry MacSweeney in another. If you aren't aware who they were and that they both died, well you should be. Even Apollinaire is just "Guillaume". It's essential to accept this idiolectic condition of James' poetry, which as well as people involves places and other things and at times approaches the arcane, to gain the reward of the poetry as an entire and integral theatre of experienced reality.

Carol Watts doesn't exactly cast off the yoke of syntax, but it is reduced to phrases, which are spaced out through the poem with only occasional overt sequence connecting them. There are structural enigmas too: the poems are in a sequence numbered 2 to 16 in even numbers then 1 to 15 in odd numbers, each set in a somewhat different manner. And there are items of very technical vocabulary to deal with. These fragments of discourse are to be read without asking the why and wherefore. It is what I call an "ungrounded" poetry: everything is floating beyond the influence of the gravity which holds us to the normative demands of the linear earth. I cannot avoid a sense of immateriality, while I believe that the (London-based) poetical connections of the author theorise precisely materiality as the mark of innovation – perhaps verbal materiality produced conceptual immateriality. The actual effect, I find, is that an intimate account or address is taking place which has to be kept secret, or at the most hinted at. It wouldn't be a critic's job, of course, to attempt to unlock this. But a great deal more work is needed before the full nature of this poem in three books is known.

THERE ARE ALSO two Oystercatchers by Peter Hughes himself, the most recent being *Behoven* (2009). He has a long established habit of writing sequences of various length, often based on external factors, ever since *The Metro Poems* (Many Press 1992)[5] – 33 poems named after stations of the Rome underground. There is one collaged from Berlioz' *Memoirs*, there are 21 poems based on an edition of *The Radio Times*, "Six Klee Paintings", several diary-like sets, a rather quirky set on facilities at various caravan and camping sites, and so on.[6] It has always been his habit to both attend to and ignore the details of his sources.

Whether sequence or poem, each work seems to locate its own linguistic condition, always recognisably his but within a range of possibilities. So while some (such as *Behoven*) sport a level of difficulty which might at least get you to the threshold of the dark room, he could also be approached through a book such as *The Summer of Agios Dimitrios* (Shearsman Books 2009), his most recent, a set of diary-poems of a sojourn in Greece, which would drag you into the light. Here the transmission is unproblematic and the punctuationless writing enacts straightforward perceptual sequences – a succession of noticings and mentionings forming a progression from starting-point to ending which is never less than thoughtful and pointed. Most of his poetry is distinctly personal but without that appeal to the reader, an appeal for recognition and sympathy, which so much marks conventional poetry these days. Rather he insists quite proudly on his own terms of cognition, including his right to the vocabulary of joke, wit, sarcasm, even flippancy, in the face of the modern world.

The Petrarch set "Quite Frankly" (that is, quite Petrarch but not entirely) shows a lot of his skills. There is no real need to read it in parallel to the originals, though to do so is certainly entertaining. He mainly follows the principal moves, ignoring what he can't use and letting the poem follow its own course where necessary. But he can sometimes take up quite close detail with great ingenuity, as in the incorporation of Petrarch's play with the letters of Laura's name in number 5. As the sequence progresses, for all his ironic modernisation and free-play, it enters deeper and deeper into a sincere realisation of the modern love-poem. The complaint against the world which is explicit (though not necessarily directly owned) in the first quatrain of number 7, informs a great deal of the writing, and both intimate affection and defiant, independent realisation of the life actually lived, are his defences against it.

It is incidentally a relief to me that this modernising quasi-translation of a classic text is conceived entirely within Hughes' own praxis, and does not follow the course of phonetic mimicry ("homophonic translation") of which we have had a lot in the innovative zones, all authorised by the American poet Louis Zukofsky, who notoriously murdered Catullus in this way in 1969. This is a mechanical operation in which the sound-values of the original are imitated as closely as possible in English whatever the result, making it a translation from Latin into nothing. The mistake is, of course, to assume that poetry's musical properties are its central value and *raison d'être*. But neither does Hughes indulge the contrary tendency favoured by a number of highly successful poets, perhaps best summarised as "Homer (Dante, Beowulf etc.) cooked up for the lads".

Behoven is offered as "registrations of the 32 Beethoven piano sonatas" and it might be possible to read them against the sonatas if your copy were not, like mine, the edition of Liszt, who put them in order of difficulty instead of chronologically. I don't know what you'd find if you did that, though there are clearly verbal hints towards Beethoven's life and music here and there. Using music as an external referent, which Hughes has done quite a lot, tends to disperse the singular location and unity of address in the poem. Or, as he says, "bring your own weather". The progressions in the poem then derive from each other, metaphors create metaphors, a single word launches a new direction. Here is number 12 (without attempting to reproduce the complex variable margins which are a feature of this set):

> / apricots & black / coffee by the mattress / on the floorboards we breathed / an aftershock of happiness // cotton refuge // glide between wing-beats // your memories coming up the stairs // O Vienna!

Here a scene, or experience, is half-established and then dispersed into particulars without firm context. It is possible, with some effort, to read it as all elements of the same scene, but it is also easily possible not to. The poem begins as personal and sexual but ends with an interjection which could, if we allow it to, leap right out of context into massive cultural concerns. To me a shout of "O Vienna!" at once feels like a reaction to the vast waves of cultural dismantling of various kinds which have swept our way from there since the collapse of the Austro-Hungarian Empire. The five stages of the poem are offered to the reader to make our own story of (as any written narrative is to some degree) moving constantly in and out of anecdotal and imaginative spheres, and this is characteristic of the whole set. Such qualities, happily keeping company with the usual mockery and verbal jests, invoke a larger sense of where we are without any loss of actuality, and within that enhanced sense of belonging the scope of our possible acts becomes more hopeful.

Long may Oystercatcher Press continue to prise poets from under stones.[7]

1   www.oystercatcherpress.com 4, Coastguard Cottages, Old Hunstanton, Norfolk PE36 6EL. All Oystercatcher books cost £5.00 including inland postage. There is a sample poem from each book on the website.

2   Parts 1 and 2 of this serial poem were published by Oystercatcher in 2008 and 2010.

3   Go to http://www.poetrybooks.co.uk then to "poetry portal", and his is one of the offerings listed there. At the time of writing the current one is about John James.

4   This concerns the Oystercatcher book *Kiss Off* by Sophie Mayer, 2011.

5   Reprinted in *Blueroads: selected poems*. Salt Publishing 2003.

6   The first and last of these, and *Behoven*, will be in his next book, *Allotment Architecture*, due from Reality Street Books early in 2013.

7   An anthology of poems from the Oystercatcher Press booklets, entitled *Sea Pie*, is under preparation at Shearsman Books.

ALISTAIR NOON AND THE ENGLISH SONNET

Earth Records.

Nine Arches Press (New Poets Series) 2012. 96pp, £8.99.

Out of the Cave.

Calder Wood Press 2011. 28pp

Across the Water.

Longbarrow Press 2012. 20pp.

Swamp Area.

Longbarrow Press 2012. 32pp.

E*arth Records.* Alistair Noon's first book,[1] begins by plunging reader and poet right into the thick of it together, with a set of 40 formally correct (or very nearly[2]) sonnets of the kind called English or Shakespearean, which supplies the book's title. It is a bold and quite defiant gesture with which to begin a first book of poems, since it at once involves us in poetry as a serious business and an acquired skill, and admits allegiance to no current school or tendency. I trust we are not so prosodically naive as to assume that forty strictly formed sonnets must be the work of some kind of reactionary mentality. In fact the poets commonly dubbed "mainstream" or "establishment" very rarely do anything like this, and when they do they often treat the form with cavalier abandon.[3] The experimenters, when they use the term, may mean anything by it.[4]

A true sonnet means something in itself and is a fine thing in itself. It is a symbolic code recognised by the reader as eliciting certain forms of attention or expectation, especially in terms of first-person involvement in the text, originally the address towards the desired person. But perhaps the English sonnet, through its less widespread use, its structure[5] and its connection with Shakespeare himself, particularly anticipates a fairly remorseless course of concerned argumentation towards a conclusion. Many other qualities may be enfolded in the idea of the sonnet, especially in terms of elegance of address, balance and fluidity, free movement among figurative modes, and the use of the final couplet as reliable verdict with or without irony. But perhaps the primary message coming through the manifestation of this ancient poem formula is something like, "You'll need to get your nose down to this". That is, the discourse will be continuous link by link across different modes of representation and will need to be followed continuously to the end to get the message. Expect then no diverting vignettes in mid-course but be prepared to follow the discourse from beginning to end, ever alert to switches of mode. This at any rate is what these sonnets expect of us.

Noon seems to have travelled all over Europe and several other parts of the world. Number 10 finds him at a major border crossing from Serbia into Hungary:

> Late at night the Balkan languages clog
> at Horgos, where they wait to gain admittance
> to the circle of stars. A see-through smog
> surrounds the returners from the remittance
> economy: static, running exhausts
> and the world's greatest mass cigarette break,

as coaches queue up for one of the ports,
bays with a quay, where the night shift's awake.
We hoot, or cheer each inch; the wise just doze.
No border guard knows the meaning of *soon*.
Priština, Niš, to Dortmund, Ulm. One
goes to Miriampol. (*O beautiful moon*
of Miriampol... Sat in East Berlin,
Bobrowski looks up). Here's Europe. We're in.

What happens in this sonnet is very much focussed on the last three lines. Before that we have a well crafted scene of the endless wait at a border crossing (a thing particularly familiar to those of us who have transgressed the former iron curtain, where a bureaucratic automatism lingers for ever among the police, but the experience is now probably just as bad on entering England). Deftly and unobtrusively integrated into the quatrain patterns, the writing remains steadily and mildly sarcastic concerning humanity forced to do nothing, marked by a scatter of little clashing verbal combinations: *see-smog, static-running*, r*eturners-remittance*, and the bays the coaches move into when it is their turn called *ports* as if they themselves feel like journey's end after the enforced stasis. It is indeed the Balkan *languages* which "clog" together; here you're either Balkan or not, queuing to get into the "circle of stars" – the European symbol, the European glamour. These are minor pieces of gentle sarcasm filling a space created by boredom. Then the poet (ever present but not mentioned) starts noticing the origins and destinations of the coaches. The first four cities named may not be specially reverberant (all massacre sites, but then so are most if not all cities of central Europe) until Miriampol is noticed and the whole tone changes.

This city in Lithuania (Marijampolé in Lithuanian) at once invokes the opening of a poem by Johannes Bobrowski, "Wagenfahrt" (Journey by Cart). Bobrowski (1917-1965) was an East German poet who should be much better known in the English-speaking world than he is (indeed I sometimes wish that some of the intense excitement focused on Paul Celan could be apportioned to Bobrowski, for they share some degrees of technique and obsession, though not at all the same fate). The invocation is rural — singing to the moon from a cart on the way home at night (shades of Mussorgsky) — and the south Prussian border zone where it takes place was to Bobrowski a sacral zone, which he created in his poetry as a kind of lost world, with its pagan deities, its histories of trespass and its mediaeval landscapes. It was also his zone of origin, where he remembered five ethnic groups living together, including Jews, of whom he wrote, "... a long story of misfortune and guilt, for which my people is to blame..."[6] Miriampol was the site of a particularly appalling Jewish massacre in 1941. Bobrowski's second use of the word "moon" in the poem is, uniting the aural and the visual, "...we heard it linger across the town, up there in the towers, we heard the Jewish moon..."

How much of all this is relevant to the ending of Noon's sonnet is largely up to the reader (and the reader's language). But clearly after three quatrains of waiting and boredom in a non-environment a quite different, poetical, place is offered. It is a written place and a place of the mind, but also the site of real longing. It is heavily ironic, then, that at just this point they get through the check-point into "Europe". The relief or even jubilation at "We're in" is surely played against the despair of those Balkan countries whose long awaited admission to the ring of stars turned out to be a welcome to economic crisis, augmentation of poverty, and impending bankruptcy. But is it not also that by the intervention of Bobrowski we have entered imaginatively into the real Europe, with its history of endless conflict and necessary expiation more important than remittance?

Noon is the most urban of poets, but without attached polemics. The sites of the sonnets are mostly such places as restaurant, cigarette factory, housing estate, road works, car park, National Museum and so on, many of them in Berlin where he lives. But his purpose, which tends to come to fruition in the final couplets, is an opening towards a wider and richer sense of the human context, by describing the urban scene with sharp-eyed accuracy but offering space to images of an elsewhere too easily dismissed as nostalgic. The sonnet (no.30) on cathedrals and the rewriting of the model city "and its pain" ends with a sudden turn away from the metropolitan to a desert where "Searching the earth between watering holes / it's the Bedouin who find the Dead Sea Scrolls." Similarly no.32, on housing ("Light has status. One pays for space and style") ends "...the place that's always free / is where the land breathes out, becoming sea." There is a sense of western vision as progressively reductive, that an exponentially rich cultural possibility in the past has been rationalised down to a thin modern discourse, and with it a shortened memory-span: "The Western memory stops / at the inventors of letters and crops." Explicitly in the opening of sonnet 23: "Artist no more in the shadow of God, / or sensing the group like a ritual dancer, / I shift my ikons." The last sonnet, which does culminate the series, announces "The constellations shift. No, it's not better / never to leave the excavated zones..." The excavated zones are what we have constructed around ourselves or buried ourselves in, in either case foreshortening our vision, and the term involves more than just physical circumstances. The sonnet goes on to propose a plethora of difference, outdated and neglected modes that we can now turn to, an expanding prospect of possibility if we cast off our dislike of the antiquated, the provincial, the foreign, finally notated as a musical and dialectal enrichment: "The magnitudes of sounds intensify. / Vowels vary their colours in the unfinished sky." (Is this also a put-down of Rimbaud's rather senseless and schoolmasterly attribution of particular colours to the vowels?)

So the sonnets do follow a course and are linked, sometimes verbally sometimes by theme or locality, and it is as if a continuous argument is undertaken through enriched accounts of forty encounters with places and structures, though not an argument that could be satisfactorily abstracted. And they are only the first third of the book.

Noon's work comes in clusters and there remain five of them before me: the remaining two-thirds of the book and three booklets. There's no need to investigate each one meticulously; outside the sonnet form Noon's normal poem is a more relaxed but pointed discourse, favouring quatrain structure but free to be unmetrical or part-metrical, rhymed or unrhymed or near-rhymed. A lot of urban and suburban scenes are investigated for signs of hope, which must always lie to some extent in the poem itself, the crafting of a lyrical structure out of the fact of the author on the ground in likely and unlikely places.

The groupings are commonly around localities, especially the kind of sadly uniform expanses of ageing featureless development you get in the former Communist countries ("All those old apartment blocks / from Magdeburg to Vladivostok / still herd mostly with their kind. / They wait in one long sullen line, / in sun and snow, hail and rain, / for a firework show of paint.") *At the Emptying of Dustbins* (second part of the book) is much concerned with these Eastern Bloc scenes.

Out of the Cave is a more diverse collection with a number of bright and witty poems of metropolitan experience, emerging, I think, from the cave of institutional discourse. *Across the Water* and *Swamp Area* are, as you'd expect, concerned with watery areas, crossed by various means and for various reasons but seriously involved in the senses of distance and the passage of time such urban-edge expanses elicit. A number of these poems are about going to work in a train in the company of others doing the same thing, thus about accepting the given terminology of society, which is thought and sung through to its crux, at which you escape from it.

I am particularly glad of *Holidays of the Poets* (third part of *Earth Records*), a rather longer set which unites the author with a lot of different authors (not all poets) as partners in witnessing a place or travelling through one, usually incongruously – titles like "Blake in Munich", "Homer in New York", "Pablo Neruda in Aylesbury"... but not always using that formula. The pairings release a lot of Noon's humour, which is always purposeful, but serious themes abound, particularly a sense of high culture (poetry) made to face the modern condition. There is a particularly delightful piece called "Basho at St Andrews", prose with haiku-like verselets interspersed, detailing two attempts to walk the coastal footpath to get to the poetry festival. Semi-wilderness beset with notices and golf courses.

There is a poetical category called "the new formalism" which I don't think Alistair Noon is. For all his belief in formal properties he is not writing in opposition or trying to turn any clock back. He does, I think, see a central space in current poetry which is being neglected or drained by extremism on both sides and seeks to regenerate it. He is just as concerned as any avant-gardist to use poetical language to reveal what lies below the surface, but does not see this as being done by negating the linguistic function itself, and thus denying cultural partnership with the reader. He distrusts the levels which the experimenter needs to excavate through, and this means he trusts perception. A good clue to the nature of his practice is given by one of the pieces of *Holidays of the Poets*, which speaks of the anthropologist Clifford Geertz and his well-known essay "Thick Description"[7]. This mode is best defined through its contrary: thin description would be an account of what is witnessed, what takes place, what is said, with no authorial comment or interpretation of any kind, and there is quite a lot of poetry like that (viz. the so-called second generation

New York school or, more extremely, the German poet Rolf Dieter Brinkmann). The classic example is of a boy whose right eye either winks or twitches, and thin description cannot say which. Thick description includes motivation, use of codes, context in general, it is the realisation of meaningful structures which are not so much hidden as understood — "to know the imaginative world within which people's acts are signs", and here it comes within reach of the possibilities of poetry, especially as Geerz goes on to describe it as the construction of a kind of fiction out of what happens – a "making". Noon brings this to poetry through his placement of the authorial self, you could say centrally but not subjectively. It is a perfectly objective attention to particulars as a means of attaching the whole ("the general makes me more specific" — Sonnet 1). *Lyrical description* is perhaps a good label for what Noon gets up to. The song qualities enhance the description and the description holds the singing to realities.

After so much fresh invention, a reviewer is reluctant to end with such a barefaced cliché as "We look forward eagerly to his second book." But we do.

---

1   There have been ten earlier booklets and downloadable e-books, three of which are mentioned later. Three of the ten are translations, of August Stramm, Monika Rinck and Pushkin's "The Bronze Horseman".

2   I noticed one or two skipped end-rhymes, and the line-length corresponds to the iambic pentameter most of the time, best measured as five stresses rather than five feet.

3   Seamus Heaney's "Glanmore Sonnets" (in *Field Work*, 1979) for instance, use half-rhyme, assonance and non-rhyme a great deal, revise the formal demands ad lib., and the line measure is approximate.

4   See *The Reality Street Book of Sonnets* (2008), an interesting chronicle of the survival of the term in Modernist-inclined writing, but in which the definition is eventually reduced to that of a short poem susceptible to a count of fourteen of anything (lines, words, streaks of paint etc.), or not.

5   Three groups of four lines rhymed (in this case) ABAB CDCD EFEF followed by a final couplet (GG). The discourse of the poem thus moves more continuously towards the ending. There is a conventional "turn" of address after line 8 which is not obligatory (inherited from the earlier "Petrarchan" sonnet). Noon frequently ends a sentence at that point without necessarily changing direction.

6   Quoted in the Introduction to *Shadow Lands, selected poems* translated by Ruth and Matthew Mead (Anvil Press 1984). This is still the only substantial collection in English, with skilful and sympathetic translations but unfortunately no text in German.

7   In his *The Interpretation of Cultures: selected essays,* 1973. The term derived originally from Gilbert Ryle.

FORMS OF DIFFERENCE

Andrew Jordan, *Hegemonick*.

Shearsman Books 2012. 114pp

Sandeep Parmar, *The Marble Orchard*.

Shearsman Books 2012. 88pp

Kelvin Corcoran, *Sea Table*. Itinerant Press.

Concertina format, 10pp. Edition of 40 copies signed.

Andrew Jordan is a scholar, magician, poet, topographer, historian, autobiographer, revolutionary... most of these and perhaps some more, but operating in little space. Almost the entire book is concerned with Portsdown Hill, a chalk ridge north of Portsmouth, one of those spare pieces of land which has fallen to the military, littered with 19ᵗʰ Century forts now ruined or re-used for military and civic purposes, and a labyrinth of underground tunnels which were mostly intended as air-raid shelters but the extent of which remains uncertain. The hill is encroached upon by apparently dismal estates and in the vicinity is an office of the "defence giant" Qinetiq, a private company who for a fee will help you to kill people and rule the world. These and other entities inhabit Jordan's writing as actors in an apocalyptic theatre.

I avoid describing the plot of this drama. Suffice it to say that it is a series of encounters with destructive forces, delvings into concealed and lurking power-focuses, confrontations with anti-democratic war machines and local thuggery and prostitution, and other scenarios. Always the author is the witness, venturing beyond the rational frontier, and he is the medium through which the "consciousness" created at these sites is articulated, for this exploration of 19th-20th Century military structures takes on, not without scepticism, the methods by which "new age" believers plotted ley lines and force fields from the forms and mappings of prehistoric monuments and church towers. The drama involves such figures as Mary Millington, "Britain's first shameless hard-core porn star" represented as a goddess who becomes the hill itself, and ends with an apocalyptic war between children and adults which represents fictively the final defeat of the destructive forces. There is a particularly effective long walk in the middle, a release of comparative calm, cultivating disorientation and vision.

But the actual discourse does not just wildly pursue alienated and paranoiac vision; it can be both subtle and sceptical, and the self-image in it is courageous and discerning in its abstract thought as much as its ventures into holes in the ground or closed military ruins, in its disclosure of institutional harm at ground level as much as meticulous detailing of topographical forms which translate into mental acts. There is also a prosody, which is not the kind of thing normally taken into account with this kind of poetry; it consists of a use of enjambement, incantatory echoic structuring and paragraphing which constantly urges the writing forward into its adventures.

There might be a problem with belief, but I don't think there need be. Some might consider the thesis nothing but hippie ravings, but that needn't matter. The author himself describes it as 'A delusional narrative, an ode to oblivion [...] a therapeutic journal [...] a decoy (but not a plan).' I read it as an adventure, a personal narrative of desperation and hope in a bid to encompass individual and total perception, and I'm happy to do so. It is a passionate writing and at its heart is the shaping power of perception. From "Theory: The Self" —

> The psyche exists within affective walls.
>
> It has a single bank and ditch enclosing
>
> a rectangular precinct surrounding a circular
>
> timber structure which may have been roofed.
>
> The latter appeared to him in a dream
>
> as a series of three concentric V-shaped gullies,
>
> the innermost containing post holes. Two
>
> large post holes flanked an entrance
>
> on the eastern side. This is where the self lurks,
>
> holy mutant, craver, administerer of small things,
>
> an addict swayed by sentiment, stupidly
>
> vain host to thoughts, this dark interior.

§

Sandeep Parmar's *The Marble Orchard* is a first book which plunges to the heart of modern poetry. Sandeep Parmar's background is Indian and her main concerns involve the treatment and status of women in her ancestral society and, echoically, here too, but boldly written into a densely figurative and syntactically free poetry. The concerns remain acute and specific but the poetical technique forces each question back onto the individual, the reader mainly, as well as building a rich and inexhaustible artefact out of experience, a bejewelled crown offered to the victim and the world.

The book begins with a prose "Invocation" which I take to be addressed to poetry, expressing her hopes for the art— 'To be of use, but nothing will decant. Perilous consonant, betrothed as fire to the ordinary. A spell; a note. Combatant of will and engraver of sighs...' The blending of disparate percepts from word to word here, constantly moving to a different vocabulary zone, is typical of her figurative language throughout. But as against this, the quite traditional function and tone of the Invocation is noteworthy, "To my muse" as it were, and there are similar instances elsewhere in the book, sitting perfectly well with the Modernistic writing, and affirming poetical writing as the "high art" which so much England-centred and academic poetry now refuses due to a panic about elitism.

Not that all the writing is dense, and Parmar is by no means committed to the modernist option. The degree of contraction varies according to the focus of the poem, and becomes quite extenuated and normative in some of them, and to my ears sometimes distinctly Shakespearean. A modern lyrical technique has been mastered in a number of short poems of tense calm, but there is a strong ambition in the book towards narrative, principally to recount the female experience in a traditional society of gender delegation and polygamy. Here the linguistic units are phrases or sentences, which stand distinct from each other, whole or broken, among silences. A hint in "Invocation"—'Poultice to the hush, to the whispers of women in corded rooms and to the glows beneath doorways' – suggests a rationale for the technique in the conditions themselves, of women kept separate and not party to the full societal discourse, but living on hints and whispers, all narrative impeded and dispersed, a condition of powerlessness and inwardness, and that this is replicated in the writing, while enhanced poetically into a telling. (To some extent I owe this interpretation to things Parmar said at a gathering in Cambridge recently.) If this is the case, it certainly doesn't close the discourse from the male reader but is transcended in the fictive mode.

In any event I think the principal achievement of the book lies in these longer poems, which also offer the reader some help in what can be a difficult discourse, by being sectioned so that the framework is clear. "Archive for a Daughter" goes through the process of opening a series of boxes and folders revealing a personal history. A particularly strong piece, "Multigravida", goes through the women of one family under the headings of their gravida codes (records of pregnancies and births) in a series of sometimes clear sometimes obscure addresses and accounts. Being myself of a fairly indolent disposition my favourite is the long series "The Wives" in the middle of the book, a perfectly clear, but no less poetic, discourse on the conflict between older and younger wives of one man (though it gets rather mysterious at the end). The more relaxed mode also allows Parmar's humorous turns of phrase to emerge ('a plague of aunties hibble and hex').

I don't want to pretend there are no problems, and certainly it would sometimes help to be told where we are and what is going on, since the obliquity of the account obviously masks a singularity, but the information is held back as if already known. But I feel this is a book that can be trusted. Here is the opening of the poem "Homecoming (after Christa Wolf's *Cassandra*)", one of the more orthodox poems in its mode of address—

> Voices spear the darkness. Troy is no more than a glint
> of departing soldiers. We pass in and out of the smoke.
>
> Soon, it is morning. It is not morning.
> The false night of forensic lamplight is the dawn.
>
> A distant wood reflects, thick with torsos blaring white, and
> hands raised, empty on the approaching shore, to deny.
>
> The light accuses every surface. All are mute:
> thorns and swollen lips stiffen the undergrowth.

I am Cassandra, née Iphigenia, Cassandra, née Iphigenia.
I have exited time, prophet and sacrifice, to speak.

§

Craft production of small poetry items is a venerable tradition and *Sea Table* by Kelvin Corcoran lies within it. The print colour is a greenish ochre. The paper is a gently off-white acid-free and wood-free cartridge. The text occupies six A5 pages concertina-folded. The heading and colophon are on two sheets of semi-opaque paper encompassing the text pages. The cover is quite thin matt card bearing a swirling sea-water design in the same colour as the rest. The binding is sewn not stapled. It is designed by the publisher, Philip Kuhn. At one time there were a lot of people doing this kind of thing on hand presses, though the production here is by adobe and inkjet. They often seemed to have difficulty acquiring some poetry which deserved the care and attention, but that's not the case here.

The poet sits in a small house in the Peloponnese at a table which he has inherited from an Oxford classicist who used to live in the vicinity. Ghosts of the prehistoric, ancient Greek, Byzantine and Renaissance past approach the table and come and go one by one, as does Ezra Pound. The table is the writing. The table is the sea. The table is the ramp down into the sea, and other images more or less without limit while the time lasts. At the end the poet sets sail on the table: "Then set said table to breakers" (that was Pound nosing in) bound for "the mouth of hell" but the ending reverses the itinerary –

> White engine of thought
> brought to the table;
> of marble, of obsidian
> the first figures stand.

— the fluid and the substantive, thought and image, held in perfect equipoise as a result not only of serious thought but also of the care implied in inseparable lyrical ecstasis.[1]

---

1   *Sea Table* has since been included in Corcoran's book *For the Greek Spring* (Shearsman Books 2013), a collection through his career of poems concerning Greece. My summary account of *Sea Table* is hopefully made amends for in my essay 'Kelvin Corcoran and Greece' in *The Writing Occurs as Song: a Kelvin Corcoran Reader,* edited by Andy Brown, Shearsman Books 2014. On "the mouth of hell" see page 80 of this book. *(2014)*

WORLD POETRY?

The World Record: international voices from Southbank
Centre's Poetry Parnassus
edited by Neil Astley and Anna Selby.
Bloodaxe Books 2012. 360pp, £10.00.

P*oetry Parnassus* was a six-day poetry festival at London's Southbank Centre in June. It was a very ambitious project conceived by Simon Armitage and Jude Kelly, to invite one poet from each nation taking part in the Olympic Games, thus an enormous gathering of "poets of the world" of which *The World Record,* which contains 204 poets, is the accompanying anthology.

I was able to be at the event for an hour and a half on my way to something else in the neighbourhood on the afternoon of the penultimate day. Having read carefully the publicity for the event I was at once struck by two things. Firstly, although there is mention of poetry being "one of the most democratic of art forms" (I don't know why that should be so), it was immediately evident that not all the poets of the world have the same status. Some got to read in the real auditoria of the complex, and you had to pay to hear them, up to £35. These were the special poets – mostly top sellers and prize-winners in U.K. The rest of the poets, which was the vast majority, gave free readings in various foyers and open spaces in which they had to contend with interference from external noise and activity, such as a large and busy bar, as well as a general feeling of camping. The other thing was that although there was supposed to be one poet each of some 200 nationalities, there were evidently plenty of back doors through which British poets could get in on the show, sessions promoted by various book and magazine publishers and organisations, probably not officially within *Poetry Parnassus* but on the ground very much a part of it and included in the brochure. These had an international content at the discretion of the editors but I reckon that in all some 15 to 20 "extra" British poets took part, some of them (Armitage, Motion and Muldoon) doing extended solo sessions or lectures. I can't help wondering whether all 200 poets democratically got the same fee, but as there's no information available on that let's assume they did.

There was also quite a lot of tomfoolery, as you'd expect, mostly in the form of participatory sessions aside from the main menu in which people played fun and games with poetry. Here's one of them:

Saturday, 6pm-9pm. POETRY PYJAMA PARTY

Bring your own torch, some pjs and a copy of *The World Record Anthology*, then crawl under a blanket and read along with poets by torchlight. Bed sheets provided. (Free).

I have known poets to crawl under a blanket with whom would be an extremely dangerous proposition for almost anybody. Less threatening games included "edible poetry" (a kind of cookery class), a mock poetry exam, a fast reading competition, the "Poetry Takeaway" (poems written for you on the spot) and so on. Of course these are all *fun* and if you complain about fun you're a dreadful killjoy, even if fun is capable of destroying civilisations.

The various sessions of rap and slam poetry and poetry with jazz or other kinds of band would to me have been a real relief after all this bourgeois fun.

But in the short time I was there I heard a poet who I thought was a real discovery. This was the Jamaican Ishion Hutchinson, at a reading for *The Wolf* magazine (which somehow got two of the extra sessions during the week). I at once thought I was hearing poetry of an enticing and rich seriousness, a finely tuned harmony of narrative and lyrical. I was so impressed that I bought his book.[1] Sandeep Parmar was in the same reading (see my review 'Forms of Difference') but neither of them is in the anthology.

The anthology, one poem by each of 204 poets from 204 nations, makes very big claims for itself, which any realistic consideration of the editorial process, that is, the sources of information required for such an exercise, will at once cast doubt on. Whatever treasures lie hidden in this book I think it's necessary to begin by pointing out what it isn't.

It is not a guide to or sampler of world poetry; it is not "a snapshot or cross-section of global poetry". It does not "uncover the world". You cannot here "discover the world" through its poets. The poetry does not "cross all international barriers" (these phrases are all from the blurb and introductions). In fact it is not a world anything; the concept "world" is quite irrelevant to this collection, as it is to the market known as "world music". It is no more than a gaudy framework on which is hung a heterogeneous collection of poems, good bad and indifferent among them, whose presence was dictated largely by available resources and the taste of the two editors ("we identified [...] poets [...] whose work excited us"). It is surely obvious when you look at familiar areas, Britain, U.S.A. France, Germany, Italy... and see that out of all the possibilities of current activity, each is represented by one poem (poems moreover rather similar to each other), that no representation is taking place at all, and why should it be any different for Djibouti? Yet representation is presented as the *raison d'être* of the book.

From far distant and, to us, remote places one might reasonably expect difference. But when I attempt to survey the contents of the book, the impression I get is of a lack of variety. It is difficult to generalise, but again and again poets from far and near, and from greatly differing cultural contexts, after they have been fed through the editorial filtering processes seem to be united in writing a poetry of prosaic declaration, generally personal and/or political, close to the most popular forms of poetry in England. The declaration is more often than not dispassionate, as is the fashion here, though sometimes a form of protest is encountered which is indeed passionate, without becoming highly individuated. It is as if a world-wide culture has sprung up in poetry which whatever the traditions of particular zones was at one time, now produces a very straightforward poetry of declarations, accounts, confessions, etc., free from interference from poetical forms, highly figurative or imaginative language, word-play or phonetic play, syntactical unorthodoxy, difficulty, literary reference, landscape, and in some cases quite free from any concept of beauty in the notion of what is a poem. Many amount to plain histories of the defeated self, especially in exile.

Among 204 poets there are of course many exceptions to this, and the fact that a number of them are essentially performance poets of one kind or another, sometimes coming directly from an aural tradition, whose works are perhaps less happy in print than in the air, must add to this sense of an ubiquitous belief in direct explicatory address as the essential mode of poetry.

And of course there is the question of translation, a problem which is rather skated over. In fact quite a lot of the poetry was written in English but otherwise it is assumed that translation effects a pure transition, that you "get" the poem in translation as you would if you knew the original language. Probably you do sometimes, especially with poems of prosaic declaration, and there are some poets who just seem to "translate themselves" in the sense that the poems are so strong that the translator can hardly seem to go wrong (e.g. in my experience Rilke, Mandelstam, Bobrowski, Lorca). But if we are fully dependent on translation how can we expect to experience the full impact of a poetical intervention into language, how can we recognise freshness and accuracy achieved by a slight shift from normal discourse, or faint echo of predecessors, values of rhythmical movement... Are we not in constant danger of losing whatever subtlety the poem has? This is not of course a problem with prosaic declaration etc., which doesn't have any. But I'd be inclined to worry about poems from places with a rich classical tradition or a more recent reputation for distinguished modern poets.

To check on this I surveyed separately the poems from four areas of the world where I would have expected to see the results of such poetical traditions, to see if they differed from the run of the world stuff and showed truly poetical qualities emerging from the translation, and what I found was—

Caribbean. Most poems written in English so none of the translation problems. Dominant mode: prosaic declaration etc. tending to a rather ponderous way of dealing with the self and the generality. Cuba no exception here, but the Cuban poet lives in London anyway. Some poems in patois but never too strong. Effective poems showing personal experience of cultural contrast came from Jamaica, St Kitts-Nevis, Grenada and US Virgin Islands. But I saw nothing as good as Ishion Hutchinson.

Arabic. Mere traces of the vast classical tradition in pieces of prosaic verse tempered with light figuration and poise. Outright prosaic for political protest. Good poems from Oman, Lebanon and Kuwait, owing something, I think, to the passionate richness of Darwish but little to the passionate experimentation of Adonis. A very nice prose piece by the London-Jordanian Amjad Nasser.

Latin America. Dominant mode: prosaic declaration etc. The rich surrealist legacy surfaces, becoming rather mechanical. The poetry generally more literary or constructed than many other zones. Impressive pieces from Mexico, Guatemala, Dominican Republic.

Eastern Europe. Dominant mode: prosaic declaration etc. Again with a "literary" leaning, in fact several poets seeming to make a point of displaying their familiarity with modern European classics. Strong stuff from Albania, Armenia, Latvia and Romania (an enlivened version of the rather mechanical joke surrealism translators have been serving up from there lately). And on p.51 the best thing I found in this vast gallimaufry, "People Talking" by the Bosnia and Herzegovinian Adisa Bašić. This is a found poem consisting of seven brief quotations from survivors of the Srebrenica massacre, apparently collected by the poet herself, delicately lineated judging by the translation, and a refreshing piece of objectivity in contrast to the many subjectified protest poems in the book—

> *Revenge*
> I know who killed my wife and
> son and
> daughter.
> I know, one of them came back.
> Opened a bakery.
> But I make sure
> I never buy anything there.

All my zonal categorisations above are, of course, untrustworthy, being based on one poem from each nation in each zone.

The "Biographical Notes" section at the back, which is of course enormous, proved to be the most thought-provoking part of the book. There are far more nations in the world than most people realise; most of them are small, and most of them are former colonies now independent. But cultural independence does not necessarily follow from political independence and it is obvious from the careers outlined in these notes that to gain eminence in poetry in these places often means directing your energies outside your country, usually to the former colonial base. Thus a remarkably high proportion of the poets of *Poetry Parnassus* turn out to live in Britain (secondarily U.S.A.), temporarily or permanently, quite a lot of them writing in English. This must have greatly eased the editorial process, though I don't know if it qualifies as corner-cutting — it must anyway have been an unbelievable headache to make this compilation. The quantity of poets employed by universities, usually western universities and often in professorships, is also high – a condition I thought was mainly that of American poetry. In fact most of the poets from small and post-colonial countries are career internationalists, floating all over the world from post to post, festival to festival, conference to conference, and few seem to live permanently in the countries they represent; in fact in some cases you wonder whether they ever visit them. It seems that few of these countries are culturally self-contained; higher education seems for many of them to take place in U.S.A. or the former European colonial capital. The list also mentions hundreds of prizes, most poets having won a bunch of them, and many of the prizes are awarded from the west.

To make matters worse, an ever increasing number of countries, not necessarily either small or post-colonial, seem to suffer from political repression and/or unbearable living conditions (now add Greece) and many of the poets collected here fled into exile. Such poets are favoured here, the notes taking a pride in our having rescued them, which is no doubt a very western view of the situation in many places, though not necessarily unjustified.

So there is an impression of an international floating poetry elite focused on the west, which must go to explain a certain standardisation of procedure in the anthology. Even the "Russian" poet lives in U.S.A. and writes in English. The only time the notes make you anticipate something entirely foreign is when the poet is or has been a state official, ambassador, or the actual president, or when there appears to be little or no tradition of written poetry in the country, and these are both very rare. With however many exceptions, there is a distinct impression that if this is "world poetry" we are mainly getting our own poetry back from all over the world. And serve us right.

This anthology is a kind of lucky-dip. You may get a certain amount of information out of it, but you'll need luck. You may discover beautiful poems from places you've never heard of (I didn't do very well in this pursuit). If you're the kind of enthusiast who buys anything with a poem by Seamus Heaney in it, be warned that it is a short poem reprinted from his *Open Ground* (1998). If you share the editors' enthusiasm for poems of political, social or gender protest there is plenty of meat for you here, if all rather standard produce. Finally, apart from Adisa Bašić's poem and, I think, thirty or forty seemingly impressive performances from here there and everywhere, I give my personal prize to the Romanian Doina Ioanid for the best of the several hundred book titles listed at the back – "Ritmuri de îmblânzit aricoaica" — Chants for Taming the Hedgehog Sow (2010).

---

1   Ishion Hutchinson, *Far District*. Peepal Tree Press 2010.

AMERICAN HYBRID

American Hybrid
edited by Cole Swensen and David St. John. New York
and London: Norton, 2009. 560pp.

It can be very difficult dealing as a reviewer with a body of poetry with which you feel you have been involved. This anthology collects poets mostly active from the 1990s to the present, with a few senior figures added, in what most people would recognise as a Modernist or radical tendency. The title claims they are middle-of-the-road but this is not generally so. Throughout the earlier part of this period I was involved in an annual gathering of poets in Cambridge, a rather chaotic affair, and in ten years we invited some 15 of these poets and another ten or so who might have qualified for this anthology. They were invited in a context of innovative poetry, and as such I listened to them, admired them, exchanged books, drank with them, showed them Wittgenstein's grave (most of them wanted to see Wittgenstein's grave), paid them inadequately, and waved them goodbye. Some I am still in touch with. There was a sense of a rather shaky solidarity of the innovative, the major flaw in which was an evident lack of interest on the part of these and other foreigners in the innovative British poetry with which we surrounded them. None of us ever got a reciprocal invitation. Ten to twenty years later it all feels rather different. If I now think there are problems with a lot of this poetry, am I betraying a trust or exhibiting my own faltering instability? Probably the latter. My strategy is to largely avoid talking of particular poets, but to speak instead of the ethos of the collection as confirmed by a majority of the poets presented, not that this will get me out of trouble.

But it goes further back than that, to 1960, when the anthology *The New American Poetry 1945-1960* edited by Donald Allen[1] appeared. This had a tremendous impact on British poets such as myself. It seemed to open a new gateway to a greater, and refreshed, sense of what poetry could be. The variety in it was wide — the global cultural excavation of Charles Olson, the poetical "magic" of Robert Duncan and Jack Spicer, the wild oppositional populism of Ginsberg, the urbane meditations of Frank O'Hara... For some of us 20th Century British poetry was herewith abandoned (though we came back to it). This opening extended beyond the book itself, back to William Carlos Williams and George Oppen, and we connected with other forms of Americana – Abstract Expressionism and free jazz. The word "open" was used a lot ("open field" was Olson's term for his practice) for a poetry which avoided literary tropes and patterning and was free to dispose itself on the page by a new rhetoric which engaged the reader directly, a prosody that was like acts of physical movement in free play. The word "objective" was proposed as counter to the presiding subjectivity of English poetry at that time, by which most poets seemed to be knowingly offering their personal qualities to the reader through a conventionalised medium rather more than anything else, anything independently observed or thought.[2] *American Hybrid* sees itself in its central content as in direct descent from the poetry in Allen's anthology, which is likewise how I saw those American poets I got to know in the 1990s. Why, then do I feel uncomfortable? Because in contrast it feels like a closure. I can but rarely see any *further* possibilities in what these poets do, any opening to the future. Allen's anthology is mentioned in the Introduction but quite unfairly as a collection of poems for quick one-off reading, as against the studied linguistic manipulations of hybrid poets; this is quite untrue.

Allen's anthology contained no professors of poetry. *American Hybrid* seems to contain little else. The poets in Allen's anthology had not won any prizes. The poets in *American Hybrid* are loaded with them. Is this perhaps a rather superficial point of comparison? Or is it a sign of what has happened to American poetry since 1960?

I feel that this anthology is constructed on a false premise. In the introductions it is taken as axiomatic and unquestionable that American poetry has for a long time been split into "two camps". The camps are of course the traditional and the innovative, conventional and experimental, Romantic and Modernist, closed and open – Robert Lowell called them "cooked and uncooked". For convenience I'll refer to these as the conservative and the radical, but these terms do not necessarily say anything about any of the writing, and there is specifically no political parallel. The idea of hybrid poetry is that this immense gap is narrowed or healed by poets who adopt features from both sides of the controversy, and thus for instance may show experimental language violations as much as plain-speaking address.

But really the two camps view, which is essential to the rationale of the anthology, was created principally by anthologisers and critics. Poets never allotted themselves so systematically, and there were never just two ways of writing poetry. Allen's anthology was not a collection of extremists on the left, its poets were not "marginal" — it represented a lot of what was worth knowing about in mid-century American poetry, and within a great range of practices, some of them mutually inimical. This indeed was Allen's intention, and it would have been clearer if he had stuck to his original scheme to include an older generation of poets: Pound, Stevens, Williams, Zukofsky etc., which unfortunately Olson forbade, insisting that the collection represent "where we are at".

This comprehensiveness is confirmed if you look at the "rival" or conservative anthologies of that time, such as Donald Hall's *New Poets of England and America* (1957)[3] in which most of the conservative American poets are now unknown names; they seem to have vanished without trace as if they never were. The conservative option rested on some half-dozen major figures, whereas the liberal option revealed a lot of very various activity among younger poets. This is repeated in *American Hybrid* where most of the poets seem to have adopted the radical option. As the radical tendency became more and more institutionalised the writing within it has increasingly catered to an academic market demand. To me much of it now seems like a narrowing, at worst a betrayal, of the achievements in *The New American Poetry*.[4]

I have to add that I find the two introductions, of which Cole Swensen's is the more substantial, and the introductory descriptions of each poet (which amount to blurbs), quite depressing. The field of American poetry is understood as a set of categories. Everything is determined by pressure from depersonalised and numinous blocs, called Black Mountain, Beat, San Francisco Renaissance, New York School (those being four categories chosen by Allen to subdivide his anthology), Confessionalist, Mainstream, New Formalism, Language Poetry, Objectivism and others. There are no people in here! just conceptualised results of former activity that can be shifted around in relationship to each other. Poets do get named of course, but like the groupings they tend to get identified by a singular summary tag. It is detached and clinical: there seems not to be, and never to have been, any possibility of being overwhelmed by an individual act of poetry. Rimbaud is reduced to the formula of "The Rimbaudian 'I is another'" which poets "take on" or "extend". The New York School is about the "diurnal" and that's that (I think Frank O'Hara was, at his best, a metaphysical poet). There is no uncertainty in this coverage, no confusion, no disarray of the senses planned or unplanned (alas for Rimbaud) — the whole thing is utterly wrapped up and ready for the classroom. Today we do the New Formalism. I was hoping that this way of talking about contemporary poetry had stopped.

It is even more depressing to see an age-old American attack on British poetry repeated as dogma. We are told, quoting Paul Auster, that "most twentieth-century American poets took their cue either from the British tradition or the French" and of course the French option is favoured. British means Romantic, pastoral, closed, conservative, "man as a natural being in a natural world, informed by intense introspection and a belief in the stability and sovereignty of the individual." (Are these all such terrible things?) The British option means traditional lyrical forms and "no radical break from nineteenth century poetical conventions". This is one of the oldest and most tiresome polemics in modern poetry, going back to Walt Whitman and Noah Webster if not further. And it is such nonsense. It is followed (p.xviii of the Introduction) by a catalogue of the shiny virtues of French poetry, all of which can in fact be found in British 19th-20th Century poetry, and the most important principle of which, a figurative freedom in poetical language which trespasses beyond social norms, has been convincingly argued (by Ford Madox Ford among others) to derive from Britain anyway, in the form of Shakespeare, whose influence on Lamartine and thus the Symboliste poets is very much to the point. And there is more to 19th Century poetry than 19th Century poetical conventions. Britain is separated from France by a small ditch, and French is still the first foreign language taught here (except Welsh for some). If anything important happened there we'd be the first to hear of it. To repeat these old saws now is extraordinary. Doesn't anybody over there actually read British poetry except in the old Oxford anthologies? And what is the logic of connecting various forms of poetical licence to a disabling of the individual? Why should anyone want to abandon, in poetry of all places, the work of the individual consciousness? The "English" problem was subjectivity, and individuality and subjectivity are not the same thing: indeed objectivity in poetry or elsewhere surely makes a particular demand on individual perceptive processes, and does not at all necessarily implicate a classroom scientism which surrenders to the collective. There is in fact a lot of trouble with concepts of the self in this anthology, on the one hand foregrounded in eccentric and idiolectic language zones, at the same time suppressed by depersonalising experimentalist conventions.

In *American Hybrid*'s field of reference the New York School was the most blatant exponent of this anti-British polemic and associated francophilia. There is a particularly dumb version of it in the biographical note James Schuyler supplied for Allen's anthology. This could be taken as just a typical flaneur's pose in a context of urban competition for distinction – expensive lunches, Broadway musicals, "art", and French poetry — but it more seriously needs to be connected to the relationship, the financial relationship, between Abstract Expressionism and French (Parisian) painting. I'll return to this.

Nobody any longer denies that contemporary American poetry is dominated by the teaching of creative writing in the colleges. The fact is now overwhelming. The great majority of these poets have been through it as students and now teach it. A recent review and discussion of the book ran through two issues of *The Chicago Review*[5] and five contributors without mentioning the poetry at all; it was all about the problems and power struggles of the creative writing courses, which are apparently in danger of swamping English studies completely, and nobody will any longer study any poetry but their teacher's and their own. (I do not seem to have mentioned the poetry myself yet.)

The effect of this situation on the poetry is unfathomable. The poets do not all write in the same way, in fact there are immense differences, but one suspects a pressure, from the schools involved here anyway, towards certain poetical beliefs and practices. But first let it be said that there is one clearly valuable result of the teaching of poetry in USA, and that has been the launching of women into the field. Quite recently the gender proportion in almost all English-language poetry gatherings was dismal. In that festival I mentioned in Cambridge, which continued into the 2000s, it was something like one in twenty, and it is still thus in most British collective manifestations, including the most radical of them. In Allen's anthology I think there might have been half a dozen women. Here there are 41 women out of 74 poets; I don't think I've previously seen a neutral anthology with more women than men. For complicated reasons, both social and psychological, women were inhibited from presenting themselves as poets in a heavily male-dominated structure. It wasn't the organisers' or editors' faults, the women poets were just "not there", though there might have been some prejudice against "feminine" ways of writing. Thanks to the incorporation of poetry writing into higher education, this distortion is finished with in America. By contrast, the representation of black and Hispanic writers is as bad as it has ever been – just a few token names (some half dozen, I think, in this anthology).

I can only wonder, in my ignorance, what goes on in these poetry writing courses, what pressures are brought to bear, what is encouraged and what is discouraged, how quality is recognised and rewarded, how much the individual teacher defines the aims, how some become stars and go on to teach the subject, how some, or most, become professors of poetry. Also how different might the results be in other universities from those involved here. The subject is not touched upon in *American Hybrid*, but I have suspicions. If writing poetry becomes a university subject leading ultimately to a doctorate, it must be required to have intellectual status of some kind, which poets have not always necessarily claimed. There's nothing wrong with the idea of intellectual poetry, but I think that the particular language-based (non-discursive) form the intellectuality takes is the downfall of much of this poetry.

What is a hybrid but a mixture of elements from differing sources? Isn't all poetry hybrid in some way unless entirely derivative? Aren't all species former hybrids? Why do the editors avoid saying "central" or "mainstream" or "middle of the road"? (because those terms are plainly inappropriate).

The introductions claim a balance between experimental and conventional which is not shown in the anthology itself, where there is a persistent bias towards a radical practice. This preference is stated or implied in the introductions and in the terms of praise used in the individual blurbs and everywhere manifest in the poems. It may well be a preference of the writing schools, and may even be developing into an orthodoxy of all new poetry in USA. There has been talk of "those who do not take the beaten path"[6] but it now looks as though this *is* the beaten path, or one of them. The central insistence concerns language. It says that language is self-substantial, that it is its own meaning. Or meaning is immanent and inhering in language, as opposed to Romantic transcendence (British of course). It speaks of the materiality of language, that language is "a social force in itself". Language is both prior to and subsequent to the poem. Poetry makes "a transformative intervention upon its own medium". In practice this means that you work with and on language rather than directly with memory and experience or any inherited sense (except very short-term) of poetical formulation. Almost all these poets devote their energies to disturbing or even eradicating language's communicative function, sometimes violently, with broken syntax and refusal of meaning, so that you are trapped in the poem with no access to the world, and sometimes by creating a transmissive discourse which doesn't make sense (Surrealism etc.) and this too is a procedure which halts perception within language. The editors seem to think that any run of readable sentences is evidence that their poet is using techniques from the conservative camp and so establishes his/her hybridity, but almost all these poets remain transfixed within language, and this paralysis is what makes it impossible for most of them to even approach the scope and clamour of poets like Stevens or Duncan or Ginsberg. It is all small-scale, meticulous. It all takes place in small corners, with or without the tenuous lyrical realisation of the local of William Carlos Williams. A lot of it is introspective in an evasive way. I think the best achievements among it all lie in a new incantatory mode of repeated verbal structures at which poets such as Peter Gizzi are adept. That is one point where the "linguistically innovative" demand is dropped, and the poetry immediately expands.

Language *carries* meaning. And for that it has to be loaded with it, and that places you beyond it or beside it, or within one language seeking to transfer what you have gained into another language. I'm not talking about translation.

Always an enemy is needed. For all the vaunting of hybridity there is clearly contempt for "the traits associated with "conventional" [why the scare-quotes?] poetry, such as coherence, linearity, formal clarity, narrative, firm closure, symbolic resonance, and stable voice." (Introduction p.xxi). After 50 years' involvement with British or any other radical poetry and its apologists you start to long for these things like a thirsty traveller in the desert. As in many previous American polemics blame falls on the "New Criticism" of the 1930s, the worst crime of which seems to have been to insist that a poem should have "a distinct beginning and end" (frightful thought – must be a British habit). I'm not familiar with The New Criticism and view it as an educational move, though I think Tate, Ransom and Bishop are poets not to be casually dismissed. I would have thought that an insistence on close reading and claims for a certain autonomy of the text were both perfectly in accord with the aesthetics of language-based and hybrid American poetry, or any poetry. Within a theoretic supposedly promoting balance the most elementary virtues and necessities of writing itself, its very efficacy, seem to be negated, all in favour of the self-substantiality of "language". And what do we get?

CONUNDRUMS TO WHICH THERE IS NO
SOLUTION ON THIS EARTH.

There is an imbalance because it is assumed that there is an avant-garde, which there isn't, and that there is an enemy conservative poetry of equal weight, which there isn't either. As in 1960 the best American poets (and certainly some of them are in this book) stand on their own ground, working from a large inheritance of disparate modes. The dull poets get more prizes (not so much more these days) and will be forgotten. But nothing could be duller than some of the conformist experimentalism gathered here.

One reason for the imbalance is probably that Language Poetry is taken seriously. Ever since it first raised its ugly head I have hated Language Poetry. It is dehumanized, aggressive and opportunistic. It's goal is emptiness. Far from being an extremist poetry it is an abnegation of poetry itself. If this serves as one of the cardinal points of the mapping there will inevitably be some very strange contours. If it is an extreme which this poetry seeks to counter-balance, that doesn't stop this poetry from itself being extremist, as most of it is. It was Language Poetry that cancelled the avant-garde by moving the radical referent right outside the field of viable poetry. Several poets are praised for their "understanding" of Language Poetry's principles, but that seems to involve subscribing to them.

This extremism, founded on an orthodox mass-decision that language is basically all there is, is what threatens to make so much of this anthology into a collection of problematic discourses. Poetry transforms language, but when we are handed the transformed artefact there's nothing we can do with it. Disruption and problematisation are terms of praise here, as if we didn't already have enough of both of them to cope with in the world. If the only linguistic transformation you can effect is disablement, rather than exploration and enrichment of language's burdens, you might as well keep it to yourself. And indeed they do.

Some of it is an intellectual poetry, some very much so. The nature of the intellectuality is frankly unwelcoming. It is specialist and seems to demand that you take a course in it, which perhaps you could. But as long as the reader remains an outsider she is made to feel, not stupid, but precisely untrained, excluded, even foreign – not knowing the language. This is not just because of the vocabulary; it is also because an abstruse discourse is further distanced by a syntax of dislocated and dislocating figurations, symbols which don't effect a correspondence as far as can be seen, tied up with other gestures of language-centering such as punning. The poetry of Marjorie Welish is the most prominent here (I have mentioned a poet by name!) and by that prominence escapes much of the condemnation. I can hardly affect to criticise her poetry since I cannot follow it, and yet it is clearly a discourse. But I can say that if I believed in language punching its way though its own facility into artistic heavens I would say she is supreme at this.[7] Marjorie visits Cambridge from time to time and we shall always be glad to see her. Another case of intellectuality is Susan Howe who leans heavily on Olson's techniques. My difficulty here is that there is a whole cultural history concealed in, rather than announced by, the poetry, and I don't think this was exactly what Olson did, who for all his hippie ravings always strove to declare himself, if in stuttered and rushed fragments. I remember a particularly moving reading she gave in Cambridge of "Morning

/ Sheet of Water at the edge of Woods". Her eccentric devotion to her inquiry was overwhelming.

It is often mentioned in the blurbs that a poet unites his art in some way with painting, by doing both, by collaboration, by writing about painting or whatever, and it is always said with approval, crossing frontiers and so forth. I don't think there's necessarily any virtue in it at all, any more than there is in my own incessant involvement with music. Abstract expressionism was held up as a screen to shield the New York School poets from all questioning. They rode it as a high tide and all the name-dropping and adoring panegyrics kept them bouncing along the pavements of New York in assured success. The realities wore through hedonistic life-styles in forms of despair and madness. The painters were engaged in a national campaign sponsored by government (I believe the C.I.A. was involved) for New York to supersede Paris as world artistic capital. It worked, and amazingly high prices obtained, and still do, for styles in painting which shortly beforehand wouldn't have stood a chance. Suicide and madness followed variously.[8] The difference between writing and painting is not a frontier, since it does not have the same form of territory either side of it. They might sometimes go well together.

The whole question of articulation is threatened by ideas about language. These poets are certainly crammed with salutary beliefs in the fields of politics, society and gender, but within the demands of radical language the manifestation of these beliefs is purely nominal. Nobody can make a statement about anything. Poets get the nod of approval because they "address issues of family and society", "address contemporary political situations". But what is this "addressing" when you turn to the poems and you are likely to find an almost total refusal to say anything whatsoever, because the influence of Gertrude Stein and Language Poetry reduces the poetry to gabble? I have always thought Stein a problematic influence to which women poets are particularly liable, especially those who propose an entire separatist curriculum which excludes all male poets, so Stein is about the only founding Modernist they can turn to. In this anthology her self-hypnotising flux of language, her grim and persistent refusal of the real in favour of linguistic surface, creeps everywhere, not only among women poets.

Occasionally, as from Juliana Spahr, we get a quite moving catalogue of political ills, accompanied by a heavy sense of helplessness and renunciation. Elsewhere it is claimed that the poetry "enacts the violence and rupture [...] inherent to identity construction." This is said of Laura Mullen whose statement is central to the whole claim to political sagacity among these poets: "There are politics involved in asking people not to make sense the way they've made sense before." This is a big issue affecting all radical poetics in the western world. Too big for any puny opposition from me. But it seems to me that in a given socio-linguistic context there is only one way of making sense and the alternative is senselessness, and I don't believe that senselessness is going to solve any problem of any kind anywhere in the world. If you can no longer talk *about*, you are silent. And some of the high jinks, the wrecked language, in this anthology is precisely an abnegation and a silence *vis-à-vis* the American public world. That entity is precisely not "addressed" and there is a sad sense of helplessness while you watch your country turning rotten and turn aside to indulge yourself in games with words.

Assuming that the selection from each poet is arranged chronologically, which I think it mostly is, I notice a number of instances of an early poetry which was making good sense and even enjoying itself in its own confidence and dexterity, which got increasingly subject to attacks of "language". James Galvin's strong wit betrayed by modernity into inarticulacy. Rae Armantrout succumbing to meaningless puns and increasingly writing as if a command not to articulate has been issued. Others too: Ralph

Angel, Mark McMorris, Stephen Ratcliffe. How does Etel Adnan get from stanzas like

> The certitude of Space is brought
>
> to me by a flight of birds. It
>
> is grey outside and there is a trembling...

to stanzas like

> altered epi/fanny. zzzz
>
> nerves—neurves. leaves
>
> in symmetry. for dorrmant
>
> lady in lace. in diamond

There is fortunately not too much in the anthology of this wringing the necks of words to force them to yield anything other than what they are. I can only hope that the future work of these poets will be able to recapture what they were capable of before "language" hit.

And that was often a kind of lightness, or as I said, a sense of enjoying yourself, which was perfectly confident that it held a serious grasp of experience at large. A poet who should have been included was Lisa Jarnot, who herself edited an anthology with a similar purpose in 1998[9], equally radical and equally "hybrid" (though the word was not used) but with only seven poets in common. Many of her poets show this lightness of touch, or an outrageous kind of wild dance in words, which would have enlivened the present collection.

These are perhaps some of the most dismaying of the exclusions, poets who would have imported some sense of free range and prance, and that includes Ted Berrigan and the whole of the "second New York school" as well as poets such as Catherine Wagner, Lee Ann Brown, Daniel Bouchard, Kaia Sand. The presence of Mary Jo Bang's closely verbal wit makes up to some extent for the paucity of humour, or the reduction of it to silliness. Poets too of a more even tenor are also strangely absent, like Lisa Samuels and Alice Ostriker. The absence of Clark Coolidge is inexplicable. And these are all perfectly "hybrid" if that is what you must be. And if we must have a few older poets as sentinels at the gate, we could as far as I'm concerned have got rid of John Ashbery and substituted Ralph J.Mills Jr.,[10] a poet who calmly and innocently transgresses all conservative/radical categories.

In Britain there are poets who base their work on myth-magic, folklorical mysteries, white witchcraft, alignments of stone circles and tumuli, astrology, dying provincial vocabularies, Celtic deities, Buddhistic detachment... They mostly live in stone cottages in the northern hills. And their poetry can be just as radical, just as intellectual and just as hybrid (sometimes just as impossible) as anything in this anthology. At least in principal, I think it has more potential than all this laboratory poetry.

I think I have been talking most of the time about some 60 percent of the poets in *American Hybrid*. I've ignored those whose presence makes no sense in relation to the editorial thesis, quite ordinary poets who sometimes commit a transgression, pleasant chat sliding into nonsense, or a wilful awkwardness introduced into a perfectly ordinary discourse. I am sometimes reminded of English "Martian" style poetry (of all things!) and its clever self-regarding metaphors, currently alas undergoing a small revival over here — "A handful of Alzheimered apple-trees" (Charles Wright). One of the results of the editorial interpretation of the hybridity thesis is that there is a lot more surrealism in the book than projective verse, indeed the "language" principle by insisting on constant verbal displacement does in milder cases quite auto-matically revert the poetry to easily recognisable surrealism in normal discursive syntax, and this is mainly the preserve of male poets.

There are some very fine poets here who form an exception to most of what I have said – to the judgements if not to all of the characterisation. There are some poets who were never going to be a problem, having always been exceptionally articulate among jabbering avant-gardists and carefully, thoughtfully, lyrical: Peter Gizzi, Fanny Howe, Jennifer Moxley, Nathaniel Mackey, Ann Lauterbach. The eloquence of these poets would grace any anthology about anything. So too would some poets quite difficult to characterise, principally Jorie Graham and Eleni Sikelianos, who hardly belong together except that they are both concerned to move into larger and more complex structures of narrative and selfhood. Harryette Mullen has a fine manner with roughly-rhymed hard-hitting verse which is also capable of true solemnity — "just as I am I come / knee bent and body bowed / this here's sorrow's home / my body's southern song" (I feel that the editors might not really approve of that stanza; they seem to think her work attacks the English language). Martin Corless-Smith's careful witty and elegant writing attaching a vast printed past in fragments doesn't feel as if it is part of the American poetry problem at all. But leafing casually through this big book when it first arrived, as one does, the point at which the writing shot out of the page and forced itself on me as something entirely authentic and moving, an impression which survived and grew, was when it was by Alice Notley. Perhaps she fits the thesis, perhaps not, I don't really care. There is a vocal urgency in it, an urgency of telling, of saying what has to be said, which rubbishes all the laboratories of silence.

> Beginning in poverty as a baby there is nothing
> for one but another's food and warmth
> should there ever be more
> than a sort of leaning against and trust a food for
> another from out of one – that would be
> poverty – we're taught not to count on
> anyone, to be rich,

youthful, empowered

but now I seem to know that the name of a self is

poverty that the pronoun I means such and that starting

so poorly I can live.

("Lady Poverty")

1   New York, Grove Press 1960. New edition with afterword, University of California Press
    c1999.

2   The only focused anthology of this phase in English poetry is *A Various Art* edited by
    Andrew Crozier and Tim Longville, Carcanet 1987. Concerning opposition to subjectivity
    see my review of *The Andrew Crozier Reader* in *The Cambridge Literary Review* no. 6,
    Easter 2012.

3   Co-edited with Robert Pack and Louis Simpson. Hall also edited *The Penguin Book of
    American Poetry* (1962)

4   Following representations from some American poets and my own reconsideration, I would
    now modify my rather extreme position in the last two paragraphs. There is more in the
    "two camps" thesis than I allowed, though I still don't think it is an entirely valid description
    of American poetry through the previous half-century. Certainly the senior figures of the
    non-Modernist sector — Robert Lowell, John Berryman, Thoeodore Roethke, Howard
    Nemerov and others — were very much a part of what was happening and have remained
    widely recognised, even if it remains true, as far as I can see, that many of the other poets
    in Hall's anthologies seem to have faded away. I'm assured that the teaching in colleges
    is still sharply divided. If you're told about Robert Lowell you won't be told about Robert
    Duncan, *and vice versa*, which is absurd. It's interesting that what is taught in colleges was
    the only reference point my correspondents could give to indicate what is now considered
    important in American poetry. My own reading surprised me at times by revealing how close
    some of these opposed poets could be to each other. There are also, and this seems to be the
    most difficult thing for the crusading mind to accept, poets who are sometimes one thing
    and sometimes a quite different thing, such as Howard Nemerov in America and Anthony
    Thwaite in UK. *(2014)*

5   *The Chicago Review* vol. 55 nos.3-4, 2010 and vol. 56 no.1, 2011.

6   By Rosmarie Waldrop reviewing Lisa Jarnot's anthology of 1998. See footnote 9.

7   See John Wilkinson's essay on her in his *The Lyric Touch* (2007) for an enthusiastic account.
    He is right to propose an "engaged and intellectually versatile public" as implied by Marjorie
    Welish's work, not forgetting that intellectual and intelligent are not exactly the same thing.

8   See *How New York Stole the Idea of Modern Art: abstract expressionism, freedom, and the
    Cold War* by Serge Guilbaut, translated by Arthur Goldhammer. University of Chicago Press
    1983., and my review of New York poets in *The Fortnightly Review.*

9   *An Anthology of New (American) Poetry* edited by Lisa Jarnot, Leonard Schwartz and Chris
    Stroffolino. New York: Talisman House 1998.

10 *Grasses Standing: selected poems.* Berkeley 2000. Mills died in 2007

ANTHONY BARNETT'S METICULOUS WORDING

Anthony Barnett, *Poems &*

Tears in the Fence in association with Allardyce Book

ABP, 2012.

672pp. £48.00

Anthony Barnett, *Translations.*

(same publishers) 2012. 352pp. £36.00

I once wrote an eight-page essay on a six-line early poem by Anthony Barnett.[1] I'm not going to repeat the exercise here, but I shall quote the poem in question:

With You

Loss.

Thank you,

Your absence. For your absence.

Thank you for your absence.

Word.

Of stone.

(p.66. of *Poems &*, originally in *Blood Flow*, 1975)

It is perhaps obvious that this poem is minimal but, if you start thinking about it, infinitely expandable, so that you could have a lot to say. Also that it is both abstract and narrative, that it suggests personal events which are censored out to leave an essential, dia-grammatic, sequence of the most telling or resonant terms. But we should also note that the condensation or stripping-down leaves room in the middle of the poem for a triple repetition, so perhaps "minimal" is not quite right. We might perceive (encouraged by the rest of the sequence) that the poet is protesting angrily at being left alone in some way, but we cannot fix that on the poem definitively because all circumstance is denied us, and the central sentence could be straight or ironic, and could be addressed to the poet rather than by him, or it could be "Loss" or "Word" which is thanked for its absence, ironically or not. When I wrote about this poem I talked about the phonetic structure, the formal drama which encloses the central outburst, the quest for emotional neutrality, the proliferation of meaning when words are viewed separately (e.g. "Word" meaning promise or troth), the suggestion of silent words which contribute to the process, and the constant halting, all directed to the paradoxical polarity of the poem – hints at urgently felt address as against the single noun with a full-stop after it which says only that it exists and ends the poem in complete stasis. I might have suggested that the entire course of the poem enacted a basic life pattern, that we begin in loss, go through ambiguous desires, and end with our names carved in stone, or I might not.

Blood Flow, a set of 26 short poems (including one which is absent) was the work which established the unique qualities of Anthony Barnett's poetry. Not all the poems are as tightly enigmatic as "With You" and the sense unfolding from the sequence becomes fairly clearly a drama of rejection, with or without rec-ompense within the narrative or outside it, though it remains always a reader's choice whether to settle for the anecdotal, and to do so risks losing the full sense of the verbal sequence. It would be better to say a drama of hurt, sometimes a drama of failure, sometimes a contemplation rather than a drama. There are some 20 more of these sequences or "clusters", of varying length, all now collected in this elegantly produced and monumental volume[2], almost always with suggestion of the same kind of drama having (probably) taken place, but with developing modes of representation towards the world.

Blood Flow established his poetry because the sequence made sense of the Modernistic, fragmented, writing he was already doing. The sense of occulted narrative made it possible for the small poems to echo and reverberate against each other within a conceptual theatre, and to offer the reader paths through the scattered instants. The first poem:

> *Woman Spoke*
>
> Very pure heart
> and maybe
> because —
>
> I have lost the courage
> or the ability
>
> give her ... keep that
> You
> who must be
> carefull.
>
> (the You is I)[3]

(p.49)

Nobody else writes like this, in English anyway. Whenever you quote a Barnett poem there is a temptation to launch immediately into a thorough explication because so many extrapolations are immediately evident. There are a thousand or more poems in this book and the reader has to be left to get on with it. I quoted this introductory poem to show how the last line may be taken as a reader's guide through the sequence to come, especially useful for *With You* which occurs 17 pages later, as well as standing for a standard feature of Barnett's style, the compounding of meaning into its opposite, leaving all the key words open to question (though less so in his later writings). But it's also worth pointing out that the mis-spelling of "careful" is deliberate, as is the minimal punctuation, and the majuscule on You. Then leaving the reader to get on with it. I'm sure the author would agree that it is a kind of game in which you are asked to participate.

The technique is a meticulously careful selection and outgrowth of words and phrases from a situation in his head which doesn't concern us. (Too many modern poets seem to think that everything about them concerns us considerably and must be expounded in full.) Every detail bears weight. The poem is to some extent conceived as a musical score in which line endings and spacing are integral, so that the text passes to the reader in a controlled order like the events of a piece of music (often, as in both poems quoted, with a crisis or conflict in the middle). But he also knows that language is not simply music but is capable of a quite different act, the access to truth, and it is not at all one of those texts which manipulates language experimentally for the sake of it. The relationships between the details of the poem have to be in some sense "true". Increasingly through his career in fact, there is worry about the possibility of extending into statement or declared cognizance of the world. So the words are set in their places one by one, always maintaining a tension, a question which must not be answered, about their relationship to experience. Authenticity is aimed at, relying on the fragmented nature of recall, both author's and reader's. One more poem from the same set, a calmer and more lyrical one, which resolves itself by image:

The City

I think of you
Kristiania, affectionately,
I must think of you

because
you become a woman

Kristin

and you are no longer
a finished name

in springiness
of a year's snow
a year's snow

(p.52)

(Kristiania is the old name of Oslo. The author lived there at the time of the events.)

So how does the snow at the end resolve what arises in the poem, about affection and incompletion? I can only suggest that it does so when the poem is envisaged as a story or scene, and this is the last, fading, frame, moving out of the poem's image-field without even a last full-stop to hinder it. So: the passage of time and recurrence (with a hint at Christmas?) and the poem simply stops because there is no more to be done, there is only "a year's snow" to be remembered, twice. And when is snow ever "springy"? I don't know. Perhaps in spring when it springs away. But "springy" means restoring itself to its original shape or condition (a hint of healing?). No possibility should be overlooked. "A year's *No*" is perfectly possible.

Not that the poet must have intended every multiple nuance you can derive from the text, in fact Barnett prefers the idea of a singular reading revealed primarily to the author, on which the reader eavesdrops. But he does think a great deal about the words in poems and translations, sometimes in terms which are not transferable, associations only knowable to himself. Since he places and separates the words so as to avoid or undermine a singular reading, it is to be expected that senses should proliferate beyond his control, but on the other hand poem and sequence both impose a strong sense of process, so that the reader's guesses are encouraged to contribute positively. I think this sense of process and thus purpose, open to the reader (as he says, quoting Celan, "Definitely not hermetic") but not tailored to that unknowable entity, is what distinguishes him from all the post-Modernist or etc., poets who deconstruct syntax negatively or randomly. There is a morality involved.

§

It has been suggested (by Michael Grant) that Barnett turns his back on England. This is undoubtedly true, in fact he says so in the interview, adding that Englishness "defines mediocrity" ("As things have stood"). I'm not concerned with the polemic here (and Barnett's opinions are usually categorical and, when negative, fierce[4]). I'm concerned to know the nature of the demand he makes of words, which does seem to be involved in foreignness and sometimes specifically Jewishness. I know that he has a personal pantheon of highly admired writers, whom he repeatedly praises, discusses and quotes, the older of which could have been formative. The poets in that category are linguistically unconventional (the principal figures are Celan, Zanzotto, Ungaretti, Sachs, Jabès, Mandelstam and Vallejo) and clearly the initial momentum was in that direction. In fact looking at the earliest work in *Poems &*, it is clear to me that he began in experimental poetry and was soon moved by the need to involve the intensity of his own feelings, to shift the experimental textuality into an expressive order.

There could be as many as fifty of these favourite authors, and the only English one I can think of is Charles Doughty (excluding Doughty's poetry), and the only ones who wrote in English Charles Olson and George Oppen (perhaps also Ginsberg). Near the end of *Poems &* is a collection of 23 commented citations, which must represent a lot of his recent reading, and not one of them was written in English. He did however valiantly publish the collected poems of four British poets in the 1980s at a time when nobody else would consider them. Jewishness is prominent in his pantheon, and these authors tend to have suffered in their lives. Probably the principal figure involved is Paul Celan. None of this is entirely exclusive, but again the options are categorical; these authors have "moral authority" and by implication those outside the pale might all be accused of "unimaginative lies".

What is the concept of truth here? It is that it is dependent on imagination, and even though many prose writers are favoured I think it is likely that the high distinction he claims for them concerns a particular language-use which achieves truth-value through meticulous accuracy and a foregrounding of language such that no term is taken for granted, but each has to be re-imagined by the writer, though it is also likely that personal issues are involved in his choices.

In his own poetry as initiated by *Blood Flow* the linguistic unit, word or phrase, is isolated. It connects only precariously or uncertainly to its neighbours, and because of this its semantic values proliferate; you are encouraged to entertain all the meanings and reverberations of meaning it could hold. In contrast to this terms are set in a sequence which suggests a narrative, that they are quoted from real events in the world, which restricts the spread of meaning to specific occasions. So there is a paradox, and the poetry is the exploration of the paradoxical way in which the particular relates to the abstract in language. Things said casually or in anger reverberate and become involved with important general terms and principles. The drama is thus enhanced but the paradox cannot be resolved. The ending of a sequence normally has a resigned tone, that in experience language fails to mend discord or heal wounds.

The mutual isolation of words to expand their signification brings him close to the methods of J.H.Prynne, but Prynne claims a scientific (e.g. etymological) publically verifiable philological process, whereas although he does use etymology Barnett's method is more in the order of "This made me think of...". And what it made him think of could be something that would not have occurred to anybody else (though I think he would deny this), so that he has to rely on his own emotive/expressive energy to integrate it into the poem.

To take an example which I find problematic – merely one word from the volume of mostly brilliant translations — he renders Ungaretti's well known mini-poem *Mattina* (M'illumino / d'immenso) as "I am blessed with light". This has always puzzled me. Apart from the complete absence of what is signalled by "immenso" I'm troubled by the intrusion of the implications of "blessed", of which he says, "...I must insist that there is no latent theology in my use of the word *blessed.*" (interview). This is justification by intent, and demonstrates that the writing remains primarily authorial, as he has declared that it should. On his advice "blessed" can indeed be read in a purer way, but the translation is sent out into a large world where the word "bless" normally carries a sense of theological endorsement in some way. Not everybody is authorised to bless, and the assumption to do so, as in the current mawkish col-loquial use of the single word in English, usually with a prefatory despairing "ah!", has a sense which is primarily passive: "May [x] be blessed" (by whatever has the right to). Barnett's justification is that he almost dreamt it – woke up one bright morning and said the sentence, only realising later that he had translated Ungaretti's poem.[5]

Such a process carried into original poetry will surely cause problems, but as I have indicated, there are forces of authentifica-tion which can solve the problems before they occur, though his greatest asset will be our willingness to read the poems as trans-figured accounts or stories, by which any unexpected intrusion can be taken as circumstantial. But where lies the "moral authority" of the poem?

I don't know. If I were to use the term myself of my own aspi-rations I would consider it to lie in the relationship of the text to realities of the perceived world and its contact with realisable prin-ciples. I can think of poets to whom it would mean something very different (e.g. the facility to scramble discourse into screaming gabble to the point of impossibility, so as to destroy Capitalism). Barnett as quoted is speaking of Nelly Sachs' poetry, that it is "not religious poetry", thereby invoking her Jewishness (a subject he rather strangely invokes when asked about his rejection of Eng-lishness) and I think he is implying poetry's power to connect to major moral issues through image and word order rather than dis-cursively, and possibly the authority which is gained by having suffered at the hands of the liars. The term is, anyway, sufficient indication of the seriousness with which he approaches his craft.

After *Blood Flow* the poems start to settle down.

> Snow falls everyday
> and does not fall.
> It is neither winter
> nor summer.
> I listen to your every sound.
> What I think is all right
> And what imperils me.
> There, a falling away.
> Surely, I am grown nearly,
> am answerable.

(p.97)

From *Fear and Misadventure* (1977), which is much more like a single poem in irregular stanzas then a sequence, though the individual pieces are indexed. Apart from having no titles they all seem to relate to the one scene and bear one mode of address, which is what Barnett's readers soon come to recognise as the usual story, of rejection. The above poem, which is not entirely typical, is close to a plain account, and openly goes through a series of contradictions until the final lines, with their uncertainty as to what is "falling away". But we should know by now not to ask that question: there is a falling away and that is what happens next, whether it is the snow, now falling elsewhere, or a wounding disaffection. Whatever it is it is what motivates the final double riposte — I am responsible / I could be answered – and the disturbed syntax and rhythm which introduces it. And as usual, if we wait, there are suggestive echoes elsewhere in the sequence – "How close is this wound, / that I thought would fall," (p.98)

Compared with *Blood Flow, Fear & Misadventure* is more willing to rest in a mildly broken but evident discourse which does not make stark bids towards abstraction. But wider reaches are hinted at throughout, becoming more prominent when the poems are considered individually. Here and in the longer *Mud Settles* (1977) the author's plea, to be taken in from the cold, is delicately modulated to suggest a public condition. In the latter book especially the constant reproving of "You" comes to intimate a mode of public address, and in the poem *After* (1979) it occasionally comes into the open: "On seven days / God is lies, also Marx, Freud, / and the Saints, smaller saint, who had half-eyes." But this declaration is still held within the fictive mode: it is integral to a plea, and a personal declaration of loss. It is encompassed by this, and cannot be argued in itself.

By the time of the next full-scale book, *Report to the Working Party. Asylum. Otiose.* (1979) it is possible to have poems such as

Committed

Flowers are blossoming

Birds are singing

Glass is lying on its side

(p.189)

Which once you have checked that you have not been tricked into reading "Grass" in the last line has only the title to disturb you, and possibly the absence of stops, making each little sentence seem preludial. Unless, that is, you are disturbed by the thought "So what?" which is an unfair question to ask of a poem obviously more interested in pondering than expounding; the question is already built into the text. (The title can only derive from the ensemble of the book, and possibly the line "Suddenly, the police" (p.179).)

Or indeed, a poem such as

Endangered Species

I have almost nothing to say.

(p.185)

...which speaks (or doesn't) for itself.

I think this book inaugurates one of Barnett's most fruitful periods. The poems are small, sometimes tiny, concentrated, variously enigmatic, and although the usual story seems to preside, sometimes starkly, there is a richer sense of the condition extending over a long period of time in which percepts deriving from many events, places and conversations are made into small poems, each encapsulating a contradiction or an enigma which is not always obviously related to the encrypted story. Some of them are simple perceptual and verbal notations. It is as if, this time, a large narrative, like a substantial novel, has been splintered into about a hundred pieces. His preference for simple vocabulary comes fully to the front here, sometimes so simple as to displace language entirely – one poem, called "Parting of the Ways", consists of two tiny drawings, of a spruce and a deciduous tree side by side (p.169).

Between the bigger books there are usually smaller items originally published as pamphlets which sometimes show him venturing into different textualities and, indeed experimenting, for in the present gap there are two collaged items, one from Doughty (though for some reason it doesn't say so, although page numbers of two editions of the *Travels* are given as titles.) and another from a technical book on forestry. These are perhaps bids to escape from the "story" which seems to hang over his writing. I have to bypass most of these pamphlets, but must note the wide choices now open to him in the contrasting nature of two sequences of 1978-9, *Blues That Must not Try to Imitate the Sky* and *Quiet Facts.* Not to exaggerate the difference, but the longer lines of the first are more evidently involved in an argument (or fight) with someone, close to invective at times, interspersed with descriptions (almost) of places, and culminating in a substantial poem. The second is one of his most delightfully tender sets of small poems, without arch concealments (except for one item which is a list of proper nouns), strong in what I like to call his "pastoral of sights and objects." No.19 reads "Gentle phases of the moon / and tides." which sweet as it is reverberates over the theme of the confrontation with the female which dominates so much of his writing, including the title of *Blood Flow.*

The title of his longest book of poems is also his longest title: *North North, I Said, No, Wait a Minute, South, Oh, I Don't Know (148 Political Poems)* (1985) which I shall abbreviate. I think that some of the Modernist cognoscenti at the time expressed doubts about this book, perhaps fearing that the writing was getting too relaxed, too little encrypted, too open to authorial attitude and opinion. They are short-line poems, mostly somewhat longer than usual, untitled but with the first word always a line to itself and indented, which I find has the effect of an opening hesitation or call to attention, like the held chord that initiates a dance number in many traditions. The writing is very much the mode he has established, rather less condensed and less lyrical, but the main innovation is that it is almost entirely in sentences, thus more explicit, both concerning the "usual story" and concerning the world at large, and with less "floating" terms introducing an incompletion or hiatus. But it is as rich as ever in the reverberation of displaced terms and in declarations necessarily clad in a deliberately "awkward" syntax, making questions out of them at the same time as statements.

I want to concentrate at this point on one stylistic feature which is not common in his writing but indicative. As the writing after *Blood Flow* became, gradually and with the utmost caution, more normalized or at least more willing to engage the reader recognisably, it also from time to time insisted on its distinctly authorial or even private condition by placing sudden blocks in what is now more like a flow: coinages, multiple puns, broken words, at which the process of assimilation inevitably halts. They are like reminders not to behave as if you're reading a newspaper. Some are quite simple doublings ("carefull", "nepotunity") but others are more formidable. In *North North* at p.350 is this poem:

> Let
>
> Inessentials pass. But
>
> if they are essential
>
> or essentials inessential
>
> give the devil
>
> his jew.

except that the last word is not "jew" at all because the W is clearly printed as an M upside-down (an effect more easily replicated in letterpress than on a computer). The poem itself, though rather bare, is typical of the talking mode of this book, but the last word stops all speech. Of course the reader's instinctive defence against this affront is to propose possible meanings which permit the reading to continue: "give me my due", "send me (the jew) to the devil" though I don't know what we do with the suggestion of "gem", and there are other possibilities. Does it help to go to the previous page and find "A // Walk though / the hills where / we is written / with a double / you." ? Perhaps. But I don't think this quest to exhaust the word is the whole answer. Somewhere

(I can't find it) he quotes from Anne-Marie Albiach, that a letter is detached from your name and you cease to exist, which shows the strong verbalism, and indeed mysticism (which I vaguely think is connected with Kabbalist practice) among these poets. So rather than a compaction of meanings perhaps we should think of the word as a spell? But my own preference is to see it precisely as a problem-word. The word "jew" is a problem to its bearer, both for obvious historical reasons and intimately as it intrudes on personal immediacies. Barnett is no Zionist, and from time to time has expressed ambivalence and worry about his Jewishness. He relishes but distrusts, I think, a Jewish intellectual inheritance, especially as it becomes enclosive. "I understand why Primo Levi rejected Celan's complexities. But I understand Celan too." (p.614). There are radical intellectuals who disdainfully dismiss Levi as simply "wrong" as against Celan. The racial concept halts Barnett's discourse at a mutilated word, as he perhaps both does and does not want it to belong there.

There are other halting words (I call them tics) especially in this central period of his work, most of which defeat me, perhaps because my mind doesn't operate in a way which could easily cope with them. I stare and stare at the line "like a staler." which ends a poem on p.91 and can only see the comparative adjective. It is a combination of the names Stalin and Hitler, too monstrous to be spoken in the poem. On p.123 "How you are an influ' / but for the good." The poem concerns crows and suggests "I altered it" for the sake of truth. Not influx, influence, nor influenza, bring me to this greater truth. In some parts of rural Ireland there is a term "flew-ins" for foreigners who have come to settle there. I'm sure the author will have a quite rational account, which might devolve mainly on particular circumstances. I think that things undisclosed to the reader are not infrequently used to arrive at a wording; he says that the word "estranged" in his poem on Celan (p.51) derived from the surname of Celan's wife, Giselle Celan-l'Estrange, to take a comparatively transparent example. We also might stumble over a word suddenly in Norwegian, obviously because that's where it happened and that was the actual word spoken at the time, or not a word at all, as there are occasional non-verbal items in the middle of (or constituting) a poem – a lop-sided cross in two strokes, an east-European diacritic in brackets without a letter to stand on... etc. Unless indicating problems which language as it stands cannot cope with, I think these are reminders, especially in a book like *North North* which ventures openly at times into the public sphere and indeed declares itself as "political" (which remains something of a mystery to me), of the essentially poetical /authorial texture which must be acknowledged by the reader.

§

If I move swiftly over the remainder of *Poems &*, it is not out of fatigue or impatience, but regard for the patience of my own readers. What happens in summary is that as the "usual story" recedes and fades away, the writing turns increasingly to prose. The last of the sets of small poems is *Little Stars and Straw Breasts* (1993) where the subsumed "story" seems to be less the anger and incomprehension of rejection, and more a rather melancholy sense of being left alone. As the pages turn and the prose increases it begins to feel like a writing project rather than a poetry project, at times like a commonplace book and at other times a collection of jottings. There is little that you would call prose-poetry and a lot which reads as casual, personal, satirical writing or various forms of self-address, still rich in word-play and with occasional tics. There is even a section of light verse and mockery concerning the town he lives in. But there are also substantial and sustained poems, most of them in *Carp and Rubato* (1995) but liable to spring up at any time. I am sometimes tempted to wish he would concentrate more on them, bright as much of the prose is. The work after 2000, especially *17 Poems of Defencelessness* and *Patricia of the Waters* (both 2011) seems to seek to unite the poetical and prosaic strands of his writing. They include some of the plainest of his writing but unpredictably various in its forms of utterance, with sudden darts shooting out into society which can be positively genial — "Everyone should know by now that the English millennium has two ns. It's taken a while." It's good to have writers around who will suddenly come out with things like this. (A quick look at Google suggests that the people who have not yet learned this are mainly in the catering and accomodation trades, and public transport.) But the general tone of the last writings in the book is retrospective and as he says—

Dishonest Poem

My memory is a slut.
I know exactly who I am.
Now that this is a closed book
I am calm.

(p.597)

§

Anthony Barnett's is a very distinct brand of poetry, only tenuously connected to the work of his contemporaries, and to very few of them. To him the works of British and American poets at large, especially those gaining big sales and official endorsement, are simply contemptible – "lies". They are lies because they are untrue to the nature of written language as a multiple instrument where sense includes silence and every item of meaning carries a load of echoes and exceptions, and they are untrue to their materials in experience and the world. We have to accept that there will be such distinct versions of poetry and that the written experience they offer will have particular validations quite distinct from those of other practitioners. We could also think (aside) that if you consider the subject or focus, rather than the manner, of the poetry, it all concerns contractual human relationships and their failures, as does the vast bulk of 16th Century British and European lyrical poetry.

The poetry is strongly centred on the self, and this whole enormous volume is in a way a monument to the self that created it. Everything arises from and returns to the self, the self is at the centre of all the action, and the language use is entirely the idiom of that self. It is not subjective: that is what is stripped away from the narrative to leave behind the pure condition of the self's engagement with language. And that actuality is surely what we learn from it, that difference.

If this seems harsh let me hurriedly add that I would say the same of Paul Celan without hesitation. His work too is a dem-onstration of language subjected to an intensity of self concern, every term broken open to find out why it did what it did to him. Everything unwinds from a deep sense of a damaged self and is likewise typically brief: smaller and smaller shards of glass in the poet's fist, clenched in an intensity of justification and helpless-ness. Barnett has pointed out that Celan had great knowledge of Jewish and German scriptural philology which must have enabled his particularly rich and potentially dignified coinage. Barnett's story is not of course that of Celan but wounding is at its centre most of the time.

The poetry resists the "big world" into which it is sent out, not only the big world of the poetry business. It views that world as decadent, or an illusion, and seeks to render it as an obedient thing in which the self's needs can be met – an earthly paradise. It hammers on the door of this place, it sings against the barrier to it. Celan too projected an unreachable verbal paradise as the echo of a mystic tongue. The writing is oppositional, in the guise of a self demanding it's due, but offers unsullied guarantees of earthly reality and a particular form of elegance in exchange – that is the contract with the reader. It can never be the only way. Explicitly expansive modes of poetry are needed if the art is to maintain a position in modernity, but the absence of exceptions such as Barnett's would be a very sad loss.

§

Translations assembles ten books or booklets, and some individual texts. Four of the authors of the longer works are French, the rest Japanese, Norwegian, Swedish and Italian. Only the Japanese acknowledges a co-translator, though numerous people are thanked for their help. The texts are hand-picked to facilitate Barnett's deployment of his way of writing. Appropriately, the French works were done mostly in the central period of Barnett's sequences, 1980s-90s; the Japanese, Akutagawa's *A Fool's Life*, in the recent prose-heavy period of his writing. But des Forêts' *Poems of Samuel Wood*, the most recent, shows how well he can cope with a poetical text which does not resemble anything he has ever written.

These are Barnett's heroes and exemplars, and the translating is done in a spirit of deep admiration in all cases, and with a sense of affinity in language-use. It must be this affinity, or his reliance on it, that applies when he quotes Yves Bonnefoy as saying that you cannot translate the poem, you can only translate the poetry. I don't suppose he would want to talk about the "spirit" of the poetry rather than the "letter", but that venerable concept is what it may come down to. It would mean, anyway, that he is free to depart from literal rendering when the poetical substance cannot be reached in that way, but in fact I think he does this very little. (It is difficult to check this because only two of the six French texts are available to me, or anyone in UK who hasn't already got them, by any means whatsoever. There are some notes at the back but they generally deal with the crimes of other translators rather than explanation of his own versions.) There is mostly no need to worry about it because the results read so well in English. And the characteristic stylistic features of two poets such as Anne-Marie Albiach and Louis-René des Forêts are clearly there in the English versions. It is not, on the whole, like reading Barnett originals, though his presence is always there. Tarjei Vesaas, Roger Giroux and Alain Delahaye seem to come off particularly well as thoughtful and imaginatively truthful writers, and Andrea Zanzotto gives many opportunities for Barnett's ingenious and imaginative workings of outlandish usage. It is interesting to have the two translations of Delahaye, who is a lost French poet, active around 1980 in Paris, but who shortly afterwards abandoned the writing of poetry and is now hardly known at all. Judging by the versions here he had a considerable talent. The Des Forêts text, a meditation on death in long periods, is full of close phonetic echoes which are dealt with admirably—

> Debarrasser, décrasser les coins et recoins
>
> Clear out, clean out the nooks and crannies...
>
> La façade en feu d'une forteresse qui s'effondre,
>
> The façade on fire of a fortress falling to ruin,...

and he evidently understands the principle of swings and roundabouts in translating poetry – that a strong poetical figuring may have to be lost at one point, but another can be added where the original does not demand it. The resulting poetical line in this version, by the way, strikes me as perfectly "British".

There are not only varying amounts of stylistic similarity between the translations and Barnett's writing in general, there are also blocks or tics, though very few. These may derive from the originals, and in the case of Anne-Marie Albiach, (a word with one letter italicised) it probably does. But in a poem by Roger Giroux "monstrueux" is translated as "terratoid". It gives him an alliteration, but is nevertheless very risqué. It took me ten minutes to find this word, which is in no standard dictionary and turns out to be a medical term used to identify a particularly nasty form of brain tumour in children. (I was not able to find out how the word was formed; if it starts with the Greek prefix tera- (marvel or monster, used to indicate very high numerical values) then I think it should have only one R.). A monstrous thing certainly, a slayer of children, but my complaint would not lie with the meanings, and he probably has other justifications up his sleeve, but that a common-or-garden word is translated into an extremely rare technical word, so that whatever else is translated, the word's status in the language isn't. It is bad of me to make a fuss over one word, but it is so very much a block on transmission. Barnett is anyway a lover of detail, in fact detail sometimes seems to take over everything, so he would probably enjoy the altercation.

1   Peter Riley, "'With You' by Anthony Barnett: Observations." *Grosseteste Review* XII, 1979. Reprinted with differences as: "The Kind of Poem that 'With You' Is", in *The Poetry of Anthony Barnett,* Allardyce Book 1993. All reference to comment by others on Barnett's work is to the essays and reviews in this volume, and all quotation of his own remarks is from the 1992 interview by D.S. Marriott in the same book, unless otherwise noted.

2   There is a selected poems available: *Miscanthus*: selected and new poems, edited by Xavier Kalck. Exeter: Shearsman Books 2005. 256pp £11.95

3   All poems quoted hors-texte are complete.

4   Apart from the interview, Barnett's opinions can be found in a recent series he calls "Antonyms", small reflective essays, seven of which are collected in *Antonyms & others* (2012) and which are contributed regularly to the periodical *Tears in the Fence.*

5   J.H.Prynne in discussing Wordsworth's 'Tintern Abbey', in his essay "Mental Ears and Poetic Work" (*Chicago Review* 55:1, 2010) magicks the word "blessing" by etymological scientism into an invocation of blood sacrifice which quite undermines the poem. This is very different from Barnett's process of intuitively sensing a verbal connection or the absence of one, but like Barnett Prynne is not too concerned about what is evident to the reader. Subconscious events are perhaps indicated in both cases.

WORKING CLASS POETRY

Jim Burns, *Laying Something Down: poems 1962-2007.*
Shoestring Press 2007. 156pp, £11.85
Jim Burns, *Streetsinger.*
Shoestring Press 2010. 46pp, £9.00
Barry Tebb, *Collected Poems.*
Sixties Press 2003. 274pp, £10.00
William Letford, *Bevel.*
Carcanet 2012. £9.95

In 2003/5 six large volumes of 18th and 19th Century "English Labouring Class Poetry" under the general editorship of John Goodridge were published.[1] With 129 poets in 2500 pages this is still only a small selection of what was published at the time in this category – a database held at Nottingham Trent University contains over 1400 names. "Labouring class" is not a very accurate term, for many of these poets were very far from labourers. They included mill operatives, domestic servants, hatters, carters, postmen, clerks, artisans of various kinds including a lot of hand-loom weavers, but the movement began with rural labourers and they remained at the centre of it for a long time. Whatever the poets were it was clear that they were of a low and poor class and more than likely that they had received no formal education. There were no fuzzy edges to the social divisions except those created by what little social mobility there was, and the fact that they were writing and publishing poetry at all was, at first at any rate, considered remarkable. The market thus formed fed on Enlightenment notions of natural genius reinforced by natural virtue in displays of sobriety and piety, as in the case of the once famous Stephen Duck (?1705-1756) an agricultural labourer who was briefly a rumoured candidate for the Laureateship. In many cases the motivation for gaining literacy and taking up poetry was one of social and financial self-betterment, which sometimes worked and sometimes didn't, and sometimes worked until the reading public lost interest. Many came to sad ends, especially when they had been raised into the status of author and then dropped, including of course John Clare, the best and to many the only known rural labourer poet.

For a long time the standard pattern was for the poet to be discovered by an upper- or middle-class person who became a kind of patron, and introduced the poet to polite society, or the edges of it, and the possibility of publication, which would be directed towards a readership among the urban educated (which did not mean London exclusively, as it later came to). But from the later 18th Century onwards "untaught" poets were beginning to show independence, addressing themselves to their own class and participating in radical movements, especially Chartism. There was an enormous increase in output after 1800, and an increasing participation of the urban poor which made the newly developed northern cities and mill towns, the "manufacturing districts", particularly rich in poets. By mid-century the working population in places like Manchester was, except for the poorest, not only literate but increasingly organised in various self-help institutions, not to mention choral societies and rambling clubs. There were poetry clubs in places like Blackburn which formed distinctive groupings (the "Blackburn school"). The original theme, of revealing to the better-off classes the hardships of labour, remained throughout, becoming increasingly politicised, but a lot of these poets were by the Victorian period addressing their fellows.

Brian Maidment, in a useful anthology of later poets[2] distinguishes three categories, though individual poets could easily belong to more than one of them. 1. Chartist or radical. Popular and accessible poems for the radical press, for chanting on marches etc., exhortations to fight for improvement and justice, but also an attempt to awaken the public as a whole to the problems of labour and the market. 2. Vernacular. Poems mostly in dialect, concerning the locality and for local consumption, many of serious purport but an inevitable habit of self-mockery or outright comedy marked the majority, and could make them popular wider afield. 3. "Parnassian". Poems in imitation of, or close to the manner of, the most admired poets among their contemporaries, especially Thompson, Goldsmith, Gray, Byron, Wordsworth and Shelley. This is probably the largest category. The poets here may be accused of betraying their class in adopting a "higher" manner, but they also served the dual purpose of bringing "polite" poetry within the grasp of their own native public by relating it to their own places and experience, and of showing that this kind of poetry was not a prerogative of the upper classes, but that the underlings were perfectly capable of grasping its technique and content, and employing it for their own purposes.

Some might find it painful to read this material now – it depends what you're looking for. There is a lot of educational and popular pressure on us to seek exceptionality in poetry, and if that is what you're after it will be hard work, though it is undoubtedly there. Only four poets have risen out of this industry to become currently canonic: Burns, Hogg, Clare and Chatterton, all of whom are probably usually thought of as isolated figures, but others, notably Ernest Jones, Joseph Skipsey, Samuel Bamford and Ebenezer Elliott are far from negligible whether recognised at large or not. But forget the quest for the exceptional, and I find there is no hardship involved in dealing with large quantities of this verse, without reading condescendingly or making allowances of any kind. Even in the mass of substantial poems in the Parnassian division, while derivative writing is common, some of it clumsy, and a lot of artificial structures are raised on commonplace thoughts, there is a sense of endeavour which is refreshing, a freedom from the hectic idealism on the one hand or sententiousness on the other, of the professional, and an unhurried pace in the careful cataloguing of scenic beauty or the narration of typically unjust or pathetic stories in uncluttered verse forms. The purpose is normally moral and humanitarian, in an obvious way, leaning into a melancholy concession that a just and equitable society is still far out of sight. And the craft is not negligible; the versification can be expertly efficient even in the most ambitious forms, such as hexameter couplets or sonnet-stanzas, sometimes developed into monumental book-length poems, of which the most renowned is *The Purgatory of Suicides* (1845) by Thomas Cooper, chartist, shoemaker and schoolmaster of Leicester; a series of dialogues with past suicides interspersed with exhortations to the working people in 955 Spenserian stanzas, written during his imprisonment for radical activities. But from here to the simple narratives in couplets, bathetic dialect verses, homely rhymes, Chartist hymns and adapted folk songs, there is a sense of venture, however faltering, into a new entitlement.

§

What happened next? The only literature explicitly marketed as "working class" in the earlier 20th Century that I can recall was in prose: Robert Tressell, a bunch of novels from the Midlands in the 1930s, autobiographical writing from the East End of London in the 1940s... In all of these the writer's origins are offered as a guarantee of authenticity. But as for poetry, from the 1890s onward the impression is that the upper classes have regained complete control, and the 20th Century development into Modernism made no difference to that. The surviving recordings of poets' voices from the first half of the century are almost all in a heavily diphthong-laden upper class accent of a kind now spoken only by The Queen. So it was with the voices of BBC announcers – Orwell pointed out that their accents made them unintelligible to the bulk of the population. But this accent too is masked by the writing hand. Poetry in this period gives the impression that education has erased all class and regional distinctions and that the written and spoken voices have become two entirely distinct things. We would hardly know where Lawrence came from if we only had his poetry, and this is true too of W.H. Davies to a lesser degree[3]. And yet the poor, the workers, the labourers, the dialect speakers, were still there, in large quantities, and are still there now.

In the Introduction to the anthology *Cusp*[4] which she edited, Geraldine Monk says, "The poetical insurgence that began in the 1950s/60s was very much a provincial one emanating from the industrial cities of the north and Midlands." I can't agree with this; I think it happened everywhere, certainly in London, and if rather late in Cambridge later still or never in Oxford, which is to be expected of university towns. What happened was not so much an insurgence as an outbreak. Very quickly, following the silence of the mid-1950s and increasingly through the 1970s-80s it became difficult to find a small town anywhere in the country which didn't have a poetry outlet of some kind, usually a mimeograph machine. It became possible to speak again of "the Blackburn poets". Easy and cheap forms of communication, materials, printing and distribution seemed to make it possible for "everyone" to be a published poet. But the main emphasis of this thrust was on the innovative, embracing every experimental or unorthodox trend that could be found, whether picked up from elsewhere or coined fresh at home, including a lot of American-influenced "beatnik" writing. The word "breakthrough" was used a lot, though what was broken through to remained miscellaneous. "Established" poetry was scorned, often as an automatic impulse without consideration of the poetry itself. Being published by Faber and Faber was enough to damn you and in some quarters still is, including sophisticated academic poetry enclaves. The whole thing was part of the large movement of alienation which gripped British youth at the time, and on the political front led to things like The Angry Brigade.

But, *What about the workers?* In spite of all the breaking through and opening up, they remained obscure. The alienist polemics sometimes attacked "the rich" and adopted leftist and anarchist attitudes, but it was nothing like a workers' movement. Any address to, vaunting or depiction of, the workers' conditions was rare and various kinds of inherited artistic elitism flourished between the staples. As in the previous fifty years there was nothing in most of the actual poems to suggest the author's class status. One of the principal reasons for this was the migration at this time of large numbers of young people into the countryside, especially to the hills of northern England and the south-west, buying cottages for a couple of hundred pounds and living there, many of them, on their wits. In this so-called "hippie invasion" the strata and traditions of society were thoroughly jumbled: people of upper middle-class origin were living in penury or working at menial jobs in mill towns. Meanwhile a poet from a small-town working class family and speaking with a West Yorkshire accent published his first book with Faber in 1957 and was to go on to become the Poet Laureate. The topographical appeal of much of Ted Hughes' work was the same as that which drew all the cottage revolutionaries to the moorlands, or the sense of place they developed once there (especially, of course, *Remains of Elmet* of 1979). But his focus was non-metropolitan, it was a farmer's engagement with earth and beast while the past (i.e. the Lancashire textile industry) fell apart all round him, and Hughes later drifted away into all sorts of strange and macabre imaginings. But some of the poets taking part in the small-press explosion were and remained concerned to demonstrate the realities of working class life in their work, and this included, in different ways, Jim Burns and Barry Tebb, though neither they nor any living poet discussed here has to my knowledge ever declared himself to be such a thing as a "working class poet".

§

Jim Burns' blurb-writers certainly see him in this light. "He writes about life as ordinary people experience it." (Matt Simpson). "Burns celebrates the North, the Unions and the less privileged of the Two Nations" (Peter Porter). But Jeff Nuttall gets it right: "...a poet whose laconic style sprang from his love of a certain American mode." This refers to the American side of the new poetry "insurgence" of the 1960s, and especially the "beat" poets. Burns is an expert on the seamier side of American poetry and has written a lot of literary journalism about American "beats", and other poets, especially the neglected and forgotten, for he takes the position of underdog as a sign of promise. With 1940s jazz added, I'd say that his attention prior to his own generation is almost exclusively American and he has been heard to utter the old American put-down: "Most English poets are social beings caught in the web of their habits." Since both sociality and the habit-bound routines of provincial life, including his own, are prominent features of his work there is some kind of contradiction here. The freedom he found in American poetry doesn't seem to be reflected in his home town of Preston, Lancashire.

Burns' position is defined not by his subject matter, which is quite varied, but by his language. His form of rebellion against established or bourgeois poetry was to reduce his language to the plainest possible, shorn not only of poetical forms but also of any kind of figurative decor, in fact any signs of poetry whatsoever. A first line like "I am standing in line at the employment exchange" is entirely typical, but not because of the picture it gives, for we could find ourselves as easily in New York ("I am sitting in the Café le Rouquet...") or Paris, London, Venice, and various other places which he may or may not ever have been to, for the speaker is not necessarily himself. In one poem he slips silently into the persona of the French surrealist poet Benjamin Péret. For while the majority of the poems appear to be local and anecdotal, it is really only the language-use which carries his attitude, which is a defiant, even puritanical (or Spartan as in "laconic") rejection of everything poetical in substance or manner. This causes problems. I remember a reading he gave in Stoke-on-Tent once, which ended with what seemed a fine piece of realist writing which I can't now identify but I remember it as having a compassionate ending. But afterwards I had to ask myself why it was a poem, since there was nothing to signal to the listeners that that was what we were hearing. On the page, apart from occasional rhyming in very short poems, there is only the lineation to make this distinction, which he is expert enough at, but does little more than keep the language flowing in conversational rhythm. In 1967 Grosseteste Press published a collection of what he called prose pieces (rather than prose poems) called *Cells*, which to me is among his best work, partly because the question about what constitutes a poem doesn't arise. But it is not included in the collection and not listed among his books. The imprint indicates, though, how seriously he was taken in the early days by the Cambridge Americanizing avant-garde, especially Andrew Crozier, part of whose quest was for the elimination of poeticisms. I believe he is a popular performer of his poetry and I can see most of his poems going down very well in that situation, for they are mostly succinct commented anecdotes with an ironic flavour which is clinched in a paradoxical ending. The realism is rarely without humour, mocking himself or society or people at large.

But this realism, insofar as it involves showing the world what it is like where he comes from and in his experience, places a heavy emphasis on forms of dereliction and social deprivation, very far from any of the joys of life, and the plain language easily becomes brutal. His discourse quite relishes banality, commonplace sentiments, cliché, cynicism, deadpan emptiness. There is nothing you could call political to offer hope of redemption from a basically depressing picture, in the complete absence of thought about causes. The workers he speaks to (normally unemployed) live a cultureless existence. Love is a matter of furtive extra-marital affairs. Academics, artists and Marxists are dismissed offhand as bourgeois interlopers. All this increases as the years pass, but the author always seems to be somewhat distanced from it all – it is not quite now, you feel it is deliberately put on, and increasingly it is a fairly aggressive gesture towards a genteel world which is not identified.

Street Scene

Two women fighting in the street,
rolling around, skirts high on legs,
and watching them a crowd of men,
making jokes and urging them on.

You can sense the tension in the air,
And guess what the men want to do
with the women when they've finished
clawing at each other. It isn't nice.

No, it isn't at all nice. Did we need to be told that? And what are we meant to learn from the whole thing? That this is what it's like out in the working-class wilderness? If so I don't believe it. Does he imagine that things like this don't take place in middle-class circles? He should live among Cambridge ex-public school boys. But it is obvious what it's for — it's a recent poem and the

American influence seems to have shifted from "beat" or Gins-bergian to Charles Bukowski, and it is a flexing of muscle. As in Bukowski the deadpan reporting displays the poet's own tough-mindedness, and there is almost a didactic purpose in pushing the reader's face into this sort of thing. Quite a lot of the later poems behave like this and unfold less violent but equally depressing scenes of urban hopelessness, most of which feel manufactured to me rather than experienced. In this he sometimes feels quite close to Larkin but less meditative, even if he does say in a more up-beat poem about his parents,

> Still, drunk or sober,
>
> I never disliked my father,
>
> and always thought that the poet
>
> who said that your parents
>
> make a mess of you
>
> was talking poet's nonsense.

It's rather pleasing that he didn't go chasing the reference and getting the quotation right, in fact his version show him modestly avoiding an in-your-face verbal vulgarity which Larkin indulged at his worst.

Generally his long poems are more interesting, if with a tendency to careless endings. Scenes and accounts are allowed to unfold unhindered and a complete picture becomes possible. But I quote a short early poem to show how he can be calm and reticent to a purpose, and with features of lineation, rhythm, and sound that clearly qualify it as a poem.

A Way of Looking at Things

> My son can see a man's face
>
> in the remains of the chicken!

Figures appear on the walls,
and (strange this) there are
cities in the fire.
Last night I saw him looking
at me. No laughter on his face.
No word spoken. Just a long
thoughtful look that I
pretended not to notice.

Whatever they have in common environmentally and however they may share a wish to demonstrate working class realities to the world, Barry Tebb is a complete contrary to Jim Burns. Reading them side-by-side makes you realise things about Burns which are not obvious on the face of it – that he is really a refined poet, a strict stylist, that the close-to-minimal language is not documentary but programmatic, that we can never with complete confidence identify the "I" as the author, in fact that the poems are spoken by some kind of ventriloquial demotic spirit who does not want to depict anything, but to cast fragments of a lost and perhaps fictive world in front of us, spells to banish delight in anything but the text, its detached and cynical obduracy.

§

Tebb is above all congenial and expansive. The poems are rough-hewn, profligate, but intense and entirely first-person, in fact the *Collected Poems* is a running disoriented autobiography – it is his voice, his life, his opinions, his perceptions, his laments from beginning to end. Not that it is unsophisticated – he displays a wide acquaintance with modern poetry including French, and is obviously well read in many departments. It is a product of the sixties, not in the sense of bohemian experimentation, but in a sense of poetry as *poetic* at every move, and an authentic authorial voice is liberated into a free-running discourse ranging from lyrical ecstasies to angry tirades.

Like the work of many poets of his generation there is a presiding melancholy, which in his case is attached to his despair at the destruction of his environment, the streets of working class Leeds where he was brought up, though he declares himself never to have been really working class because the family had no roots there. Poems with this tone are interspersed variously among other occasional and lyrical poems, including far too many complaints about the power structures of the poetry scene (but some sharp and entertaining encounters with local officials – apparently he was known to the local poetry-promoting staff as "the dreaded Tebb"), but it dominates what I think is his principal achievement, *Bridge over the Aire*, a poem in six books, each book a sequence of short poems of very varied import, which occupies the last eighty pages of the book.

This is principally a lament for a lost childhood sweetheart with a constant re-visiting of former haunts, both urban Leeds and the stone cottage up on the moors, always with a sense both of personal failure and submission to a destructive policy of development. But what makes it engaging (and so different from what Jim Burns might have done with a long poem, not that his aesthetic would have permitted such expansiveness) is that there is no sense of narrative relevance in operation. These mostly short and short-line poems may depart into almost anything, it seems, but without losing sight of the accumulating purpose. This freedom allows him to spread, rather than follow, his narrative, and to include all sorts of frivolous moments, childhood erotica, detached descriptions of places, as well as some items which seem to have no bearing on the main issue. The personal narration expands effortlessly into something wider as it progresses. One moment leisurely nostalgic glimpses —

Middleton Woods took me by surprise
Drying the tears of my eyes one Saturday
In late August, in fields of carnations
Below the faience tiles of Kirkgate Market
Dahlias and chrysanthemums, pink and maroon,
The lemon yellow sheen of the sun.

(IV/18)

Next a seeming irrelevance—

John Dion, I prefer
Wordsworth's daffodils
To your's, they are
More rare and far
Less dear.

(IV/20)

and suddenly a kind of poetical credo—

I want a poetry
Bitten back from the tongue
Or spat like phlegm
Into the fire back
In a language that has
Metamorphosed through
Centuries of speech Burned into a tree
Bark and exposed to
Weathering like stones
In hillside farms.

(IV/28)

and back to Leeds in a little outburst of ancestral tropes—

> By the Hilton Hotel
> I sat down and wept:
> They were burning the sleepers
> Under the rusting crane
> Making a pyre so hot and red
> I thought the very air had bled
> (IV/35)

Bridge over the Aire stands comparison with Barry Mac-Sweeney's *Pearl* as a poem of lost hope focused on a childhood affection. It has less sense of a demonic force tamed by fondness, less desperation, but gains a kindred sense of redemptive memory.

The poetry world has not treated Barry Tebb kindly. He is still his own publisher, calling his press The Sixties Press "in disgust at the state of poetry publishing in England" and the book shows its amateur provenance in such things as an almost complete absence of page design — all text just runs on until it reaches the bottom of the page, and the very long sequence at the end doesn't even get to start on a new page — and a liberal scattering of misprints such that at times you feel you can't trust the text.[5] But as a "neglected poet" he is in good company in 20th Century British poetry.

Neither of these poets matches well with the categories of labouring class poetry in earlier centuries. I suppose both could be "Parnassian" in writing from down-under in contrary versions of late Romanticism. But there is no sense of a working class being addressed, or even existing – they both stand as individuals. Burns sends us snapshots of mostly dismal environments and life styles which seem things of the past if they were ever real, and don't add up to a whole; they remain fragments like shards of prehistoric urns, valued for their sharp edges. Without saying so Tebb laments what has been called the "emptying of the north", the drainage of cultural value to the south-east as a result of social mobility and laissez-faire economics (a lot of institutional reparation for this has taken place in the last twenty years, some of it far too late) but centred on the self, with no sense that he speaks for or from a kindred body of any kind.

§

When the Scottish poet William Letford comes along the categories seem to revive but then crumble to dust. *Bevel* is his first book and he is by profession a roofer, a fact which is made much of in the publicity for the book and his successful reading tours. He writes directly of this and other facets of a working environment, and some of the poems are in what I take to be a Glaswegian dialect, so he should be "vernacular". But it becomes complicated when he is a roofer with a M. Litt in Creative Writing from the University of Glasgow, recently back from a residency in an Italian village, poems from which are included in the book.

Letford does not lament anything, beyond the kinds of misfortune a young man is apparently liable to in a place like Glasgow (being head-butted etc.). There is none of the bitterness and regret which in different ways haunt Burns' and Tebb's poetry, there is no sense of belonging to an oppressed or disregarded category of humanity. In fact there is quite often a sense that he's enjoying himself and this includes the way he evidently takes delight in handling language, not as an elevated poetical idiom, for the terms are mostly quite plain and the substance mundane, but distributed on the page in a variety of different ways with a sense of game-playing. Most are short and carefully crafted pieces without punctuation so that the words shape the syntax themselves.:

We are

inside the kick

and crunch of colour

where autumn's taken its

dagger and opened up a vein

so the pavements aren't so grey

our heartbeats are not so

bleak and this kiss holds

more than warmth

and blood

The metaphors are strangely violent but strangely unthreaten-
ing, and here as in a number of other poems he shows a determination to push the sequence of thought and image beyond the
obvious or mundane requirements of the scene (I refer to the last
line). Possibly a metaphysical streak occasionally suggests itself.
His repertoire of informal patternings seems determined by the
ambience of each piece rather than imitative experiments (though
the name of Edwin Morgan occurs to me as a possible precursor).
Sometimes the lay-out is bizarre. This poem—

coffee-shop window

only children brave enough

to return my stare

is a perfectly measured haiku in exactly the haiku manner of
so many modern orientalising poets, though why each of the three
lines has to be printed alone in the middle of a page I don't know.
Some pieces are not much more than novelty items, or bits of
whimsy, but we are again and again brought up against a stroke
of sharp observation which is actually a verbal skill, an ability to
carry the reticent, detailing lines to the heart of the matter by the
right and often unexpected image which clinches it.

Winter in the world
The old lady struggles, footsteps careful, leaving
shuffle marks in the snow. No shopping bag, so
maybe it's church, or maybe not. Perhaps she is
out for a walk
because she can, and the night is spare, and she is
undiminished and harder than bone.

You can't call this "slight" just because it stays with the particular and offers no political or philosophical gestures, nothing shouted from the hilltop. The terms "because she can", "undiminished", "harder than bone" carry implications and, the last in particular, an irony which doesn't diminish the subject. It could not be true to say that in these poems, which are almost entirely restricted to particulars, there is no culture, and no history. Centuries of developing poetical language lie behind them, and the whole story of the entitlement of the workers to subtle and sophisticated poetry.

There is no focus on the workers as a class at all, but there is on *working,* and a certain defiance in the freedom with which he disposes his poems as suits him or as he finds the world, reminds me sometimes of the defiance with which Clare pursued the particulars that interested him rather than agree to the more 'philosophicall' writing that his patrons would have preferred.

§

There are plenty more poets who could be enrolled as working class heroes if we don't look too closely, both avant-gardist and mainstream (as it gets called). There are poets from the north-east, Tom Pickard and the late Barry MacSweeney, with their culturally aggressive stance (though the latter's working class credentials are doubtful) and the aggressive but populist Tony Harrison from Leeds. There's Michael Haslam, who forsook the middle-class and his Cambridge education to live in west Yorkshire on the edge of the moors, almost in the footsteps of Ted Hughes, has worked as a roofer and many similar jobs, and writes a densely sound-conscious personal poetry in quite Shakespearean rhythms. And of course the likes of Simon Armitage, who has gained immense success by trading in northern laddish energy and reductions of literary classics to low-grade understanding. In all these the "class" element is largely irrelevant or fake.

The quest ends inconclusively. But anyone who thinks that all these problems, depictions, complaints or particularities concerning the working class and its poetry have outlived their validity and that the category no longer obtains, could do two or three thing. Firstly, get a job as a roofer (Letford gives good advice on how to cope with this – "know which way to fall"). Or visit any of the depressed and poverty-stricken areas of Britain. There is plenty of choice. The former coal towns of the valleys north of Cardiff would do well. Just stand there and look around you, or try to buy something other than a packet of cigarettes or some low quality comestible. Or stay at home and note the tone of comments from our metropolitan authorities, such as James Campbell of *The Times Literary Supplement,* in the middle of a recent account of one of Jim Burns' books: "Mr Burns, who lives in the unlikely setting of Cheadle, Cheshire..." Cheadle is a commuting suburb south of Manchester, a large spread of fairly uniform house rows, which perhaps still has daily morning and evening interminable traffic jams on the Manchester road known locally as "the Cheadle crawl". How could a *poet* possibly bear to live in such a place?! Blatant snobbery from the south-east is far from extinct.

---

1   *Eighteenth Century English Labouring Class Poets 1700-1800* general editor John Goodridge. Three volumes, Pickering and Chatto 2003. *Nineteenth Century English Labouring Class Poets 1800-1900.* Three volumes [same editor and publisher] 2006. See also *British Labouring Class Nature Poetry 1739-1837* by Bridget Keenan, Palgrave MacMillan 2008.

2   Brian Maidment (editor) *The Poorhouse Fugitives: Self-taught poets and poetry in Victorian Britain.* Carcanet 1987.

3   Davies' success was as part of the vogue for tramp writers (or writers who claimed to be tramps or became tramps for the purposes of writing a book) in the early years of the century, which was itself part of a vogue for countryside writing, serving a readership to which anything beyond the city walls was obviously a mystery. Most of this was in prose and W.H. Hudson is the acknowledged master of it. *(2014)*

4   Shearsman Books 2012. *Cusp* is a collection of statements by poets mostly from the north of England, including me, on how they first became involved in poetry and were liberated by innovation. It is issued as a challenge to the hegemony of London and Cambridge in the advancement of new poetry mid-Century.

5   In the poem "I want a poetry…" above, probably "Burned into tree" should occupy a separate line, since it is not Tebb's habit to introduce upper-case initials for common nouns mid-line, but it is printed as shown here.

THE YOUTH TACTIC

Dear World and Everyone In It.
New poetry in the UK, Edited by Nathan Hamilton.
Bloodaxe Books 2013. 336pp, £12.00
The Arcadia Project.
North American Postmodern Pastoral, edited by Joshua
Corey and G.C. Waldrep. Ahsahta Press (Boise, Idaho)
2012. 574pp.

§

Dear Nathan Hamilton, You do know don't you, that the tactic of announcing a new, fresh, lively, optimistic, young poetry which will replace a stale, gloomy, heavy, old poetry, is as old as poetry itself? Of course you do.[1]

§

Not then "new" meaning recent, but a new *kind* of poetry is proposed, and it is proposed as a *hybridisation* of two opposed and extremist modes of poetry writing. And yet there are lines like

> In Wallace Stevens' poem 'The Public Square'
> a languid janitor bears his lantern through col-
> onnades and the architecture swoons. I cannot

read this poem without being struck down with

vertigo...[2]   (Oli Hazzard)

and there are lines like

all forgetting hemp day, you must hocus-pocus with fenugreek

all holding all butt holes open with your hand, f*ck doggy for

you allgot to get f*cked in curry...   (Jo Crot)

than which it is difficult to imagine any more extreme or opposed ways of writing. So clearly something in the rationale is skewed.

This contrast is evident in a lot of the poems in the book; they conform one way or the other rather than agree to the editor's hope for a unified new poetry. On one side unproblematic deployment of explanatory, chatty or story-telling language retailing anecdotes of the self or symbolic narratives, on the other disrupted syntax, impossible leaps, ill-fitting words thrust together. On one side a deliberated placing of counters, on the other mimicry of uncontrolled mania. On one side a plain often child-like vocabulary held close to a conceived subject, on the other a barrage of obscenities, remote technical and academic terms and names, and interventions designed to destroy any subject-matter. Where then is the hybrid centre? Sometimes these contrasted modes seem to be straining to meet each other, which insofar as it happens is the point of the anthology, but the stubborn oppositions remain more evident to me. Could it be that the centre is in fact not hybrid, that poetry is not best defined from its outer limbs?

§

Don't be misled by the sentimental title. There are some very fierce poets in this book.

§

The "youth" tactic is a clearing of space. It always has been. It's a binning of senior and threatening poets and editors in order to create a vacant space where youth can mount the stage and claim its audience. The platform on which it is done is perhaps invariably one of the ability to comprehend and cope with a changed world. I remember doing it myself in the 1960s. We binned people like Ted Hughes and Dylan Thomas and claimed a new dispensation. Some 70-year-old poets are still doing it, to their everlasting shame.

§

Dear Mr Hamilton, If I were you I wouldn't have mentioned so many prizes in the biographical notes. They are still not generally trusted in this country, and their proliferation might seem to undermine the anthology's claim to youthful independence of movement. Many of the judges of those prizes are among the "old editors" you attack in your Introduction. Perhaps particularly the Eric Gregory Award... But more of this later.

§

In the month before the publication of this book I received two or three e-mails most days "inviting" me to the launch in the Royal Festival Hall, London. This building has a capacity of 2,500. Once again the celebration of the poetry is rather more noticeable than the poetry itself.

§

Dear Mr Milton, For all the talk of youth and political opposition, among these 74 poets there are by my reckoning:[3] two Asian, one Caribbean, five Irish, one Welsh, one possibly African (and for some reason four or five Americans). So, as often in recent anthologies, the gender proportion seems to be the only one you need to worry about, the only one where you need to protect yourself against campaigns of vituperation. But perhaps this disproportion is not very surprising. Perhaps poets from places like

Jamaica have no need of distrust of language, nor of faux-naïf posturing, in order to locate a style, but inherit a tradition of centrality in connection with an audience. I.e., they are used to people listening, perhaps people whose minds are open to what we used to call "imagination".

§

Whatever common ground can be claimed among these young poets there is no doubt that they are stretched between two opposed positions which will never see eye to eye. These, the polarities of the ensemble, are conveniently identified as ex-Cambridge poets, and what I call the "Gregory Trail", with a number of volunteers from elsewhere in each camp. The contrasting versions of what poetry is, its purpose and its nature, are severe, and the whole anthology partakes of it in various degrees of strength or dilution. The oppositions outlined in my second paragraph are basically those of these two camps.

Those who have passed through the poet processing plant at the University of Cambridge generally come out angry and riddled with beliefs about language which, at the extreme, abhor meaning as such and place all the power of poetry, a world-saving power, in word-by-word problematisation, an occulted guerilla campaign to displace and corrode the language of the enemy. The enemy is the world we live and communicate in from day to day. This is a crude summary, but the useful thing for this anthology is that this tradition now seems to produce two contrasting strands which are considered complementary. I think it would be perfectly legitimate to call them "masculine" and "feminine" in the familiar literary senses which have nothing to do with gender, but for the sake of safety I'll call them "hard" and "soft" (not that that will get me out of trouble). It is of course the hard strand which hurls obscenity and scatology at us and lectures us on the betrayal of the revolution and rejoices in its own paranoia, ably represented by Joe Crot (who is a committee) and Keston Sutherland, who contributes a13-page prose rant which feels rather antiquated (full of highly symbolised entities) and which at the end seems to crumble back into the remnants of a lyrical poem. The "soft" strand is inclined to be more intimate and particular, more reflective and considerate, or simply quieter, in short lines with each word carefully weighed, while the poets remain fighters. Women poets do seem to be more attracted to this mode, thus giving us the thoughtful and disturbed meditations of Emily Critchley and Amy de 'Ath. But I'd put Michael Kindellan in this division and Marianne Morris mostly in the hard-line party.

Semi-detached from Cambridge is a grouping recognisably "London" which is influenced by all the promotional teaching of experimental poetry which goes on there in three of the colleges, stemming from the legacy of Professor Eric Mottram, which has encouraged all and any forms of unorthodoxy, from a purple letter upside down in the middle of the page, to hopping up and down making strange noises. We do not get either of those here, but experiments with typography, visual word-patterns on the page, performative tactics, broken words etc. show the connection.

But if we recognise "softening" tendencies among these (and other) avant-gardists, this only superficially aids the hybridisation theory, partly because the "softened" poems retain a great deal of the edge-sharpness of the Cambridge connection, partly because the prize-winning alternatives are mostly so dull and superficial.

§

The Eric Gregory award, which was instigated in 1960, has always been a kind of stamp of approval from the establishment on young poets. I call it a trail because it generally starts from a magazine which carries some prestige, goes into the award, and, for some, on to greater things, such as Faber and Faber and/or top prestige in general. It is a career boost. None of the poets I would designate "Cambridge" or "London" has won it, nor any other prize, with one exception. But no less than 18 of the poets in the anthology have won the Gregory prize, which is really a very high proportion, and their number is swollen by poets who conform to its expectations but somehow failed to get the trophy. However well-meaning, an anthology like this cannot gloss over these differences in the way poets are treated and encouraged to align themselves, or the nature of the career envisaged. I should add that the Cambridge/London axis generally does very well for academic appointments, which some might think of as potentially damaging to the poetry as anything else.

I think the Gregory Trail is the principal weakness of this anthology, one which it was lumbered with from the start by its connection with *Rialto* poetry magazine, which conspicuously feeds poets into this prize. It encourages a poised, theatrical, self-conscious poetical performance, a posing before the reader. Clever metaphors, ungrounded pseudo-allegory, little suburban scenes gone awry, easy irony, obliquely deflected chat, often in a tone and vocabulary suitable for addressing an infant class. Any cultural critique there might be tends to be rather coyly wrapped in a sense of careless chat or fabricated figuration; there is little real anger or concern, though there is sometimes a sense of helplessness. The editorial weakness, I think, is in not recognising how so many of these poets teeter on the edge of conservatism, and how similar, or identical, a lot of their writing can get to the stuffy old poets they are supposed to be displacing. Or how the society in which the poems belong is no healthier just because it is full of bright young things. Not that there is complete uniformity, and some of them certainly distinguish themselves in various ways. The sardonic wit and craft of someone like Sam Riviere, who is well advanced on the Gregorian pilgrimage, cannot be denied; indeed within the terms he sets himself he is exemplary, and there are others, including the ones I failed to notice.

§

If there are conflicts between old and new poetry, as people insist there are, that is because poetry has become such a competitive activity, where, as in the visual arts, the question of what is good is inextricably tangled in the question of what is advanced. I take this to be something inherited from the late 19th Century. At the same time the poets gaining most institutional reward for their work are mainly valued because they are not too advanced —just a flurry of it, new but not disturbing, politically correct without getting too excited.

§

Dear Nathan, I'm glad you say that this is not an anthology of the "best" young poets (a word which in poetry publicity has become a meaningless slogan, along with "leading"). You're right to say that it is impossible to edit a representative anthology of young poets in UK and that it is impossible to be impartial. Likewise it is impossible to review 74 of these poets, many of them writing in manners alien to me and to one another. How should I know which to nominate other than by the insignificant process of what appeals to me immediately? What I mainly see is allegiances and tendencies, and what I can say is, "I wish they wouldn't go in that direction" or "I wish they'd escape from those conventions", which is what I do say about both of the outermost warring camps here represented. For I do think for instance, that the best of the "Cambridge" phalanx are those who withdraw themselves to a greater or lesser extent from the group aesthetic, which is mainly a matter of establishing some kind of calm which will open vision beyond the confines of the evangelical channel. Similarly perhaps those within the Gregory fold who are willing to dwell more on single words.

§

In fact I think that there does seem to be a new, characteristically youthful mode captured by this anthology among a number of its poets, which shows a willingness to engage with unorthodox procedures, a contemporary poetry not necessarily with any sense of inheritance from the old avant-garde but probable respectful towards it. The young avant-garde represented here is only one corner of it, nearly all from the south-east. In fact there is an anti-northern bias in the whole anthology. But I refuse to believe that the liberal distribution of unendorsed texts on the Web has been responsible for a spread of unorthodox modes as against the control exercised by "old editors" on printed distribution, as the Introduction proposes. This ignores all the small-press activity of the last fifty years, of which there has been a great deal more than the ancestors of "ex-Cambridge". .

What presides over the greater part of the anthology is the preponderance of a clever and zany prosaic patter, obliquely twisting ordinary percepts this way and that, as an exercise in its own right. Perkiness. Finding ways of not quite making sense. Messing around with the superficies of language. Perfectly ordinary discourses with little arresting features attached such as inappropriate diacritics, or unnecessary foreign words. Name-dropping or collage from cultural history. But none of the melancholy which has dominated 20th Century lyrical poetry, thus rejecting the modes of big-name poets such as John Burnside or Carol Ann Duffy. The recent distressing revival of "Martianism"[4] in young poetry also seems to be ignored for the most part. No prosody, and a lot of prose. No history either, not of poetry anyway, beyond immediate precursors and basic 20th Century European masters. It is a poetry which is very much at home where it is, mentally and culturally, and happy to stay there, sustained by verbal jolts now and then like shots of whiskey after work. It is no doubt "cool" but I fear it is often "square" (if anybody still understands that term).

However much I like to make fun of the terribly earnest young ex-Cambridge poets and their theoretical certification, they remain virtually the only ones on show here to display a passionate concern for the world riven deep into the language, and also to show a serious involvement in the long-term history of poetry.

§

The poets that most appeal to me in this assemblage are not strung on a washing-line between two inimical walls, they come from their own places. In this context they offer a sense of relaxation, of not being in a desperate hurry to grab the next telling word immediately, but letting the poetry unfold while avoiding clichéd linkage. Young poetry suffers a lot from tightness, and ex-Cambridge can be tight to the point of asphyxiation.

James Wilkes, for instance, his spoken phrases flowing smoothly from line to line across major disruptions and building into a scenario—

> we are speaking to you
> from the fireside
> from the bottom of our hearts
> from a bunker several miles
> beneath the smoking ruins
> of chicken cottage
> on Tottenham Court Road
> as was
> from one machine to another
> from the cosmic ether
> we are speaking to you
> yes, just you...

Likewise the poet known (on this occasion) as Mendoza, his lines widely scattered across the page and with the rhythmic pointing of a performance text, but at the same time maintaining gravity in echoes of the most serious ancestry. The result shifts between bright and weighty as no other that I know.

> from the wilderness   I defy sudden corrections. I could
> build on these species but I wait for an observation
> of self-   awareness   or
> purpose   or
> evolution:
>
>
> Thus I, like Earths topography kiss the chorus of years

Kai Miller, amazingly the only Caribbean poet to get into the anthology—

> A light song of light is not sung
> in the light, what would be the point?
> A light song of light swells up in dark
> times, in wolf time and knife time,
> in knuckle and blood times; it hums
> a small tune in daytime, but saves
> its full voice for the midnight.

This lyrical strength is not simply a product of his ancestry, but garners its resources internationally while standing on a solid ground. It's the first of twelve stanzas which hold onto the lyrical structure through ever widening fields of concern. I never saw anything less hybrid.

I have written previously of Sandeep Parmar in *The Fortnightly Review*. She is represented here by four strong poems from the book I then reviewed. I'm struck by how unafraid such poets are of recognising their lyrical responsibilities, and to do so in all seriousness, as in this ending to an elegiac poem—

> ....that day of chaos

where you are still sounding your warning
(though I was too young). To be left with the bitter
heaviness of song, its chaos.

And at least one of those I've classed as ex-Cambridge, Amy de'Ath. I can't easily use the word "soft" of her writing as represented here, for it displays a sharpness, and a vocal insistence which drives the poetry forward through all kinds of thickets. But a few lines show her capacity for a lyrical tenacity which weaves an enigmatic texture entangling public and private images, but can be broken through to direct appeal.

> Then paint me the sum of polygamy.
> Tender brawny snippets, pear pips
> & a drainpipe running down to the
> sea. Not you not me.

> With night you come stomping,
> It's kristallnacht in my dream—
> why did you shave our heads?
> When will we reinvent love?

I wish I could say that these quotations are typical of the entire collection. I rather think there could have been a lot more poets like these five included if the editing had not been fixated on binary opposition and how to appease it. But the anthology is welcome as it seeks to break the mould of adulation, to steer aside from the senior "best poets" publicity and all the attached routines, and offers a lightening of the popular concept of poetical substance which will encourage the admission of the unorthodox.

§

You can tell at a glance that the American anthology is a different proposition. About twice the size, a bigger page, 102 poets, utilitarian presentation — it's meant as a college course book. Its theme is again one of mitigation. The term "hybrid" is not emphasised, but the concept is present; the stress is shifted onto "pastoral". The anthology claims to represent a thoroughly modern poetry which has turned its attention to what I may be forgiven for still calling the natural world.

This is a good idea if it seeks to reclaim for poetry a function it has had, in the west, since the 18th Century and for millennia if you look eastwards, which has only recently been called into question, of meditation on the rural or natural scene as in various ways a counter to urban enclosure, perhaps a recompense or consolation, but potentially a more positive and far-reaching thing, an acknowledgement of human and earthly distance, a means of attaining a sense of the total. But there seems to me to be little attempt here in either the presentation or the texts to achieve that scale of engagement with the world, and I think the reason for this lies in the insistence on the "postmodern" subtitle, which can hardly be distinguished here from what is commonly called "experimental" or "linguistically innovative". An insistence on more or less dysfunctional language in the poem which obscures the message and shrinks the scope. In fact the Introduction can only be called complacent in its cultural ahistoricity. The term "postmodern" is used as a given without any attempt to define it, and we are told at one point that nothing is quite the same after Language Poetry. I think there should be prizes for ignoring Language Poetry.

The word "pastoral" runs through the entire history of poetry, and it has developed a large array of significations, some of the greatest seriousness. In the hands of critics such as William Empson and Northrop Frye it has become virtually a term for the entire process of transfer in script, the "elsewhere" held up before the reader as the mirror of society, or the artifice against which we stand accused. Such is the only true "Arcadian" sense. I think that among many young radical poets these days it has degenerated into a term of abuse, representing a turning away from the real world in search of a comfort which is blind to politico-economic realities, a fantasy time-lapse which is actually dangerous. It means rural watercolours by Churchill or Hitler.[5] The word "lyrical" has, of course, been treated in the same way. *The Arcadia Project* espouses neither the comprehensive nor the reactionary sense of pastoral, but it is difficult to know what actually is meant by the word here, for on the one hand it seems to signify no more than bits of nature, and on the other its meaning is dispersed until there is almost nothing left of it. Certainly there is nothing of an historical sense which would make any work with Virgilian or ecclesiastic connections, such as *Songs of Innocence,* relevant to the enterprise.

The thesis of the Introduction (by Joshua Corey) is that the postmodern pastoral engages with the quiescence of the pastoral mode in order to undermine it, and that this intervention will open perception to the real and the future. American prosperity is a bubble due to burst: we live in an Arcadia, he says, which is becoming obsolete as it slowly and piecemeal destroys the earth. It is time yet again to be ejected from the Garden of Eden. The conflict in the poem, "the intersection of the present tense with historical and ecological knowledge" forms an interruption of the dream and connects it to reality. Pastoral is a simulation, a theatre, which "contains within it a kernel of negativity that, when properly activated by poet and reader, promises to put us in touch with the reality, or the realities, of our contested world". There is obviously a serious intent here, but it remains sectional and, as so often with Introductions to heterogeneous anthologies, leaves major question unanswered. Ecology is placed at the centre; there is no suggestion that economics, for instance, might be a major player in the despoliation. Nor is there anything to explain why poetry will enact this confrontation and contribute to a kind of intellectual rebirth better than mass education or prose expertise — how anyone coming away from this book with a head full of disturbed language will necessarily be empowered or enlightened. This last bit is, in fact, always missing from the apologias. The artistic need to claim your space by being advanced is always too precious to be forfeit to all the good causes which are invoked to back up poetry. Too often the reader is urged to trust that a healthy message which she cannot see, is somewhere present in a cluster of language which refuses, or is not allowed, to say anything.

To me the most promising idea in this rather homiletic disquisition is that of the bringing-together of contraries. Mr Corey points to the integration of nature into the modern urban space (not that it was ever absent from ancient urban space — the force which first closed the gates on it was surely the working environment of the Industrial Revolution) and says, "To write the postmodern pastoral poem is to write from consciousness of this ultimate yet elusive reality, to be a digital native with dirt between ones toes. These poets are flaneurs in the country, naturalists in the city, zoologists in the suburbs." These reversals could be the impetus to a lot of sharp writing, including comedic and parodic genres, and could prompt the opening of perception beyond habitual confines. But there is not much dirt available to the toes in university offices, and I don't think that the poetry collected here does, on the whole, grasp the potential of the paradox. One reason might lie in the statement, "Postmodern pastoral retains some allegiances to the lyric and individual subjectivity". This conventional belittlement or rejection of staple conditions of the short poem is where contemporaneity sticks the spanner in the works, for poetry cannot escape from song and remain poetry, and the personal (which does not have to be labelled "subjective") is at least one of the forces that keeps it alive. This is why we do not get the opening or the realisation promised us, because forces inimical to the fully realised poem intervene. And here the plot thickens as it is revealed that natural imagery (which dominates the book) is not necessarily part of the process at all, for we are told that any object of attention even urban or electronic is material for the pastoralist, "...celebrity websites and abandoned factories and *telenovelas* and the New Jersey Turnpike are all eligible objects of postmodern pastoral's dialectical nostalgia, sites in which the human and the unhuman mix and collide..." So any percept, it seems, not necessarily even approved, any earthly thing, can form the Edenic enclosure from which the poet will eject us by tracing the negative kernel. Here we naturally wonder if any modern poem has ever not been postmodern pastoral.

But this thesis on the collision of human and not-human could bring us close to the heart of modern poetry. If (and it is a big if) the modern poem embodies a conflict, possibly an unresolvable conflict, which figures the "contested" condition of the world, then it does indeed hold an honourable and salutary position as guide to reality. Is this then what the challenging texture of so much contemporary poetry is all about? Does this account for the way poets say and not-say at the same time, deliver a message which is unreadable, wrench words out of their syntax, make meanings into blanks, offer their personal perceptions of the world while invalidating them, and generally take with one hand what they give with the other? The formula *human / not-human* hardly seems adequate if by "non-human" is meant no more than physical properties of the earth which come into conflict with the "human". The conflict must lie deeper and spread wider if a world condition is to be attached. It has to be there in the language itself.

For whatever the Introduction says, the inner conflict of most of these texts is between saying and not-saying. And while we can understand the necessity for the human to confront the non-human (or the self the not-self for that matter) it is harder to accept that language's transmissive function must, in poetry or anywhere, be distorted or negated because of the condition of the world. There is obviously nothing about the proposed existential conflict which absolutely necessitates any distortion or disabling of language, of which we get so much. No justification or theorising of this is offered (though no doubt in the classroom a lot is said about it). My own understanding of the dialectic set up here is that the "human", understood in this narrowed and comfortable sense, is what is heard in normal or communicative language, while the "non-human" is heard in its opposite, and the conflict between these two is what produces the strange object in front of us on the page, in which "...words and syntax, like the pastoral itself, form a hybrid terrain of human and nonhuman elements to be negotiated and explored."

But is the poem, or the world, necessarily conflictual as is proposed here? Certainly the media would have us believe that the world is, and the governments who so stoutly defend us from the enemy outside, and the revolutionaries, so angry with the enemy inside. Do we not rather choose such a reading ourselves? Are the lives lived and the choices made in them necessarily determined by conflict? Do we seek conflict as our solution? Couldn't the process of the poem be expressed less as *human / not-human* and more as *human / more-human* ? Then the peculiar textures of modern poetry might arise not from a conflict of meaning but from an excess of it? This does not imply a "subjectivity" which subsumes physical reality to its own theatre, but rather recognition of the extent of human cognition as it faces all that resists it. Is it not a specifically human act to recognise every stone on the shore and to donate their "meaning" whether friendly or inimical? The conflict could be *within* humanity as most fully understood, rather than a threat to it. And are not the acts of humanity themselves among the greatest threats we know? Does not the entire history of poetry present us with an enormous quantity of valuable constructs produced entirely out of the condition of being human, with all that is entailed therein by the complexity of the selfhood and all its fields of action and reaction? The difficult and threatening things of the world (stone, wars, decay, etc.) do not have their own language; they use ours, they are already part of the "human" and as such need to be confronted. I don't know any reason to believe that a language of reduced or eliminated efficacy is the best tool with which to do this. What we mostly get from this "postmodern" textuality is a constant halting and reversal of the discourse prompting emotions of worry, doubt, or exclusion. The lone self is frequently the terminus of events, left helpless and silent.

Could there not be a modern poetry which is as complex and difficult as you like, and as fiercely and specifically directed towards the world's ills, while inciting emotions of consolation, exhilaration, pride, and so forth, *positive* emotions, rather than being restricted to pricking the reader with the sharp points of homiletic contradictions? Well indeed there are such, and some of them are in this anthology, among a great deal of studious and sophisticated writing unable to escape from an oppositional despair — that is to say, puritanical writing.

§

I have manifestly been reviewing the Introduction to this anthology and not the poems. I have not named or quoted a single poet. But there are 102 of them in 500 pages, and the poets are far from offering anything like the unity of manner and purpose which the Introduction suggests, though there are majority concessions. The principal criterion of inclusion is very much reference to the natural world, though it can be minimal — mention a birch and you're in. It is quite commonly, though, impossible to see a trace of anything which could remotely be identified as pastoral, and these must be the poems which occasion the Introduction's excursion into the dispersal of the pastoral concept, where any earthly percept will serve.

Does the inclusion of words like leaf and earwig really make such a mix of poetry styles all subscribe to one thesis of pastoral, as if they are all engaged in the same process? Although most of the poets must be young (the information is not given) there are a dozen poets approaching seniority whose concerns are well established and whose presence can only be an asset, though they are not all well represented on this occasion. I'm particularly glad to see Jack Collom, Merrill Gilfillan and Lisa Robertson included among them, poets whose reputations have perhaps suffered from their distancing from the academy. Otherwise there are poets who could be characterised as surrealistic, religio-ecstatic, gobbledegook, objectivist, minimalist, collagist, discursive and all sorts. I was quite pleased to stumble, on page 145, upon a textuality which could almost come from British "New Apocalypse" poetry *circa* 1940. But what there is a tremendous amount of is a spaced-out punctuationless texture scattered around the page or in columns, floating particles of language, white paper between more or less unlinkable entities from diverse vocabularies, always avoiding sentences, involving fragments of landscape or details of natural phenomena. This is clearly the orthodoxy of this department.

I could spotlight some thirty names for special mention but I'll restrict myself to one. In this context it was a great relief to come across the long poem by Juliana Spahr. We are back in a world in which human beings wholeheartedly offer language to each other for mutual help and understanding. It is a passionate outcry of engagement with earthly existence which becomes complex and crowded but is not afraid of simplicity of utterance, in a chant-like mode resting confidently on its non-western affiliations.

The anthology is divided into four sections with titles which are nowhere explained and which mean nothing to me. A class project perhaps?— Find out what the sectional subheadings mean. One of them is *Necro / Pastoral* which to me means village funerals.

There could also be a class project to find out who all these people are. Faced with a new anthology, especially one of this bulk, I usually turn first to the section of mini-biographies to get some sense of where it all comes from and possibly some interesting detailed information. The section "About the authors" in this book could be the most boring and uninformative of its kind I have ever seen. Almost all entries begin "(xxx) is the author of..." and all you get is a list of books followed by a list of prizes and then usually which university the poet teaches at. We are not normally told which generation a poet belongs to, what part of the States she comes from, her ethnic background, beliefs, anything. Nothing is spoken of except success in the eyes of the institutionalised world, and only the few poets who do not fit the standard academic career pattern get any contextualisation. Is this what poets have become over there — production and reward machines?

1   This review mimics from time to time the mode of the quite engaging (but evasive) editor's Introduction, a collection of sparsely connected short passages, many of them addressed to the world or various poetical persons.

2   From "a janitor..." to "...swoons" is exact quotation from the Stevens poem.

3   I can't vouch for the accuracy of these head-counts as the information is mostly not given, but I don't think they can be far wrong.

4   Martianism was a mode pioneered by Craig Raine and James Fenton in the 1970s which rejoiced in clever, self-regarding, metaphorical tropes and nothing much else.

5   I was once present at a lecture on W.S. Graham in which it was suggested that to live in a ramshackle cottage near Land's End was in itself somehow to subscribe to German National Socialism

EDWARD DORN: RELENTLESS FURY

Edward Dorn, *Collected Poems*
edited by Jennifer Dunbar Dorn. Carcanet Press 2012.
1023pp. £25.00
Edward Dorn, *Two Interviews*
edited by Gavin Selerie and Justin Katko. Shearsman
Books 2012. 102pp, £9.95

A *Collected Poems* of Edward Dorn, the American poet who died in 1999, is a necessary and overdue publication, and, whatever the circumstances, the fact that it was not published in U.S.A. suggests that there is something very wrong with the local culture over there, a fact which Ed Dorn was very much aware of. In fact most of the time it dominated his writing.

It has often been said that a "Collected Poems" is a dreadful thing, and when it is 1000 pages long it is certainly a daunting thing, and there are all sorts of problems in how to use it. When Frank O'Hara's *Collected Poems* appeared in 1971 I got rid of all the original books, and now can't find a poem I want unless I can clearly remember the title or incipit. The first collected poems of Charles Olson (*Archaeologist of Morning*, 1970) had only a non-alphabetical chronological list, no indexes, and above all no page numbers (pagination being evidently considered bourgeois) – I had to pencil my own in.

Dorn's *Collected Poems* is very professionally edited and produced in these respects, indexed and sourced, everything dated, and the original volumes are kept distinct, so the reader's conceptual problems are reduced to the effects of sheer bulk. For me the principal of these is that a poet's entire work over a long period (in this case 55 years) becomes one solid lump (or "Sllab" as Dorn might have called it). You don't of course have to read it from cover to cover – only the hapless reviewer has that obligation – but nevertheless it is formed into a unit and will be thought of as such whether in adulation or doubt. Everything however various becomes equally validated, and the extremes of the writing are inhibited from challenging each other.

There are some poets (e.g. W.S. Graham, Pierre Reverdy) whose work tends towards a sense of unity because it is the product more of a single-minded drive, as if attempting to write the same poem over and over again. Edward Dorn is not one of these. There is an immense variety of modes, scale, and pitch, from high elegiac seriousness to casual jokes, and from lyric to narrative and polemic, and there are both latent and manifest contradictions. But all these strategies are conjoined in his insistent purpose as poetical radical, hater of establishment and commerce, towards which verbal projectiles of many kinds never stop being directed, bearer of a fury which never relents.

In many quarters, Dorn has become a hero of the new, and the adulation is total, "a master among masters" as Iain Sinclair says in his blurb. Although younger than most of them his reputation sits comfortably with the poets of the "new American poetry" of the 1960s – Olson, Creeley, Duncan, O'Hara, Ginsberg et al., inheritors of the techniques (modes of attack) and purposive scope of Ezra Pound, but never of his politics (though sometimes of his disdain). These are the masters he sits among. And for all their differences they do stand together in opposition to the entire drift of American politics and society in the 20th Century [1], none more so than Dorn. Naturally in present conditions, many poets and readers experience a dependence on these pioneer radical poets which makes them sacrosanct, just as for many of us the light beaming towards us from Americans such as Dorn in the 1960s seemed the only channel to a future for poetry worth thinking about, however much we later learned what our native strengths were.

A think that in Dorn's case this was justified, and much of the work he did up to and including his first move to England in 1965 could well bear the adulation. He went into Black Mountain College at the age of 21 and was taught there by Olson, but the manner he developed in the next two decades was his own, obviously influenced at first by Olson as well as Williams and Stevens, but not drawn into Olson's cultural agendas, nor apparently tempted to run for the academy. In fact for a decade he moved around in the western states, which is where he came from, getting various manual labour jobs. The poetry comes straight out of this.

> Now it is winter and the fallen snow
>
> has made its stand on the mountains, making dunes
>
> of white on the hills, drifting over
>
> the flat valley floors, and the cold cover
>
> has got us out looking for fuel
>
> "Los Mineros" p.85 (1960)

So evidently not in a great rush to be an avant-gardist, nor to rush the poem through its own excitement, but happy and able to take on a centuries-old calm elegance of landscape conjuration which you'd think any well-read young poet could do at the drop of a hat, but they strangely don't. Nor is it without verbal subtleties (contrast of fallen / stand, and an ABAB quatrain end-rhyme in vowels only). It is an introductory passage, and the poem goes on into a more prosaic realist account of the failed quest for coal, ending

> Madrid is a gaunt town now. Its houses stand unused
>
> along the entering road, and they are all green and white,
>
> every window has been abused with the rocks of departing children.

That's Madrid New Mexico by the way, which judging by Google Image hasn't changed all that much since then except that the coal miners have been replaced by "artists" (This sarcastic tone is something you pick up easily if you read a lot of Dorn) . The discourse is still plain and still hinting at its ancestry (loose Alexandrines?) but also pointed. These conditions of stasis and decay frame the central discourse of the poem, which consists of the silent questions of a critical and knowledgeable mind busy noticing details — the ethnic sources of labour for the mines, the disasters, the depression. An awareness of history informs the poem in a tone of reluctant, fated recognition. Dorn's tone is normally angrier –

> That any slob can suddenly ride up in a limousine
>
> and tell us anything, is
>
> one of the world's wonders.   p.94

but still deliberate and measured. An undetached calm is the signal feature of his poetry in the first half of the 1960s, as he carefully learns to hold language and syntax in his own terms, and the instances and concerns of the provincial and unprofessional life he lives are more and more projected outwards towards the reader and world as linguistic vectors. He is clearly moving, in no rush but determinedly, towards a version of the local which remains local but of greater reach. He remained local for ever; even on the other side of the earth thirty years later he is the semirural westerner peering into what went on in the 13th Century through the lens of a burning sense of justice betrayed.

The book *Geography* (1965) is the summation of this first phase. If anyone were to propose it as his best book I might not disagree. It achieves a fine balance as it moves the poetry forward into a fuller engagement of earth and psyche. The writing is more weighty, more intricate, of larger breath, reaching towards declaration – uttering pronouncements on the world but always focussed on America, which is relished geographically but otherwise abhorred—

or of how we might

plead our case in the face of Sartre's observation

that this is a nation where those who care

are the damned of the earth   (p.144)

This condemnation is repeated in similar terms among his last poems, of 1999. There is an increased scope of learning and reference, as here, but still governed by passionate speech – indeed the virtual elimination of punctuation means the poems' periods are articulated entirely by the syntax of speech. The delivery is in some ways plainer while the intellectual substance and the figuration are both more involved, so that we are more warmly invited while made to think harder. Yet our thinking can hardly be distinguished from our appraisal of the man in the narrative of his life on the ground.

Periodically among the poems of this time one will appear entitled or subtitled "Song" (and there were three little books of them) which are concerned, nominally, with more intimate matter, specifically created because "You see, one of the feelings about my work all along has been I haven't really felt comfortable with very personal statements like, say, domestic poems."[2] If the work was to be a narrative of his life, as he said it should, he couldn't avoid this challenge, and it produced some of his finest short poems, in a mode he called "lyric" but which hardly differs from the manner of his other poems except in line length. Sometimes, as in the splendid political poem "Song: Venceremos" (p.196), there is no trace of these motives. "Song: Heat" in *Geography* shows how far he has brought the writing of immediacy (and love) towards what some would call visionary, and also how the writing now operates as an unmediated transmission to the recipient of dramatic speech by rhythmic lineation and spatial disposition—

Massive time

the pacific controls our continent

but what controls me is far

less in size than that and far

more burning, oh heat

a continent is my forge

buried deep in the caloric inside

is our relative, the fire

    the twin bellows of love

        cavity of the chest

in the mountain the door

on the lips the red explosion

in the valley the unlit incubator ...   (p.188)

This writing is virtually uninterruptable. No matter where you end an excerpt you cut through the process, and there are three poems 15 pages or more long.

But the old facetious humour is not lost—

I am not amused by

your speech

don't grate my ear
with thin brilliance.

And stop spitting peanuts
into my drink
as you say you adore
poetry.   (p.188)

—which is only the beginning. Dorn pursues his victim through
another 50 lines in terms of a false internationalism and senti-
mentality intimate to the social and economic depredations of the
country. But the critique or complaint is not constant, as it later
became. He will also acknowledge the liberal refuges of the local
and the operations of small-scale virtue –

Goat cheese and greek olives. The owner
is sullen and friendly, he calls the black women sister
they come and go inside his grocery, one thing at a time
it does not pretend to be a small supermarket.
Cold air, clean glass. We rest and watch.
The occasion for this excursion is in the selected strings
of a life gone terribly lonely. It will be a march.
A frail cloud moves with silence into the window.
No sound in the store. No bell on the door.   (p.169)

The intrusion of the self is not allowed to swamp the description. But the unexcited calm here, a mental calm which allies with
serious thought, is something which later disappeared from his
poetry.

§

Things now start to happen. In 1965 Dorn took a post at the University of Essex and lived in England for most of the next five years. His next book *The North Atlantic Turbine* appeared in 1967. What exactly happened is beyond me to say, but the book begins with a particularly strong poem, "Thesis", which is set in a small settlement in the Canadian Northwest Territories peopled largely by Inuit. It begins—

> Only the Illegitimate are beautiful
>> and only the Good
> proliferate only the Illegitimate
>> Oh Aklavik only you are beautiful
> Ah Aklavik your main street is dead
>> only the blemished are beautiful only
>>> the deserted have life made
>>>> of whole, unsurpassable night
>>> only Aklavik is life inside life inside
> itself.　　　(p.233)

At about the time Dorn must have visited the place (if he did) the Federal Government attempted to close Aklavik down and built a new village in a more practical position, Inuvik, referred to later in the poem: "Simple fear compels Inuvik, her liquor store / lifts the darkness / by the rotation of a false summer. / The Children of the Sun never go to Inuvik, on bloody feet, half starved...". Aklavik survived due to local organised insistence but it sounds as if this process was not concluded at the time of the poem. It is a long poem, and the as-if uncontrollable passionate outcry on behalf of another version of "the damned of the earth" never relents.

It's worth pausing here to consider what kind of poetry Dorn's is, what really goes on in it, especially in "Thesis", in view of what he was to do later. It is obvious that "Thesis" is governed in its making by personal declaration, "from the heart", reinforced by the unorthodox lineation and syntax as the messages fall over each other in their urgency to reach us. Also that this passionate speech is irrational and extends its vocabulary far beyond description or any parameters which would normally be considered to constitute relevance. It cannot of course be true in a general sense that "Only the Illegitimate[3] are beautiful", in fact by normal canons of veracity it is obviously nonsense. But such usage of truth and generality here would be scorned. (I have a vague memory of British poets who were reading Dorn in the 1960s speaking with contempt of "truth" in such a rational therefore "mean" and "false" sense.) What it can be is *true to* the poet's inner vision or (better) his soul. And in realising that truth which is both internalised and extended the poet reaches out to the earth, connecting the immediate with geophysical distance and the extremes of human emotion. So shortly after the opening quoted above, the hyperbolic insistence produces this—

All life is

in the northern hemisphere turning round

the radicals of gross pain and great joy

the poles of pure life move

into the circle of

our north, oh Aklavik only

the outcast and ab

andoned to the night are faultless

only the faultless have fallen only

the fallen are the pure Children of the Sun

  ....

It is a theatre: Aklavik is the only place, "all life" is before us on this stage, and it defines its terms as it goes along by metaphors which reach beyond any function of comparison and are perhaps not metaphors at all, but, within the theatre, literal terms. There are more extreme figures than this, two of which defeat me: that the Children of the Sun, the Aklavikians wrapped in semi-permanent night, are said not to permit the "intrusion of food", and the blackflies which evidently infest the place "form a core and critical shell of inflexible lust". The poet is obviously risking everything, including the appearance of sanity, in the furore of expression which bids for a unity of disparate perceptions which is close to systematic, though he is in no way indulging allegory or symbolism.

Similarly in the part of "Song:Heat" quoted above, organs and acts of the human body (lungs, kissing) are immediately mountain, valley, ocean (quite interchangeably, I think) – "a continent is my forge" and that heat is love. It is not aggrandizement; it is intensity. It does not say, "My love is as vast and hot as the continent" but rather "My love is made on the whole continent."

"Romantic" might not be an entirely inappropriate word here, thinking particularly of Shelley and Blake. In its manner it is a product of Olson's teaching, who placed the self as the one reliable access to humanity, earth and cosmos, to be represented in strings of semi-autonomous phrases. But this kind of high figurative discourse has been cultivated widely as a reaction to 18th Century rationalism (which Dorn later became very interested in) and in the 20th Century was particularly strong in British poets such as Dylan Thomas and those he influenced. The distinguishing question, though, is exactly *how* the observed details or the particulars of perception are made to become global or cosmic terms. Here it is by sheer pressure.

I find Dorn's course as we have seen it so far, on the edge of the next phase, quite exemplary, because there was no bullying involved, no heroism, and no movements were launched. With Olson's discoveries at the back of his mind he pursued the realities of the life he lived and patiently sought a writing which would evince a unity of being comprising at least history, politics and geography as intimate to personal experience. It was ambitious, but he kept it literal and was always ready to embrace calm and circumspection. There is arguably a shrillness in "Thesis" which means he has pushed out to a limit. The aroused self is the sole authority, and such an exclusive foundation might not bear much further pressure. To me this is why, among the twelve substantial poems of the book of which "Thesis" is the first, you do not have to go very far before meeting what I can only view as his first major collapse.

§

Dorn himself was dissatisfied with *The North Atlantic Turbine*, mainly because most of it is concerned with England and he recognised a failure to "perceive things English" —"...there's a harping note in the book because it's vague and unfocussed." (*Interviews* p.24). Most of his work heretofore had come from a particular locality which he knew intimately and here he was floundering in a foreign land. This worries me less than what happens to the poet's voice. There is in fact a lot of fine writing in the book, particularly when it is bound to his own questing experience and allows of his innocence. But there is also a lot of pontification, all rather monotonously extremist, which seems new to his poetry. The title-poem, also called "A Theory of Truth", is a solid nine pages of it, all from a position of total cynicism.

Dorn's position facing the world here should be made clear, for it informs just-about everything he was to write from now on, involving some tortuous difficulties which badly need the clarification. "Thesis" was extremist but it was a poetical enactment; in "A Theory of Truth" and elsewhere in the book he expounds his position baldly as he had not done before, and makes it clear that as far as he is concerned the entire civilisation he inhabits, and probably a lot more than that, is simply "crap" or "Evil" and always will be ("permanently intended disablement").

The condemnation is total; it is in the last analysis the world itself which is reviled — not just capitalism, though commerce and finance are the principal destructive agents, not just war and exploitation, but the very buildings, the objects, the people and everything they say or produce, art and all. The world is totally degenerate. This cannot be taken for any kind of leftist agenda, for all the "politically correct" attitudes and all practical approaches are equally despised (civil rights, education, socialism, opposition to the Vietnam war, ecology...). As for art, "The fact is there is no art /no vision in the West[4]..." The Renaissance "...is simply expanded commercial enterprise", the Ghiberti doors on the Florence Baptistry "are the doors to the biggest bank" (they "would fit Chase Manhattan as well"). There is no discussion, no justification, the word "bank" is enough to spotlight the core of Evil. There are two interesting lists of places and things which should be bombed or "blown apart", which include the Empire State Building (I seriously wonder what he would have thought of 9/11) but also the back passages of elephants in zoos, all computers, all internal combustion engines, anyone possessing more than £5, and so on. "Finally the earth as a primary object must be destroyed" and indeed "life on earth" is itself an exploitative trick played on us from birth. The question of how serious all this is doesn't of course arise. Obviously it cannot be totally serious, but neither can we treat it as pure comedy, which would leave us free to be amused by the stand-up audacity, because it is too insistent for that. And certainly there is a reality to which Dorn points his finger, one which has become exacerbated since his time. But there is mainly burning resentment and impersonal hatred behind it all and, increasingly, a sense of election.

These pronouncements are offered in a tone of public address without public accountability, and all the demands that that would make of the poet's knowledge or realism are bypassed. The public world is a complete fake and nothing is owed to it. And what is the "theory of truth" here? Is it that truth is created purely by strength of feeling, that truth is essentially negative, that truth lies within untruth, that truth has died the death because of commercialism..? But there are several hints that the singular figure of the *poet* is the central depositary of truth and the only citizen to have the chance to be liberated, by dint of the inversions and distortions of poetical language, from the untruth and Evil which absolutely govern this society. This lionisation and privileging of the poet seems to be something he picked up in England, and it had an increasing influence on his subsequent writing, mainly in a deliberate hardening and dehumanising of the voice, and, eventually, a miniaturising of the vehicle of address. But first there is an interruption, a very big one.

§

In the late 1960s Dorn began work on *Gunslinger*, a long narrative poem which was published in something like its final form in 1975, in four books and two episodes. It has been described as his *magnum opus*, the epic of America, a poem which creates a new era, a "masterful critique of late twentieth-century capitalism"... , but whether you agree or not you'd have to add that it is never for a moment serious. It is certainly not "epic", in fact "anti-epic" might be better. The often quoted outline of the narrative situation makes this clear enough: an unlikely trio consisting of "Gunslinger" (i.e. killer cowboy) who is known for his wisdom and spends a lot of time expounding elliptically, "Lil" who is some kind of saloon madam picked up at the start of the journey and whose role is mainly to add zest, and a talking horse called Claude Levi-Strauss who is remarkably cool. They are joined by others, notably "The Poet" who seems a naive figure but very adept at evasive obscurity when on a platform. They are supposedly roaming the south-western states in quest of the millionaire Howard Hughes, thought to be concealed in a hotel in Las Vegas (or to have bought Las Vegas to hide himself in), but they seem not to get that far. But off they go and various things happen, but not many, and mostly they talk. The talk is a very slick and knowing kind of banter and is loaded with constant reminders that it is all very intellectual and serious, that it uncovers the structure of the mind itself (words like "ontology" bandied about, the name Heidegger dropped now and then) and at the same time that it is nothing of the sort, but rather three or four dope-heads rambling through complex vocabularies not at all sure what they are talking about, as indeed where they are actually going seems normally to get forgotten. This outline gives a false impression of an easy read, but you could make it a lot harder for yourself to read *Gunslinger* than you need.

The 1975 edition (then entitled *Slinger*) bears three blurbs on the back cover, two of the "American masterpiece" kind, but the one by Richard Brautigan seems to me to be the most accurate and reassuring: "I wish to thank Edward Dorn for taking me along on this poem. It was a fine trip with some splendid scenery." Not that it's just fun, but it is essentially comic and should not be allowed to cause readers' headaches in search of abstruse significance, however hard it tries to. The nominal references, for instance, seem to be purely decorative. The horse's name means nothing in relation to Levi-Strauss or his anthropology. The pre-Socratic philosopher Parmenides makes an appearance (or rather his name does) several times and there is a cryptic message from his "secretary", but Parmenides' actual beliefs are beside the point, and chasing them will not help with the poem. These names are there because Dorn likes them.

The way the poem works is that of any other comedic narrative: by setting up a narrative scenario with contrastive elements (or characters) in it but of no significance in itself, which then becomes the vehicle for acts of conflict and accident, verbal and otherwise, which are the centre of the construct. This is how a good Laurel and Hardy film is structured. There had been a lot in

Dorn's writings about roaming round the American west haunting saloons and viewing the locals. Now Dorn can make an entire comedy of it by displacing reality into a filmic setting, leaving him free to work with the comedic details. All sorts of wit and wisdom might emerge from it (or remain forever concealed within it), especially given Dorn's attitudes concerning the relationship of language and reality, which is of course invariably erroneous in common usage, and which Gunslinger constantly mocks and corrects. The public voice is repeatedly turned back on itself to reveal its own mendacity and everyone's common speech with it.

Dorn called it a "psychological drama" (*Interviews* p.49), as if it were an interior portrait of himself. All the voices, he said, are his voice, and perhaps its success lies in the multiplication of his own voice so that it is no longer the single pontifex of 'A Theory of Language', but his own questions are stooges to his own answers and a whole drama is set up out of the furniture of his mind. "Interior" here is specifically not subjective — that "I", it is made clear, is dead — but represents a big field of objective vocabulary, wit, and stagecraft, at the disposal of the self from its own resources. In its particularly obsessive way it worries about the world, not about the self. As such I think it is a fine read, though I leave it as an open question whether the plunges into writing of great difficulty which happen from time to time bear the same tongue-in-cheek function as most of the text, whether the obscurity is in fact mocking itself, which Dorn implies it is. But I also think that in order to read this work successfully you may sometimes have to put Dorn's tongue back into the cheek it has slipped out of, that is, to read the open declarations into dramatic irony. The following from Book III, for instance, is perfectly straight, but to my ear it would serve very well as a speech from one of Molière's self-deluding dandies. —-

> To a poet all authority
>
> except his own

> is an expression of Evil
>
> and it is all external authority
>
> that he expiates
>
> this is the culmination of his traits.   (p.516)

When it is read to him during an interview (*Interviews* p.52) Dorn just says "I believe that".

The writing of *Gunslinger* does in fact change during the course of the work. By at least half way through one notices a more recherché and erudite diction, more abstruse references, clouded narrative transitions and generally an augmenting sense of disdain for common humanity and its language, along with a sense of in-group address. These latter traits lead straight into his subsequent writing. But it is an enormous work; there is a lot more in it than I have touched on and there are more problems than I have tried to resolve. But I do think it is the major achievement of Dorn's later career and that once you have grasped the major aspects of its mode there is a lot to be gained from it, whether you are prepared to join Dorn in his insistent and lordly oppositionality or not.

§

The post-*Gunslinger* Dorn, of which there is about 300 pages, is something at which I tend to wring my hands in despair. This is partly because there are such displays of wit, humour, acuity, such craft in the writing, such evidence of an active mind, which I sadly find I can't connect to, because it seems to me that the attitudes are fixed and predictable, the approach insistently casual, and the poetry's scope drastically reduced, mainly by the elimination of the personal. I also find intermittently a sheer carelessness, a willingness to indulge trivia, and very occasionally an outrageously provocative piece of inverted demagoguery.

There are particularly about 350 mostly very brief poems of a very casual kind which Dorn called "satire" but which are not substantial enough to be satire, they are mainly just jibes aimed at all the falsities of language and power as he comes across them, in the news, on the TV, in the streets and shops, anywhere. I believe there are several hundred more not included in the book, not because they were rejected but simply because of their bulk, which would have necessitated a two volume edition. There is also obviously an unclear boundary between casual notebook jotting and finished work for publication, in fact the distinction is eliminated. The tone of these squibs is consistently flippant. There is commonly a sense of cruising around noticing the corruption of civilisation as it passes by, or spitting jibes at the road-side peasants, and some sets were in fact composed while driving a car with one hand taped to the steering wheel, the other free to write on a pad.

It is easy to see in them the kind of force that *Gunslinger* has, but stripped of the coherence that narrative gives, and pulverised into a mass of separate sneers and scoffs. Many of them will escape any non-American or even non-local reader because of the references, but the bulk of them are addressed with unerring aim at a true cultural problem (or disaster) which is still with us, and is not only American, concerning such matters as the swamping of the public voice in commercialist duplicity and fantasy, not to mention the devastation wreaked all over the earth by foreign policy in partnership with certain industries, and other matters of equal concern. I can at least half agree with Amiri Baraka (in his Afterword) about Dorn's "piercing understanding of where we all are...", his spotlighting of verbal abuse; rather less so with the outright condemnation of the total: "...this place, its fakery, its malice..."

Slow Coup
If voting changed anything

it would be illegal   (p.867)

This is surely the kind of thing you are cajoled into agreeing to at once, but might have second thoughts about on reflection; it's what in Britain we call "Private Eye" humour, and the majority of them are like this, though some have more specific and substantial point to them—

What Will Be Historically Durable

About Nixon[a] there was
Something grandiose
Although this peevish society
Failed even to blink at it.

Nothing illustrates this
More than
When he stole the post office.

a. Yet, it is too easy to use one whose very name is
a satire upon all government
(taken from Junius)   (p.603)

Obviously one could take a lot of this kind of thing, and there is a lot, though we might still wonder, eventually, what became of the poetry. But in filling up these writing-pads anything goes. What has happened to the "great American poet" who commits things like—

Proposition 13

> People who associate themselves
> with dogs
> are basically dishonest.   (p.636)

or gems of wisdom such as—

> next year will be the 100th
> anniversary of 1877   (p.638)

Such pieces are not typical, but they are there. We can be sure that there is a hidden agenda to such empty writing. Somebody is being attacked, somebody always is, and there is always the possibility that it is you.[5]

I feel that these missiles are issued from a well-protected position. Rather than speaking out as he stands, Dorn clearly writes from the shelter of a supportive "educated community" as he calls it; the address is to an in-group. In fact I am sharply reminded in trying to wade through many pages of the stuff of a very different milieu. I am constantly beset with the image of a bunch of public schoolboys (in the British sense) cruising around the provinces making fun of the locals (the "plebs" as they would call them), punning on the quaint place-names, laughing at people with dogs, mocking the entire culture they inhabit from the safety of their group superiority and privilege. Too often it is exactly like that. And the seriousness of the pandemic threat against which it rails doesn't change the picture. Another thing I'm reminded of is Baudelaire in Belgium.

Who exactly is under attack? J.H. Prynne (in the other Afterword) calls them "the power people" but Dorn's resentment spreads well beyond any actual wielders of power and implicates all the shoppers and holidaymakers who just can't see that they are being exploited in every moment of their lives. The insistence on language itself as the principal bearer of harm opens the accusation out to the totality. Everyone, and the human condition itself, is to blame, with sole exception for a small band of aficionados speaking poem-language. Somebody, as I said, is always under attack even if we can't identify who. The reader's defence mechanism against the unavoidable suspicion that it is in fact him/ herself is to apply to join the club by agreeing to the thesis of universal rottenness; perhaps Dorn relies on this.

The nature of poetry itself becomes problematic as all the received conditions of poetical language are jettisoned. The poetical afflatus such as Dorn was happy to indulge in "Thesis" vanishes, leaving only a thin, hard and univocal line of clipped discourse, without intimacy. In 1965 Dorn went a tour of parts of the American west in search of the Shoshoneans, a native American people now dispossessed and scattered, and the results (with photographs by Leroy Lucas) were published as *The Shoshoneans* (New York 1966). Writing of this book Martin Thom[6] suggested that Dorn, faced with the damage itself, stricken with pity and shame, and with the Vietnam war raging, felt unable to sustain the role of ethnographer, accepted his demotion (especially when the Shoshoneans allowed his photographer, who was black, to participate in the dance but not Dorn) and fell back into being a private person without role or authority. Such was the account he wrote.

It could be that in these last writings Dorn felt unwilling to sustain the role of poet, which he would recognise as it was practised at large to be complicit with the power structures he so much hated. But that would be a paradox since he insisted all the more strongly that he was writing "poems" and believed in "poet" as pretty-well the only honourable occupation left in the world. But this privileged sense of the poet would comprise mainly himself and the "community" of his contemporaries, the support of which made his self-confidence possible: for the rest the role was abandoned. He didn't seem to realise the precarious position this left him in. Statements in "Thesis" may not be justifiable from a rational point of view, but they are wrapped in royal robes of rich figuration and rhetorical gestures. Now the poems broadcast the author's opinions unconcealed, and all the more starkly in the modes of irony and sarcasm he adopts. They are largely bare too of all sense of place as landscape with or without human figures — all we have is mockery in a desert. His extremist or hyperbolic statements now stand exposed to anybody's questioning, of which "Is this actually true?" will always be the most damaging. The wit and the deftness of script discourage us from asking the question, but it cannot be kept at bay for ever.

One particular poem has been pointed out to me as raising acute concerns about Dorn's political sagacity when he extends his reach beyond his familiar field, "Open Letter to the Apache Nation" (c.1999). Again it is not typical but it is there. It begins as a commiseration addressed to the Apache nation for its virtual destruction in the 19th Century, but then turns to another people considered in the same light, the Serbs. Dorn takes entirely the Serb side in the Yugoslav wars of the 1990s. Others have done that with equanimity but, typically, he knows no restraint

> The Serbians have every right
> to expunge their invaders who are
> the issue of Turkish Eunuchs
> and who have always attempted
>
> to yoke the people of Constantine
> to their pernicious and vengeful religion.
> (p.887)

So much for Islam. And, he adds scoffingly, "all in the name of a cure for 'genocide.'" meaning either that there was no genocide (but there was) or that to educated poets genocide isn't important. The reason for this kind of position is clear enough —

> I'm with the Kurds and the Serbs and the Iraquis
> And every defiant nation this jerk
> Ethnic crazy country bombs...

> ... it would take more paper
> Than I'll ever have to express how justified I feel.
> (p.894)

This is politics reduced to a temper tantrum. The motivation is an absolute belief, cultivated throughout his career, in sheer oppositionality. Everything without exception that the USA power structure does is and must be Evil. You know this before you start. For the kind of poetry Dorn chose to write latterly this is particularly damaging as it automatically casts doubt on many of his other, more agreeable propositions, if it becomes obvious that neither knowledge nor thinking is actually considered necessary.

There are other things among the last writings which are more substantial and connected, though the language remains prosaic compared with his earlier work. They are mostly projects tackling particular subjects, several of them unfinished: the Apache, a literary conference (kind of in-house poetry), various journeys, the Cathar persecutions. *Languedoc Variorum*, which resulted from a one-year appointment in Montpellier, is a set of calm and deliberate poems going through the Cathar history without adding anything new but reflecting seriously, and extending into neighbouring zones. It would perhaps have been better without the addition of two parallel unfinished prose texts, one of them a mass of opinion-ation about religion and oppression of various kinds, the other one of his mock texts in the manner of telegraphese or breaking news. Dorn's version is elaborated but simplified, even to black and white, but there is a particularly effective comedy poem on Simon de Montfort. A lot of Dorn's concerns in his mature poetry are framed in terms of religion, in which he fervently declared himself a heretic (but was he not more like a gnostic?). His espousing of the Cathar cause was entirely predictable, but who would not? His belief in poetry was pseudo-religious — poetry was the work of an evangelical sect, and the poet was a kind of priest in it, indeed one of the *perfecti*.

I must cast a glance at his last work, *Chemo Sabé*, which chronicles his treatment by chemotherapy for pancreatic cancer in 23 poems. It is remarkable, and a sign of the versatility of his poetry, how it can face any mundane thing directly, that he could turn it to this subject at all. As might be expected in the situation, the way is clearer here, the contempt is less bitter, though the poems talk much as they have been doing, constantly extrapolating from the particular towards the body politic, and the very drugs themselves become abstract dramas of conflict. And the old political obstinacy is just as strong (my last quotation was from here). Elegiac calm is only reached in the last poem.

But I'll end with what I think is the best of these, *Recollections of Gran Apachería* which was written during the final phase of writing *Gunslinger*. The result of a course on Apache history, it is written as a dignified and poised consideration of the long war against the Apache, in which the stories are woven into the meditation, which analyses the conflict in terms of different modes of perception. Several ventures are made, modest but committed, into the Apache mythos, and the sequence ends with a particularly fine piece, "La Máquina a Houston" which I might prefer over "Thesis" as a less madly impassioned but as moving account, in its careful detailing, of the last indignity suffered by these "damned of the earth" — the transportation of a crowd of Apache into exile in Florida at the end of the war, their final defeat.

§

Dorn was a great talker and left behind a whole trail of interviews, in which the questions always focus on his writing career but his answers may end up anywhere. *Two Interviews* captures interviews from 1971 by various hands, and one in 1981 in London by Gavin Selerie which is rather more substantial. This latter is particularly informative on Dorn's meeting with English or European thought and culture, including his interest in the 18th Century which obviously informs the later anti-poetical writing and, not surprisingly, his dislike of the Romantic poets, a misjudgement he shared with most of the innovative American poets of the twentieth century. In 1971 he seems somewhat inhibited facing questions from students who do not exactly speak his language, but Selerie is very much on his wavelength and releases quite extended disquisitions. Selerie also contributes a long introduction, and there are some unpublished texts from the years of the interviews. Dorn's unorthodox and intelligent understanding as reader and thinker is fully in evidence.

1   This includes Frank O'Hara, in spite of a lot of coterie cuteness, in his quest for authenticity and fidelity to the actual as it is lived, in a language-use outside literary norms, though not I think, in the sectional market of homosexual discourse as is sometimes claimed.

2   *Interviews* edited by Donald Allen, Bolinas 1980, p.23. All other self-comment from Dorn is quoted from this book unless otherwise stated.

3   It is at this time that Dorn begins a habit of upper-case initial letters on nouns in defiance of normal usage, often for the purposes of emphasis, but not necessarily. Sometimes it seems like a donation of status to the word and its subject, at other times I am at a loss to know what the result is.

4   Usually when Dorn says "west" he means the western states of America but the context here makes it clear that he means Europe and the whole "western world".

5   I think Dorn had some sort of mystique about dogs. There was an interview about them in an anthology called *Dog Stories* in 1993, which I haven't seen. I doubt that in the 1970s public culture was run almost entirely on anniversaries as it is now, but that would be a possible explanation of the 1877 piece.

6   Martin Thom, "The Poet as Ethnographer" in *Poets on Writing* edited by Denise Riley, 1992.

THREE NEW YORK POETS

Barbara Guest,

Collected Poems edited by Hadley Haden Guest. Wesleyan University Press 2008. 558pp hardback $39.95.

Joseph Ceravolo,

Collected Poems edited by Rosemary Ceravolo and Parker Smathers. Wesleyan University Press 2013. 592pp hardback $35.00. Also available as an eBook.

James Schuyler,

Other Flowers: uncollected poems. edited by James Meetze and Simon Pettet. Farrar Straus and Giroux 2011. 238pp hardback $28.00, paperback $18.00.

As soon as Barbara Guest's authority in poetical writing is established, which is in her first two books, there is an evident urge to tell the story, to push a discourse forward; there is an unfolding, a characteristic pressure towards completion. The poems are *tellings* and she wants them to tell *in full.* She wants the poem to reach its conclusion, beyond which there is only silence. I think this condition holds through her entire career in spite of her development of an increasingly experimental writing which eliminates all possible subject-matter as well as any possibility of a connected narrative or location, or any form of address — the poems become collections of disconnected mentionings separated by empty space. But I maintain a faith (and faith is sometimes necessary) in her determined drive to completion in the working of the poem, and that as the silence after the end of the poem is incorporated into its structure the floating fragments remain meaningful as they interact with their surround, and that the primary vehicle of this is an intense condensation of figurative language so that from one point to the next an extended and often unknowable process has taken place whether of event or of thought.

Not that the early work is conventional. There is a range of commitment to unorthodox procedures, some original but many of them related to the New York poets she is mainly associated with (Frank O'Hara, Kenneth Koch, John Ashbery and James Schuyler) and their attachment to earlier French poetry, especially in her case Surrealism. She was in fact the eldest of these (born 1920) but didn't publish her first book until 1960. But always, even in the most New-York-ludic pieces, there is a sense of pressing forwards quite earnestly, both in the progress of the poem towards a true ending, and in metaphors that reach further and further out into the unknown. Even the most unproblematic writing, such as this very early example—

> I just said I didn't know
> And now you are holding me
> In your arms,
> How kind.
> Parachutes, my love, could carry us higher.
> Yet around the net I am floating
> Pink and pale blue fish are caught in it,
> They are beautiful,
> But they are not good for eating.

even here, there is a reticence, an unwillingness to present a given situation, a disregard for circumstance, a delicate disconnection at times, and somewhat strange moves such as the ambiguous syntax of the sixth line, which may or not be figurative, and of course there is the bathetic caution about the inedibility of the fish. These mild disjunctions and distractions are held in a steady verse movement, and one feels that a series of poetical moves is given priority over any full account, or emotional declaration, while the tone remaining authentic, and this is confirmed in the paradoxical ending to the poem: "I am closer to you / Than land and I am in a stranger ocean / Than I wished." The comfortable surface is rippled throughout by signs of uncertainty and apprehension but the poem is more than the depiction of an emotionally ambiguous condition because of curtailments (such as the first line) and excrescences .[1]

The first two decades of her writing produced a collection of attractive poems varying among themselves in the degree to which they transgress rational discourse, some of them outwardly straightforward, some decidedly dark, and all of them rewarding in the detailed skill of the writing, the just word-placement, the intuited metrics. They mostly mimic the speaking voice, giving an account which claims and then abandons its own intent and transcends its own singularity in search of a truly poetical and artistic summation. Increasingly punctuation is abandoned and the lines crowd the saying into a continuity which defines its syntax by words alone. What is happening is that perception is being brought to serve an abstractive formative process like an abstract painting; the necessary details of experience are so combined and transgressed as to create an elsewhere which is the poem itself as a finished artefact, an addition to the world rather than an event in it, no longer beholden to it.

The book *Moscow Mansions* (1973) in particular is full of solid, outwardly and deceptively discursive poems. The opening of the poem 'Red Lilies', from this book, shows admirably how her pursuit of such a course is, as it often is, carried into something like a comedy which loses control of its own imagery—

> Someone has remembered to dry the dishes;
> They have taken the accident out of the stove.
> Afterwards lilies for supper; there
> the lines in front of the window
> are rubbed on the table of stone
>
> The paper flies up
> then down as the wind
> repeats, repeats its birdsong.
>
> Those arms under the pillow
> the burrowing arms they cleave
> at night as the tug kneads water
> calling themselves branches
>
> The tree is you
> the blanket is what warms it
> snow erupts from thistle;
> the snow pours out of you.

The metaphorical extensions of a domestic scene are pursued until we don't know what exactly is happening, but the pursuit remains warm and serious. Is "the snow pours out of you" a notation of joy or dismay? We can't know, because what is happening is that the scene of some kind of failed dinner *à deux*, whatever it was in reality, if it ever was, is being made into an independent poetical and linguistic construct in order to liberate the verbal possibilities. This can only really be shown by quoting the whole poem, where the metaphors (if such they still are) constantly gravitate back to the mundane and rebound into high flight. The poem ends

> The pilot light
>
> went out on the stove
>
> The paper folded like a napkin
>
> other wings flew into the stone.

This both consummates the details of the scene and extends into an independent image transaction. The last line is still an account of what happened, but blended into what happened in the writing of the poem, and thus the reality is enhanced beyond the occasion. You cannot say it is an interiorized representation of what it felt like, and it is not symbolical in any explicable way. It is more like a theatrical projection: the pilot light explains the accident in the stove, the errant paper becomes a dutiful accessory, all is reconciliation and then "other wings flew into the stone". What was obdurate becomes permeable. This is the kind of process Barbara Guest went on to develop for another 400 pages. It never becomes possible, or desirable, to say what the newly hatched images, here wings, "are". They are the word at its fullest reach — they are the winged word showing how it can subdue the hardness of stone.

The almost constant levity, or twinkle, in her diction doesn't alter the fact that in her sense of mission Barbara Guest was the most serious and the most difficult of the New York poets of her generation. Not for her the jaunty "I-do-this-I-do-that" mode cultivated at times by O'Hara and Schuyler and later seized on by Ted Berrigan and Ron Padgett. She doesn't refer to Broadway operettas or night-club jazz, but there are several mentions of Schoenberg. The impression is of someone involved in leading a civilised existence focused on the arts, with quite a lot of globe-trotting (but did she actually go to all the places she mentions?)

ever suave and discerning, with none of the Bohemian rau-
cousness so common on the other side of American writing at
that time. Within this ambiance there is a rich investigation of
experience through scenes and people, fictions, paintings, and
sometimes narratives, dedicated not to revealing their meanings
but to uncovering the verbal possibilities of their existence, which
is a meditational process seeking to hold them against the world
itself through language.

The book *Defensive Rapture* (1993) most clearly marks her
arrival at a technique of spatially separated disjuncts which
dominates the rest of her career. But I think that before that there
were at least two instances of remarkably strong works which
could be said to represent a step back or a pause in the development of her manner. One is the long poem *The Türler Losses*
(1979). This actually is about the loss of two Türler[2] watches on
two occasions — though it tries not to be. It shoots off in her
usual unannounced way into image zones both near and remote,
credible and impossible, but the losses keep insinuating themselves into the texts again and again, sometimes merely as words
associable with time and clocks, as if defying her wish to forget
them. So the text, rich as it is in material, constructs evasive tactics
which fail. Loss itself is enjoined, including death, but in the same
easily distracted mode, and a whole emotional life is drawn in as
a source of the images which circulate around these losses. There
isn't a singular summation to these processes; they occur all the
time. One of them is—

> A child entered the room
>
> wearing a clock costume
>
> A child of pygmy size
>
> unmodified by time's blisters
>
>
> And time's throat burrs and time's screens

across which time's numerals

Flash ruptures

The depth of these lines is surely obvious, achieved in some measure, I think, by the classical feel to the lines which augments as the end approaches, but also in the noun/verb ambiguity of some of the words. The whole poem is a moving compilation of such moments focused on instances of memory and loss and it is striking how disparate images are held in the poem's memory — it will not perhaps surprise anyone that it begins with the cry of a night hawk which seems to die in flight, and this is probably answered at the end in "A wrist for every watch / releasing doves". But in miniature too, the reach of the verse can be extraordinary. The entire process of this long poem could be contained in the phrase "Loss gropes towards its vase." which occurs very early on. The word "vase" is unprepared and thus all the more free to suggest Keats' urn or any other signification we find useful, whatever receptacle we wish to store our losses in.

The first poem of the book *Fair Realism* (1989) begins—

> Wild gardens overlooked by night lights. Parking
> lot trucks overlooked by night lights. Buildings
> with their escapes overlooked by lights
>
> They urge me to seek here on the heights
> amid the electrical lighting that self who exists,
> who witnesses light and fears its expunging

and goes on from this evocation of isolation and distance, into a comparatively straightforward account, without excursions elsewhere, of removing an abstract painting from a wall and replacing it with a scene from *The Tale of the Genji*, a moving encounter between Genji and his son at which "each turns his face away from so much emotion". The poem is manifestly a different proposition from her usual: poised, deliberate, connected, laden with content... and stands out as such even though the whole book tends in that direction. It is also unmistakeably hers, and has become probably her best-known poem. There is a hint at a personal involvement in the story of filial encounter which perhaps motivated the piece but more importantly the whole poem is a meditation on conditions of light and darkness. It is an unusually orthodox treatment of the kind of material she usually handles, but it does extend out of the field of recognised discourse when it reaches for its ending—

> The light of fiction and the light of surface
>
> sink into vision whose illumination
>
> exacts its shades,
>
> The Genji when they arose
>
> strolled outside reality
>
> their screen dismantled,
>
> upon that modern wondering space
>
> flash lights from the wild gardens.

You could write reams on any of Barbara Guest's successful poems, which is most of them. It is not only image, vocabulary, and figuration; it is also syntax, rhythm, form, lineation, sound values... and, as here, a kind of emblematic construction is formed which remains gently shrouded in the evident reality. There is something approaching a theme: singular light falling on wild or alien places, then an open, abstract landscape of widespread sea and sunset colours is replaced with a depiction of a human relationship... and then the ending. The message is that it is we, the human, who create the darkness as we play our light of vision onto these static frames, and finally in our minds liberate the figures from the realism of the picture, and the world at large (wild garden) flickers both light and dark... The descent from the totalisation of the abstract to the human particular (a chiaroscuro which permits the figures to avert their faces) opens the way to an extended sense of home, of what we inhabit... Well, something along those lines, but how much more engaging it is at it stands, showing lights *on* the wild garden (etc.) worked through to lights *from* the wild garden, a turn from direct to indirect perceptive process.

In the later work, from the mid 1990s, the floating, spaced-out settings donate a certain serenity, but the linguistic displacement can become extreme to the extent that outlandish word choices make it impossible to follow her. To choose one of the most puzzling passages I can find—

> more liquid
> than eyes adulterous surface —
>
>
> the bruised arch — a sting
> severely clothed — rich in dynamite —
> cord to shallows —;
>
>
> a fluid haze divides —
> the rhythm vault —
>
>
> — single movement — topped with purple hills —
> contralto shift —.

Obviously the relinquishing of subject matter, depiction, story, discourse, speech, and more, has reached an extreme. And when you do eliminate all those things what are you left with? Words. The words do occur in small groups but even there the mechanisms of connection which govern meaning can't be trusted. No apostrophe on "eyes" so we have to break that line in two. "rhythm" not "rhythmic" so that that noun and "vault" merely stand in apposition. And we start to mistrust even the connections we are given: consider "the bruised" as standing for a plural noun and "arch" as a verb. But the worst stumbling blocks, of course, are completely unprepared context-destroying words such as "dynamite" and "cord".

One thing that puzzles me about a passage like this is why I'm not annoyed by it, as I usually am by such things. One reason is that there is no hint of alienation or protest as the motivation: she is manifestly not tearing the language apart because it is the weapon of the commercial or political enemy. She is doing it out of a belief in the value of art as the creation of a self-sufficient world which has to be separated from the traits of normal (or "empirical" — see below) discourse. Another reason is that I have come to trust her poetical procedures even when they defeat me. I do believe that each of those impossible transitions is likely to be arrived at as a result of careful thought as well as associative flare, and that she is seriously concerned to enact these terms within a context which doesn't distinguish between the immediate (experience) and the acquired (reading etc.). These scenarios are basically episodes of her life.

There are also contextual conditions which on the one hand offer to bring some coherence but can also feel as if she is deliberately laying a false trail. The above is the first section of the poem 'Expectation' subtitled 'Erwartung: Schoenberg'. I have followed the whole poem against both the music and Pappenheim's libretto without locating any structural connection whatsoever. There is no chance that the poem follows a parallel course, of image, mood, or anything. All there is is occasional words or short phrases which seem to refer to music or possibly to moments of the libretto — "arch" and "vault" because in the monodrama a woman is groping though a dark wood at night looking for her lover, and "adulterous" could be relevant. For music: "the rhythm vault", "movement", "contralto" (but *Erwartung* is for soprano), and later "Chromatic rise" and "littered octave". That's about all really, which is almost nothing. The first section of the poem is followed by four more, headed "variations"; but *Erwartung* is not in variation form. So it seems we are offered the connection only to be denied it, and this is inevitable: we must not read her poem as a version of some other artifact or as saying anything at all about any work or experience but its own. *Erwartung* is the source which is erased in the writing, the "absent subject" which leaves only its scent behind. And yet there are clusters of metaphor, especially at endings, which might well be the conclusion of the quest, not as summaries of the source but as the poem's own discovery in relation to the source. In this case "littered octave — disrupted — [...] spells the translucent." But my ellipses conceal two further terms ('knee-bound" and "mutinied") which seem entirely to deaden thought.

There are other apparently false trails laid — a group of poems entitled *Dürer at the Window, Reflexions on Art* and a much longer work, *Rocks on a Platter: Notes on Literature.* In neither case of course do the reflexions or notes conform to normal expectation, but the latter in particular is a finely wrought accumulation of quotations, epithets, references and Guest-type poetry hovering over the possibility of notes on literature, reaching a kind of plea for depth in the recovery of mythical vision—

Where are they, *wood nymphs and the glittering*

Beings — do they overstep each other...?

The Dolphin God — does he swim on the page?

The sections of this work are headed by quotes from, among others, Hegel and Adorno, which might give some indication, if we need it, of the rationale behind the poetry in an attachment of European idealism, a rejection of what Hegel called empiricism. But I am unconvinced that the poetry was conceived according to these precepts and rather suspect that they were attached at a late stage. More telling is a short prose piece from *If So, Tell Me* (1999) concerning the necessary absence of the subject—-

> It can be seen she encouraged the separation of flower from the page, that she wished an absence to be encouraged. She drew from herself a technique which offered life to the flower, but demanded the flower remain absent. The flower, as a subject, is not permitted to shadow the page. Its perfume is strong and that perfume may overwhelm the sensibility that strengthens the page and desires to initiate the absence of the flower. It may be that absence is the plot of the poem. A scent remains of the poem. It is the flower's apparition that desires to remain on the page, even to haunt the room in which the poem was created.

This seems a thorough and honest account of her poetical method. But we should notice that what is recounted is not a cold manipulation of the text but a part-regretted perseverance motivated by the need to cope with absence. Perhaps we could even suggest that it represents a hope rather than a secure platform, and recognises that the problems created by subtraction as a creative method could be interminable.

There is an essay on the late poetry by Majorie Welish[3] which describes very precisely Guest's poetical practice, defined quite correctly, I think, as "lyric" (e.g. "syllabic acoustic relations at the expense of given subject matter") and as a form of literalness. For me the most disturbing sentence in it is this one: "She leaves traces of lyricism so imaginatively acute that a moral rectitude is the precipitate". Insofar as I trust the late phase of Guest's poetry I would agree at least to hope that such is the result and justification. It would be a welcome resolution if this emergence of moral rectitude could be demonstrated by close analysis but I doubt very much if that would be possible.

Barbara Guest's *Collected Poems* should on no account be missed.

§

I find it hard to think of a chronologically ordered collected poems which begins so impressively as Joseph Ceravolo's does. Wallace Stevens' occurs to me as one such. This consists of the small book *Transmigration Solo* dated 1960-1965 but not published until 1979, some thirty poems written in his late twenties. They take on the full possibilities of "New York" outlandish figuration and non-sequitur but held in a strongly vocal rhetoric, emphases and repetitions which signal a human presence bearing a tense emotional charge—

Migratory Noon

Cold and the cranes.
Cranes in the
                    wind
like cellophane tape
on a school book.
The wind bangs
the car, but I sing out loud,
          help, help
as sky gets white
          and whiter and whiter and whiter.
Where are you

in the reincarnate

blossoms of the cold?

Whatever awkward questions arise — What kind of cranes? How can either kind resemble cellophane on a school book?... their awkwardness is held in the urgency of the voice, its distress and its confrontation with contradiction.[4] A drama is in progress, there is not *time* for the suitable metaphor and this speed delivers us into a more challenging place. A stanza from 'Pain Songs'—

> The path, the path is where?
> It's the cow's, o but
> to be near the cow.
> Let's be near some old
> realization that just died.
> Near some depowdered
> head that comes round
> the horseshoe curves of sense.

The sense of desperation is typical, typically crossed with the rhythmic and imagistic confidence of the writing, the strong syntactical engagement of the self with scene and object and the imaginative leaps from figure to figure. So too is the dramatic repetition and re-starting, many poems having governing words repeated through the text as impulsions to continue. How a dead cow comes round to being an archaic head moving in ellipses to create sense is not for me to say, but it does.

Ceravolo is generally mentioned as a "second generation" New York poet (born 1934) and obviously he found his initial impetus in the procedures established by the older poets, indeed he attended a writing class run by Kenneth Koch. But he also kept himself to some extent separate, not least by living outside the city and being employed all his life as a civic engineer. The question of how he would develop the mode of *Transmigration Solo* thereafter raises itself acutely, but unfortunately he didn't. He shot off into something completely different, in the long text *Fits of Dawn* which was actually written in 1961, therefore concurrently with *Transmigration Solo*. It's all like this—

> mumbbler of gash-
>
> compel
>
> Rice! hold you
>
> festive running   Choose!
>
> Leap confide ballad
>
> positional
>
> ashame, oh stump!
>
> moons of drimp confuse.
>
> Tiens corner tien
>
> shed compel[5]

I generally find it best not to comment on this kind of writing, which many still value highly, except in this case to note that the emotional charge now has to be supplied by exclamation marks. It is anyway clearly a move to push the volatile figuration of New York poetry as far as it will go in the wrong direction, where no thought process can possibly take place in either poet or reader and no autonomous artistic "place" can be created except one which is uninhabitable. Such is obviously the intention (rather than simply the failure) and it is astonishing that he located from somewhere (Dadaism?) this extreme textuality at such an early date, before even Ted Berrigan's *Sonnets* (1964), the "classic" second generation work of wildly disordered language which is actually far less obstructive.

Ceravolo's progress after this shows a slow and faltering return to modes of address, in increasingly open poems intermittently hindered by experimentalism, bringing him to *Spring in the World of Poor Mutts*, actually his first published book in 1968, which was awarded the Frank O'Hara prize and at once established a reputation for him which was more than local. There are many vagaries of manner in this book but it does recapture the skill shown in *Transmigration Solo*, generally in a calmer tone, though there is normally a sense of emotional struggle. The life hinted at behind the verbally led texture becomes familial, a child is involved and the child's voice is repeated in the text. There are even some family scenes, but always within the tense uncertainties of a poetical voice which holds the language unto itself, denying the reader full entry into the experience. There is, for instance, this startlingly candid sexual poem uniting male and female involvement in birth, but in which we have to go through an enigmatic episode towards an ending which is loudly glad and suddenly inconclusive. But these are, in principle, precisely the moves which make the poem an enactment of the particular rather than a question of any-man and any-woman.

Pregnant, I Come

I come to you
with the semen
and the babies:
ropes of the born.

I rise up as you go up
in your consciousness.
Are you unhappy
in the source?

The clouds sputter
across the ring.
Do the birds sing?
Is the baby singing in you?   yet.

I'm also struck by short poems of perceived nature marked by the decision not to extend, not to devolve perception any further, but to trust it as it appears to be, in sharp contrast to the distrust of unmediated perception in much of Barbara Guest's work.

Dusk

Before the dusk grows deeper
Now comes a little moth dressed in
rose pink, wings bordered with yellow. Now
a tiger moth, now another and another   another

I think this book will remain Ceravolo's principal achievement, but there is a lot to follow it which is by no mean negligible. There is first a poem called *Hellgate* filling 28 pages, which starts very well but later takes some banal routes and is plagued by the bardic tone of a "spiritual journey". It is a plea for authenticity, of great scope and an impressive performance, but something has happened. With *Hellgate* Ceravolo's relationship to the reader changes, and this concerns all the many (over 300) poems which fill up the rest of the book. Up to this point even the plainest writing (such as 'Dusk') is rendered as a verbal proposition, and so relates primarily to the reader's experience of language, constantly tested against recognition of the actual. In this way, you could say, reader and poet connive in the realisation of the poem. Subsequently the poet undertakes to declare himself to the reader directly, most noticeably in the involvement of his religious beliefs, and this spreads into a deliberately artless offering of bald statements about a world he finds misconceived ("this vampire, America"), as well as reflections on his reading, which seems to be within the "general knowledge" area, and the voicing of an evidently disturbed private life from within a personality which seems to have been hard work. But the change is not absolute. He vagarises constantly between wilfully artless writing and all the poetical expertise he has gained, switching between them from poem to poem or in the middle of a poem or innocently blending the two.

So the book ends with this large collection of poems which I find intriguing as we constantly witness this veering to and from poetically conceived writing, and if the retreat from New York poetry can produce distressing commonplaces it can also release disarming simplicities, as well as moments of complete candour. The art he renounced is in fact never very far away and can be servant to startling episodes of plain speaking.

One of the most interesting parts of the book is a preludial assembly of about 90 very short poems entitled *INRI* published in 1979 (described in the introduction as 20-syllable poems, but some of them are twenty-word poems and some of them are neither. There is nothing in the book to relate to its title.) Ceravolo here comes to a perfect compromise; the poems are entirely evident in their purpose and address, even epigrammatical sometimes, but the brevity brings out all the skill he had developed in controlled wit and the handling of image and sound, and produces an uninterpreted but carefully placed detailing, low on active verbs, which begins to feel quite Chinese. Two examples:

Spring Breeze

Clean cutting breeze:
a little brutal too much.

Spring trees
My child asleep
in my arms

Runs Me Over

Sometimes when I sit here
eating in the hot sun,
a great sadness
runs me over

Ceravolo's *Collected Poems* is in some degree a surprising event — I would not have thought his reputation had reached this stage yet, though I am glad it has. It was thus a bold venture on the part of editors and publisher. It is also a revelation of a body of work of which the most meticulous devotee can hardly have suspected the bulk or the range.

§

James Schuyler's *Collected Poems* was published in 1993 as a volume of 430 pages, and *Other Flowers* is a book of additional poems which escaped the collection. The first thing to be said is that there has been no barrel-scraping. These are all finished poems from right through his career preserved by Schuyler but never published, and discovered in his archive. They stand as equal to most of his previously known poems; perhaps only the very long *The Morning of the Poem* (published 1980) represents an order of achievement not represented here.

People generally turn to James Schuyler with a sense of relief and admiration; it is felt that his poetry is highly achieved but does not present problems. He wrote a lot of conversational poems which read like diary entries (some of them were originally diary entries), or missives to poets and lovers. The admiration is for his impeccable craft in forming these poems, which however casual they may be are never facile, but by sonic and rhythmic detail, by bathetic wit or its opposite, and by the art of pressing on regard-less, always become seriously engaging. The throw-away ending which returns us to actuality was a speciality, but he could also begin a poem, "A nothing day full of / wild beauty and the / timer pings." This is not actually bathetic at all; it places two notations, large and small, on the same plane, as continuities. There is a poem, 'The Smallest' which is a disquisition on this question of scale: the smallest "contains alphabets" and "is infinite". There are many disquisitions on given topics working quite logically through to a conclusion, or just as likely to throw in an ending which turns the whole thing upside down, both moves governed by a sense of the quality of perception amidst the clutter of living or the hurts which pierce the fabric of enjoyment. Everyday living is woven inextricably into his poetical textures but it is not the whole story; he is basically a serious poet exploring his own distress. The new book is full of the sense of personal address which is his principal vehicle, so it is perhaps salutary to remind ourselves what else he was capable of—

Blank Regard

Crystal flesh, starry lice,
gilded silver scows, ivory
death-mask fall feathered,
wrists' anemones, eyes' dials,
a viol slashes currant-red
damask love-seats and lapis
spittoons. Riots. Axes drip
drip, a basket of heads. Of
embassies, of retaliant tunes,
hawkers, harpers, chronicle.
Dusty oxen scamper in hills,
green, spiked, wheel cut.

Time, bite your tail, hoop

snake the steak-sliced neck.

Surely this poem too offers no problems, unless we demand
them of it. It is a list of the attributes of an elsewhere, somewhere
in the bejewelled past, ordered so as to pass into tokens of harm
(mainly in images of cutting), ending in a plea for protection from
the ellipticality of time.[6] Many of Schuyler's surreal or cryptic
scenarios, meditations on paintings etc. are similarly harmless
if you don't ask the wrong questions. But happy ending are not
common, and even what is manifestly a joke poem will refuse
one—

Duff's

The sky in here is very blue

and made of wood.

You are very great,

I think.

Ruth is great.

Have a brandy.

Nobody lives for ever

and it's a fucking shame. [7]

There is felt to be something elusive about the quality of
Schuyler's poetry; more than once I have seen the question put
"How does he do it?", especially regarding the unfailing vitality
of so many poems. I can't answer this question but I can suggest
two possibilities. One might lie simply in the qualities of "good
writing" as such, in prose or poetry, which he could have mastered
early in his career and never abandoned — his first published
book, in 1958, was a novel. This would be a matter of clarity and
completion in large or small, helpfulness towards the reader, the

dramatic organisation of a sentence or passage to project its point, and so forth.

Secondly, *Other Flowers* by presenting more of his work from the 1950s than we are used to, shows that among the various Modernistic or New-York-ish forms he practised there were also intermittent exercises of a different kind, such as the poem 'Beautiful Outlook' (1953), which begins—

> Passersby see it as prison, grave or den
>
> into which their fear of what they fear lurks there
>
> could drive them. Within, the walls are hung with light
>
> like any room, meals are punctual and time
>
> speeds, goes slow, does not exist, to suit the need
>
> of each victim of the other side of love.

This is a direct address on a given subject, concerning one of the hospitals which Schuyler periodically had to enter because of his mental ill-health, a subject from which it does not deviate and behaves in just the writerly way I have spoken of. It shows, of course, how outright in his discourse and thoughtfully serious he could be, in this tone as in others. But if the lines have the feel of a classical measure, that is because it is the first stanza of a formally perfect sestina. There are two other sestinas in the book, a "sonnet" in couplets and other incursions into traditional form, some fragmentary. You do not, I would think, write a poem like 'Beautiful Outlook' without studying formal metrics and it is arguable that this reveals another source of his notable confidence in moving around within a poem. The poem ends in the obligatory triolet—

> A hospital is not a den. The men in there,
>
> the sick, saw light shatter, heard the tick of time.
>
> Each man had his ugly need, each deserved love.

§

The artistic and poetical boom in New York from the 1950s onwards for, at the most, three decades, is a strange and in some ways artificial phenomenon. The poets built their success on the backs of the painters, of course, and they in turn built theirs on the backs of the Parisian art scene earlier in the century. Almost all of the poets were heavily involved in the art world and devoting energy to constructing a parallel or consanguineous relationship of the two activities. Poems were conceived as being structured as an abstract painting was, or a poem was a description of a painting, often undeclared, or sometimes a tension was created between a real subject and the painted one ("an evening real as paint on canvas" as Schuyler put it). This relationship is often offered as the key to understanding the more difficult poetry, though I don't think it is. The poem will always in the end have to stand alone. The poets also mixed with the painters, indeed lived with them — Schuyler lived in Fairfield Porter's family for eight years, O'Hara was a curator at the Museum of Modern Art, Guest was herself a painter, and so on and so on. They all (except Koch) wrote art journalism and the take-up of French poetry was entirely in line with what the painters had done (and incidentally produced a rather unhelpful anti-British polemic).

New York's largely successful bid to become the modern art centre of the world was specifically designed by dealers and officials, rather than the artists, to replace Paris when the latter was disabled during the occupation and many artists were fleeing to the States from Europe, and it is said with authority that government funding, including C.I.A. money, went into supporting this drive with publicity, including the funding of European exhibitions. This does not devalue the New York paintings nor the poetical association, but it was not a spontaneous flowering. Kinds of abstract painting one moment considered beyond the pale, a small minority avant-garde interest, were suddenly worth a fortune, and I note, without understanding it, the apparent strain placed on the artists in terms of breakdown, suicide, drugs, and alcoholism. A lesser pain seems to have spread to the poets, where drugs and alcohol were commonplace, and I wonder sincerely what mechanism dictated that male homosexuality should have such dominance among them. These things may be seen as a product of a particularly fervid local scene, and yet very much the same description would apply to the smaller poetry scene in San Francisco at the same time (Jack Spicer, Robert Duncan et al.) so perhaps some larger and more mysterious force was at work in a national spasm of late Romanticism.[8]

The New York poets saw the support and promotion of the painting as part of their function, in poetry as much as in prose, and took pride in dropping the artists' names in their social poems. There was obviously a pressure to innovate in the art/poetry context which for the poets meant a careful violation of what was considered the proper (weighty) substance of poetry, by intense, "abstract" configurations as much as by anti-poetical everyday banter. I find it impossible to know what the balance will finally be; between recognition of the remarkable, original, moving and sometimes profound poetry made possible in this unusual context, and a verdict which considers it as all little more than a set of aestheticist gestures, 1890s style, thrown up by a manipulated market. But there is no doubt that all three of the poets under review used the situation they were in to extend the conceptual bounds of poetry on the basis of quite traditional lyrical skills which always show through the dazzling web in one way or another. For me, Schuyler's work might in the end prove the most valuable as, having grasped the opportunities of New York poetry in a virtuosic but entirely genial way, he then cultivated the art of staying where he was, while the other two were pushed further and further into a linguistic avant-gardism turned to an intellectual purpose (Guest) or tangled with the need to escape from it (Ceravolo). The opportunity offered by these books to obtain a comprehensive view of what was done is invaluable.

1   The fifth line (parachutes) is also the title and is emphasised by occurring twice during the poem. I leave in a footnote my uncertainty about the fact that parachutes are generally intended for descent rather then flight, and if one carries you into the stratosphere something has gone seriously wrong — is this another of the poem's submerged questions?

2   My research on EBay shows that these Swiss watches can be very expensive — thousands of dollars — but are not necessarily so.

3   Some at least of this can be read on the web as "The Lyric Lately" in the periodical *Jacket* http://jacketmagazine.com/10/welish-on-guest.html   At the end it says "to be continued' but I know of no evidence that it was.

4   My experience of cellophane on school books is that it tends to lift and peel off with an effect of whitening the tape, which sits well with the imagery of this poem, but to each his own school books.

5   There are no typographical errors in this quotation.

6   There is a note by Schuyler among the annotations at the back of the book saying how this poem was made from a book of pictures concerning Marie Antoinette and "the late-eighteenth-century vogue of wearing a red ribbon à la guillotine", etc. This does attach the poem to a real history, but I prefer it in its own light.

7   Duff's was a New York restaurant at which the poets used to gather. It is now a heavy metal bar subtitled "Duff's alcohol abuse center". You have to be over 17 to enter their website. Sic transit...

8   On the topics touched on in this paragraph, see Serge Guilbaut, *How New York Stole the Idea of Modern Art* (1983), F.S. Saunders, *Who Paid the Piper* (2000), and *The Cultural Cold War* (2001), and http://www.independent.co.uk/news/world/modern-art-was-cia-weapon-1578808.html The more recent commentaries treat the CIA's intervention as more directed against Russia and Communism than Paris.

POETS WITH ZIP

Simon Smith, *Mercury.*
Salt Publishing 2006. 180pp paperback
Simon Smith, *London Bridge.*
Salt Publishing 2010. 84pp paperback.
Simon Smith, *Gravesend.*
Veer Books 2011. 56pp 16x16cm stapled. £5.00
Sam Riviere, *81 Austerities.*
Faber and Faber 2012. 128pp paperback, £10.00
Antony Rowland, *I am a Magenta Stick.*
Salt Publishing 2012. 96pp hardback, £13.00

Three young British poets — under 55, which is young enough — all producing in different ways a poetry characterised (in their blurbs if not elsewhere) as fast, urban, witty, youthful, immediate, accessible, playful, risqué and all the rest of the adjectives that offer relief from staid, serious or pastoral poetry. All of the blurbs on these books include the word "funny".[1] Certainly humour is involved in all of them but the term is misleading to various degrees, most extremely when the publisher describes *London Bridge* as "accessible, funny and immediate", as if we might expect some kind of a stand-up comedy script. Parts of the book, and most of *Mercury*, are in their way difficult, disturbing, and at first unyielding. All three poets have a seriousness which underlies or subverts what could be called their *zip* (defined as "informal movement at high speed").

Simon Smith's poetry seems to be changing, increasingly agreeing to a cohering transcription after a period of linguistic disruption which is most marked in *Mercury*, all under the banner of a presiding nervous urbanity. Since the 1990s he has developed his own manner of swift-moving unpunctuated poems which veer constantly towards and away from a sense of telling. Verbally centred, disjunctive, constantly starting and stopping, they view the world as at once a real and a written thing, and set their aims at making a sharp-edged rhythmically lively construction by means of verbal wit and the fragmentary incorporation of circumstance. All these statements are liable to exception and contradiction in particular cases, but perhaps one of the most important principles is that there shall be no predicated vocabulary, but all terms are to be found on the ground wherever the poet is. The vocabulary is wide open from Odyssey to DNA to ketchup, though he maintains a sense of privacy and carefully marks out his own ground in this welter of words. If there is (he says there is) a politics beneath the surface it must operate at least partly by breaking down the comparative class or high and low status value of English words. The routes taken among these fairgrounds of word and percept are both smooth and disrupted, forming in many poems a list of semi-connected items patterned by the lineation, with a taste for the daring which makes him translate 'La Jolie Rousse' as 'The Auburn Stunner'.

Mercury may represent a limit, in the degree of disruption, non-sequitur or countering which takes place, and which is even expressed formally — the line of poetry is emphasised by upper-case initials and double-spacing throughout, while at the same time the most outrageous enjambment can take place across these reinforced lines, quite likely to disorient the reader. In this way and others the writing constantly offers a place, and so a route, and so an understanding, and then takes a sharp turn into a side-road or cul-de-sac. A poem begins as one thing and becomes something different, all within the parameters of his stylishness—

Mending Wall

> Frost said free verse is like tennis
> Without the net, well fuck that poetry's
> No game, it's a way of life we are
> Calling to each calling hat on heart
> Hand on hat, Ideas by any other
> Form of phoneme: hill Hell tell
> Trail pill till chill feels heels heal
> And anything that means you
> Take the ch

The "ch", which for some reason I want to read as "chicken", is not a typical act. It either conceals a Frostian reference which escapes me or is there to cause trouble. But in spite of the switch from subject-matter to word-list there is a kind of argument pursued throughout, which passes over a serious appeal in the middle before ending up jabbering. There are other places where Smith continues to fight the old free-versus-formal battle, rather surprisingly these days, but I suppose the drift here is that the free and meaningless play of echoic sound-values is a contrary to Frost's formalism, perhaps itself satirised rather than advocated, a reactive collapse or an ethic reduced to rhyme. His own position lies in the central balance or a reciprocal critique. It is by the way typical that chasing Frost's poem "Mending Wall" gets you nowhere, especially as it is not rhymed and the only formality to be found in it lies in the easy-moving, unstrict pentameter line. It is also not in this poem that Frost made the remark about tennis, and if the wall as a barrier is considered important let us remember that Frost saw both it and its annual repairing as unnecessary. Smith's poem is far more involved in Smith's thoughts and conditions than in Robert Frost.

This poem belongs in a group which opens the book concerned with American writers (Spicer, Updike, Frost, Pound, then Spicer again, pp.4-12). Rather than studies of these subjects they are more like quotidian events, what he happens to be reading today, for a constant "hodieism" as some anthropologists call it, pervades his writing. There is throughout a sense of picking up on whatever happens from day to day, and thus on the details of where he is (London, south-east England, Kent) — scenes, events and people of concern to him, freely including what he reads or studies, and propositions wherever they come from which have flown across his sight, and these percepts are weighed and extended and ignored, always in quest of a bright and often deflective construct, summated in the rhythm of the last line, sincere or casual or flippant or broken as it may be, but always with a phonetic finality about it. In *Mercury* more than anywhere else, particularly in the first section of the book, this process leads to some defeating for- mulations, where in some cases not the source, nor the nature nor the progress of the event which got the poem going, is evident—

> *First Aid Box*
>
> You you you and you in this instance
> First mirrors then coat pegs where we are in this sentence
> No single one alias my mirror first mirrors first maybe we do maybe
> We don't don't we make lists seep edges

If this is a problem there are two possible answers. Firstly, something is taking place in this poem: seek it. (Maybe a lot of reading of people like Saussure and Derrida would elucidate

Smith's forays into perceptual disorder, though personally I'd rather have a puzzling poem than either, and so I think would he.) More broadly, there is especially in this book a sense of the sequence of short poems as a diurnal continuum, approaching a journal or even a narrative, in which phrases and images recur close at hand to suggest a temporal phase, though not by any means plentifully. (The previous poem contains a version of the third line, without, I have to say, revealing anything to me but contributing to a sense of a domestic context in which an emptiness, a white sheet, a "sound you can't open" becomes a mirror and the poem passes on to a list of worldly differences.) These echoes or recollections from poem to poem, usually occurring in clusters (as the American poets do), don't of course create any actual elucidation. The texts remain ever shifting and evasive; they refuse a contextual summation in favour of a verbal one or a gesture of dismissal. If nothing else they allow the reader to stay in the same place in the company of the poet, and to assume that the words mirror a version of what happened on different levels or under different aliases. The author helps by worrying about this himself—

> *Thump*
>
> This is one of my poems that starts serious and high
> Then tails off. Do we have a story or a plan?
> Do we have a story then? So up it pops as soup
> Soap. Breathe overall finish with a sign
> Like a sign a dead body away from this side on this
> Occasion finish with

I find this a more satisfying performance, where as with the Frost poem the address is abruptly terminated by unconnected words, soup and soap, which are presumably what happened next while the one seems to derive from the other, which is one of his methods of progressing through a poem. I suggest a serious intimate condition as the resolution of this poem, as of most of them, in which the "we" is you and I, in which "sign" and "side" are echoes of absent "sigh" and "sighed" and the tone is regretful and final— it is finished (for now anyway).

Mercury is in three sections in which the degree of hinting incompletion (which is also to say the degree to which I am reminded of the work of the senior English poet Tom Raworth) is progressively diminished, though the sense of masked intimacy is not, nor all the worry and concern which spreads out from it. At the end of the book there is recurrent imagery of stars within a reversal of scale —

> *Constellation*
>
> Cello and cellar
>
> They don't know and I don't
>
> A black hole would make good a necklace of significances
>
> Maybe the consolations remembrances they are the stars

and he ends a poem with "We are the absent star // Boxed outside the skylight" — surely a perfect notation of distance as confinement in an unspoken sense of loss. In episodes like this I find that the seemingly impertinent phonetic play, the silences, the reversals and the whole craft of it form a truly dramatic writing.

Smith may consider *London Bridge* a lightweight production, a miscellany, of distinct pieces of various kinds without aspiration towards the large-scale (but with Smith large-scale can be small-scale). But I warm to it rather more than to the earlier book, and think it consummates many of his former modes and influences. I also find that the writing of one substantial poem can be an operation of grander scale than a whole book of fragments held together by intuitive echoes. Smith's typical gestures are still here: the shifting/shifty obliqueness, the quasi-epigrammatical endings (that is, sounding like the final lesson but not saying it), and all the speed and urban zip he has cultivated for so long, but held in poems which welcome the reader and may even conform to recognised purposes: topographical, satirical, occasional, personal, and one permutational. But there is still the sidewise lurch, the wry diversion, or the shift to the unpredicated, through which he tracks a course which remains calm and thoughtful. There is a poem, 'Least Most', of quite straight socio-economic comment "...a world where gambling means saving and Nectar points / Mean prizes and prizes mean." which suddenly ends "As the details speak for themselves I realise orange rhymes with language."— of which make what you will but it clearly could be the last line of a completely different poem. It is a complete turning away from the subject, with no hidden agenda attached, no ulterior back-reference. It does not answer the preceding problems, which remain, as they probably should. Contrariwise, there is a poem entitled 'Ode on a Grecian Urn' of which the first line is "I'm wearing odd socks nobody can tell, but I know." and then launches into all sorts of diverse matter, so that the title seems merely an excuse for outrageous bathos. But then the poem turns to admiration of personal beauty and at the end comes round to the long postponed Keats within a kind of apologia —

The synchronicity of it:

So Chance and Procedure are file-sharing with Truth and Beauty,

'To see how things go' is one incredible finishing line, and all you need to know.

— all the diversity and disconnection through the poem, from socks onwards, is unified in all being *now*, which is always his domain. You cannot catalogue the now, there is too much of it, but Smith's strategy is to build up an ensemble, often quite short, of salient and contrasted points which he refuses to resolves except in the shape of the poem.

This writing is frequently on the edge of satire; the world is viewed with tongue in cheek. Sometimes this emerges fully as in the poem 'Text' which I take to be a satire on linguistic philosophy, lining up four continental magi against four top prize-winning British poets as if in some game (implying an equivalence) and shortly afterwards—

> A tale to share over dinner,
> *Once upon a time, the text*
> *was unhappy, boo-hoo, boo-hoo* .
> 'The slippage of the signifier
> Across the signifier makes
> The signifier the signified
> For another signifier.'
> But the modern poets left no message
> [...]
> Meanwhile on the ground
> Les Tricoteuses knit one pearl one knit one,
> 'Di Dum, Di Dum, Di Dum, Di Dum, Di Dum'

The small book *Gravesend* [2] is actually programmed, as other texts may be without our knowing it. The poems were written on a regular train journey between London and Chatham and there was a rule that they should contain whatever occurred on the train or out of the window at that point. This does not in fact make a lot of difference, they are still very much Simon Smith poems with the quotas of diversity and irrelevance we might expect with or without a programme. You could study an Ordnance Survey map of the route or you could make annotations concerning Dickens' association with Chatham and many other points, but Smith's skill in assimilation will always be ahead of you, partly because it assimilates ruthlessly to his own present tense, and partly because total assimilation is refused in favour of sheer presence.

I finally think that any clear-cut categorisation of Simon Smith as urbane, fast, zippy etc., misses the mark. You could say that Smith takes a particular line out of modern poetry, involving poets such as Frank O'Hara and John James, who are openly acknowledged. But he also talks to different poets such as Jack Spicer (in *Mercury*), and anyway such categorisation doesn't entirely fit either O'Hara or James. His translations in *London Bridge* include finely crafted versions of Martial, and Propertius, as might perhaps be expected in terms of urbanity, especially the preference for Roman over Greek, the avoidance of the mythic load (he has also translated Catullus). But there is this poem in *Mercury*—

> *Theseus' Dad*
> Black sail, white sail light wing as easterlies drop canvas
> Billows light as light Aegeus reaches out for silence

which if you know the story is a fine gloss on it. Apollinaire is also present which might seem again to confirm the anti-formal stance as against the classical basis of Baudelaire or Rimbaud (schoolboy winner of prizes for Latin poems) but Smith also translates a major poem of Rilke, and is perfectly at home with it, and has translated Reverdy. When he comes to Apollinaire's "La longue querelle de la tradition et de l'invention / De l'Ordre et de l'Aventure" his version seems to show some impatience with the formula: "This interminable argument the formal versus / the free-form Order V Adventure". All this confirms to me that there is more in Smith's verbal play than the usual labelling permits and much of it deserves a slower and more considered reading than the zippy epithet encourages.

§

It's surprising that Sam Riviere's poems should have an affinity with Simon Smith's, because in many ways they belong on the opposite sides of The Great Divide. But they do, perhaps most evidently in the fast unpunctuated patter with comparable habits such as a vocabulary of the moment and the liability to lurch into different tones and image-zones. There is a similar unwillingness to interpret or explain; experiences and allusions are left as he finds them ("I hate when life like an autobahn explains itself"). I find him closest to Smith, and generally at his most effective, in smaller poems—

The Handsoap Cares

It's stopped snowing as bedhead comes on my headphones
On the top deck I'll have to walk home in the cold again
just like last time I should've brought my bobble hat
but feel bad seeing jenny wearing the hat emma
knitted me so it's started snowing again

— and this includes the fact that, as with Smith, the title often seems oddly detached. But only rarely is there any sign of a real enigma such as this one —

Too Poetic

*{Poetry}, or a relation thereof.
*{Anthony_Ian_Berkeley}, a deceased rapper and
hip-hop
producer, or a relation thereof. [3]

More normally there is smooth-running talk, skilfully crafted to navigate through the syntax without punctuation, forming accounts and addresses of many kinds and there are longer poems (such as 'Regular Black' p.51) which become perfectly serious through, or in spite of, the acerbic jocularity and shifting attention, as an account of cultural change.

Being much more open than Smith in its declarations, the poetry is much more involved with apparent authorial attitude and opinion, and there is an inclination to strike poses, especially masculine poses. Love is here a matter of "girls" who sometimes get addressed mistrustingly, and are not infrequently deprecated at the end of the (?love-) poem ("& I thought I would be glad / you called but I'm kind of not"). We are told at one point that "being from the north" is "way outmoded" which is pure poseur material. Like his lines his world seems a lot less cluttered than Smith's, and he is more evidently pleased with himself and his zippiness. The poems move to conclusions which stay within the theatre of the poem, without offering anything conclusive except gesturally. In spite of his publisher and his habit of picking up prizes there seems little to connect him with the practices of the poetical "mainstream" except for the habit of setting up an authorial figure for admiration and sympathy, frequently tempered in his case by the restlessness of the discourse and moments of self-deflation.

I would have said that this poetry avoids politics, but the blurb denies this.[4] Apparently the book was originally conceived as a response to the "austerity measures" introduced by the coalition government in 2011, hence the title. I would say there is little trace of this intent left in the majority of the poems or if there is it is well disguised. But given this hint it is possible to notice connections, such as the poem 'Help Yourself' (p.107) which must be a parody of the questionnaire forced upon recipients of benefit about which there has been much complaining recently. There are a few others, but otherwise if we allow this aspect of the poems we must see it as contributing to the generally sardonic tone, which is normally personal in effect. His best is his contribution to the long history of realist casual anecdote poems —

Chocolate Milk

The sort of really attractive junky sitting

THE FORTNIGHTLY REVIEWS: POETRY NOTES 2012-2014

on the wall by the Magdalen Street
drop-in centre who said I looked
4-dimensional and asked me
to dance in the gorgeous
level light of 5.45

There is a kind of appendix at the back, little prose comments on the poems which I find add well to the genial aspects of the book, including self-doubt and light-heartedness, but would contribute more if the poem referred to could be identified with greater ease.

§

Antony Rowland his plenty of zip but is a very different matter. There is for a start a clear subject-matter to each poem, of great variety from local comedy to the Holocaust, and with that a range of genres and especially of vocabularies, many of which are rarely found in poems. He ruthlessly exploits idiolect — language use of a particular group defined by association, age, relationship, occupation etc. — and the text is liberally scattered with names that very few will recognise. It is possible to become quite comboblicated (a word he uses himself) and anyone under 45 is at a disadvantage. Nothing, whether a foreign word or a remote provincialism, is ever explained.

The effect is often enough comic but a seriousness also pierces through the vocabulary and in connection with this there is also (to make matters worse, as it were) a poetical figuration which can be both dense and tense, with abstrusely conceived or risked metaphors, sometimes a touch "Martian" ("the bar taxidermy of pickled eggs") but normally more resonant. The opening of 'Little Germany'—

Rugby posts cloud the evening
wireless tuned to squatch

in a box room thinking

of the beck's dip, shuttle
terraces and the geography
of the park, us frozen in.

and later——-

Pace out
the rubble wound: we are sorry
to announce a lease heritage
of before and absence, like

white Sowerby hill-slicks.

Explanations? Little Germany: the old business quarter of Bradford (where he comes from) of Jewish foundation, which is probably important because later we get "I hooked an arm around Nazi punks in The Rawson Arms". squatch: don't ask me I'm over 45. beck: stream. shuttle: probably thinking of industrial looms with their rows of shuttles. Bradford was once the trade centre of the northern wool industry. lease heritage: probably thinking of the leasehold system, one of the curses of England. Sowerby: old mill town in the Calder Valley about twelve miles from Bradford [5]. But quite apart from the local vocabulary, there are questions such as how rugby posts "cloud" the evening, how a "lease heritage" gives us "before and [after] absence" (perhaps because in the leasehold system there is no "after": you buy a house and eventually it reverts to its original owner). I think that such questions represent a use of Modernistic figuration (of the British kind) which is meaningful when investigated, whether thought-out or risked in the moment. This is often where the poems command attention, giving us in this case a serious topographical reminiscence, acutely identifying the signs of change, refusing to go into generalising terms. This is what he does best, half concealed, as it were, behind the peculiarities of his style and thus all the more engaging.

Most of the poems in the book come in unannounced groups. There is a topographical group which includes 'Manchester', which is like Ginsberg as a northern comedian — a genuinely funny poem (but you need to be under 45), and there are groups concerning food (gravy, beer, pudding, sausage), zero-star hotels ("I do not like the biting animals in the carpet /and, overnight, the chocolate in my dressing gown / had been eaten by something...") and there are poems determined by their particular idiolect (toddler-speak, English as a foreign language, and recurrently the dialect of city youth). Some are entirely subject-bound as much as any 18th Century poem on sheep-rearing: 'Sausage' runs through all known types of sausage, with stray comments, and then stops.

Rowland's idiom is not exactly difficult or exactly obscure in the sense of concealing, and it is apparent that what he does is done very deliberately as a tactic, a use of modern poetry with serious implications. He himself supplies the word for what he does — *awkward*. He is the author of *Holocaust Poetry: awkward poetics in the work of Sylvia Plath, Geoffrey Hill, Tony Harrison and Ted Hughes.*[6] I am not involved with this book here because the poets he discusses do very different things from what he does. But in it he expounds his definition of "awkward poetry" as a way of subliminally referring to the Holocaust among these poets in various kinds of disturbed language: stilted grammar, conceptual juxtaposition, subversion of tradition, domination of authorial idiolect which rejects objectivity, moral ambiguity, etc. — a self-conscious, self-doubting, means of relating poetry to the Holocaust without appropriating it for self-serving artistic ends. It is an anti-aestheticist position devolved from Adorno's prohibition of "poetry" after Auschwitz and the related comments of people like George Steiner, interpreted as meaning that poetry has to change its face rather than cease.

I think this awkwardness is what he does, and deliberately, not with the same specific historical reference, but as a critique of the socio-linguistic condition he inhabits, especially kinds of standardisation and corruption, implying that to speak of the world in the standard modes of poetry would be to condone, not by beautifying the damage but by appropriating it to an artistic purpose. That such a serious idea should produce some comic and grotesque poems is quite in order, since it is important to steer away from the central reservation at all costs, and anyway few of them are without hints of past or present atrocity. Even 'Sausage' has one.

I was surprised to encounter this ethic in such a place, since I have long been accustomed to a more extreme version of it from the militant avant-garde. Similarly owing a lot to Adorno, these poets will deliberately focus on atrocity (British treatment of Iraqi prisoners was tremendous meat for them) as the stage on which to uglify both poetical language and the human image to the point of repulsion. Rowland is of course much milder (which to them would mean complicit) and spreads his vision more widely, viewing the social theatre at large rather than through highlighted instances, but the principle is similar if not the same, for both found their systems on reactions to major atrocities as forms of opposition to the artistic, and at times the language use is comparable, though Rowland will locate his avant-garde idiom in such zones as the practical world of people trying and failing to speak English.

This attitude comes into its own in the last three poems of the book, collectively titled 'Führerhäusen', recording visits to three of the death camps. The perilously ambiguous position of the tourist is quite delicately dealt with, as is the whole question of preservation and display, the ethical meaning of neat lawns in such places. Guilt too is handled with care rather than being plastered on every watercolourist in sight. But above all the experience is authenticated in a poetical diction which is at many points deliberately "awkward" or unyielding, and indeed there is a lot of local language which is not translated, but by current standards it is not rebarbative, rather an original and thoughtful handling of a major European Modernist mode which predates the Holocaust and in its faltering meditational discourse accepts calm noticing as at least as authentic as violent anger. It is an enhancement of perception. From 'Birkenau' —

> After Kraków's holding beers
> a skylark in throttle
> over Zauna,
>
> full ubiquitous yellow
> butterflies padding
> historical ponds,
>
> a birch woodpecker couched
> in red, a light trick
> of the crumbling orb,
>
> and terminal moraine:
> brick chimneys maroon
> absent wood aesthetics.

§

The public presence of poetry such as Smith's and Roland's has owed a lot to the work of Salt Publishing, who for all their banal terminology in publicity (everything always "exciting" and usually "funny") have specifically encouraged such writing from both experienced and new poets and worked tirelessly to promote it, as well as publishing precedents in an older generation such as the Collected Poems of John James, of John Temple, and of David Chaloner. They recently announced that they will publish no more books of poetry (except annual "Best of..." anthologies, which don't really count), so this phase is now ended.

---

1   *Gravesend* does not bear a publisher's announcement, only three commendations from others but they too, like most of the blurbs, mainly attempt to entice the reader with fun and obliquity more than anything else, or by emphasising quirky references. From the blurb on *I am a Magenta Stick*: "...these poems always tackle the important questions. Where does beer come from? Why was Shakespeare fond of gravy?..." etc. Don't worry, it seems to say, this is not really poetry.

2   *Gravesend* now forms about two-thirds of the book *1178 W. Sunset Boulevard* (Shearsman Books 2014). The blurbs on this book do not contain the word "funny". *(2014)*

3   It must help to know that Mr Berkeley's professional name was "Poetic".

4   Smith too, as I have mentioned, claims a political import which is not at all obvious. For any young or youngish poet to deny any political content whatsoever in their poems these days would be a form of career suicide. *(2014)*

5   Sowerby puzzles me. There are quarries but it's not a limestone area and their offcast is not white. Perhaps something I never noticed.

6   Edinburgh University Press 2005.

POETS AND THEIR STORIES

Aidan Semmens, *The Book of Isaac.*

Parlor Press (USA) 2013. 84pp paperback

Paul Brown, *A Cabin in the Mountains.*

Reality Street Editions 2012. 114pp paperback, £9.00

Catherine Hales, *feasible stratagems.*

Veer Books 2013. 68pp paperback

I suppose that the writing of narrative poetry became a lost art around 1925-1935, last seen from such poets as Yeats, John Masefield, Lawrence Binyon, E.A. Robinson and Robinson Jeffers. That is, real narrative poetry in the tradition filtered down from Homer, and not including accounts of personal experience, transcended or symbolised or interior narratives, anecdotal verse such as Edgar Lee Masters and Osbert Sitwell wrote, or very long poems from Scotland saying what's wrong with the world. It wasn't just so-called Modernism which banished narrative by abhorring explicit continuity; most of the respected poets of the first half of the 20th century settled entirely for the short, lyrical/ meditative/depictive poem (Sassoon and the war poets, Lawrence, Auden, Spender, Graves, Edith Sitwell et al.). There were exceptions — Patrick Kavanagh's *The Great Hunger* is perhaps one, though it is a surprise to find what the subject matter actually is if the title leads you to expect an Irish historical narrative, and there were occasional later essays in ballad form (Dylan Thomas, W.S. Graham, George Mackay Brown etc.) which tended to mask the story in the verse technique. I think that in the first half of the 20th Century the pervasive influence of French poetry as well as the way the concept "myth" was understood both militated against narrative. Probably the most valiant foray into the latter tangle was the short poem (in this context) *Aristeas, in Seven Years* by J.H. Prynne (1968).

Yet there remains an urge towards narrative, or at least the scope of narrative, in much recent poetry, especially among the practices known as "innovative" or "Modernist". This is hardly surprising, since it is only in these zones that any real attempt seems to be made to reach further ranges of thought, to touch on the forces which govern the politico-cultural world or any large-scale comprehension of humanity and civilisation, even if conceived as necessarily fragmented or wrapped in forms close to mysticism. Conventionalist poets are mostly entirely happy with accounts of the self in social and personal terms handed down from Romanticism. [1]

Aidan Semmens has a story to tell, a big one. It's about his ancestors in an important Jewish-Russian family, especially his great-grandfather Isaac Hourwich (1860-1924), economist, lawyer, journalist, Marxist activist... who like many radical Russian intellectuals at that time was imprisoned and exiled, to Siberia and then America, then back and then back again. He was the author of *The Economics of the Russian Village* (1892), *Immigration and Labour* (1912) and translator of Marx into Yiddish. [2] His biography covers a major slice of European and American history, and other family members make an appearance, including the wife and children Hourvich left behind, from which Semmens is descended. This branch includes the first leader of the Communist Party of the United States.

From this rich material Semmens has made a sequence of 56 sonnets (though sonnets only in having 14 lines), drawn from archival sources including Hourvich's own writings, but which he describes as "distressed" or "damaged" sonnets. So, apart from two end-pieces drawn from The Book of Esdras, the texts are all to a greater or lesser extent disrupted by all the disruptions and irregularities of contemporary poetry. There is almost no punctuation, the periods get lost in broken grammar — tenses, plurals and grammatical connection get violated, and what is said is again and again subjected to moments of unyielding stutter, or a disorder as if the speaker has not mastered English. Yet there is a constant sense behind it that a weighty discourse is intended:

> radicalism is not your mistake
>
> your tub is poison & the stink of later
>
> is very deep dark & all unseen
>
> the name of a flower is a name
>
> of something else, respected citizens...

This is what makes this in parts a particularly difficult text, as rather than the disconnected and floating bits of language which you get in a very different kind of contemporaneity, the manner and context lead us to expect an argued and narrated discourse of which we are frustrated. It may sometimes be a matter of abandoning the reader to a word-salad but normally it is a serious discourse which doesn't quite fit together, rendered more serious by a scriptural tone which is never far away. If it is garbled it is sometimes a garbled psalm:

> I conducted you through & sea, at the beginning
>
> gave to you soft passage, Moshe for the leader of
>
> & Aaron for the priest; I gave to you light
>
> in the first, great interests they have made I among you,
>
> but for forgot me & is triumphed not in my name

for destroying your enemies;...

which will sometimes emerge unscathed, as in the continuation of the above:

> I had a pity on your mournings,
>
> gave to you a bread of angels, cleft the rock for
>
> your water,
>
> covered you with leaves; I shared among you the
>
> fruitful earth...

These incantatory passages are from near the start of the sequence, which is soon involved in more detailed documentary material. Whatever difficulties are encountered, the theme is clear throughout: a man a family and a culture of integrity beset constantly with opposition, suppression and conspiracy, as well as their own internal conflicts, and at the same time praise for the context and continuity which enabled serious and informed radical discourse and campaigning to grow to such strength in the exiled Jewish communities.

But what of the story? The story is a difficulty, because sometimes you get it and sometimes you don't, but more often than not you don't. Among all this impressive contemporary poetical textuality, the figures of the story come and go like shadows. We cannot always know what person or event governs a particular sonnet or why. There is a tone of connected intellectual discourse but propositions seldom emerge intact. Each poem is obviously viewed as a self-sufficient entity. There are notes at the back, one to almost every sonnet, which "...provide context and the means to make coherent sense of whatever might otherwise be difficult or unclear" (blurb). This isn't quite true. Very little is actually explained in these notes and many provide only asides to some of the names involved without saying why they are involved. There is some very interesting material in the notes such as the verdict on Pound, who does not figure in the text ("Thus an anti-Semitic windbag is a significant figure in the development of a partly Jewish aesthetic tradition.") and on Adorno's famous proscription of poetry after Auschwitz, which "...would if followed hand a small but crucial victory to the Nazis (It is for this reason that Adorno himself later retracted it)." But this is rather curiously in the note to a sonnet which ends with Adorno's proscription verbatim as if endorsed, unless we are to read ironies which are not self-evident. [3] The general effect of the sequence is of two recognisable forces struggling to emerge from a Modernist text: the story and the psalmic cadence, neither entirely succeeding.

However much I admire this writing I have again to ask myself the question that has haunted me since I took to reviewing Modernistic poetry. What is gained by subjecting the text to this damage and what is the principle at work? It is only partly answerable. Treated as it is here the text escapes the story and the history, and is obviously a reflection on the current condition, including the author's. It becomes a critique of our culture through disrupted language, which is a thing we quickly read into such usage. So the damage is not enclosed in the history but spreads out towards us, but losing a firm grip on the history in the process. The theme of the book becomes the destruction of the city and everything of worth, of Jerusalem in the Book of Esdras, of Moscow and New York in the story, and all round us.

This is, I think, a better account than the one given in the blurb, that the disturbed textuality "embodies ...the theme of migration and dislocation, and the experience of living in societies whose language is not wholly familiar to the user..." The text creates "misunderstanding" and (as if automatically) "new understandings." This is a Modernist principle which I have struggled with for a long time, finally becoming convinced that a story such as this would be far better "embodied" to the reader in the wholeness of a coherent and connected narrative, whether in poetry or prose, without constant distraction by linguistic pitfalls.

As regards the process of distressing, the author declares that these were at one time "more-or-less regular sonnets" which he disrupted, and the process is more fully described in an interview in the Salt blog [4]. His original texts were in fact put through translation software, more than once I think, producing poor translation and mistranslation which determined the final condition of the text. I think there is more to it than this, for there are things such as incomplete words which are unlikely to have been produced by this method, and I'm sure the author interfered further with the sonnets, probably to increase their distress. One of the purposes may be that Hourvich was a hundred years ago and the broken text serves to remind us of our distance from him, of how he is becoming more difficult to see as he recedes in time, while determined to represent him, or as if the disruptions we now inhabit interfere with our understanding of history itself.

The Book of Isaac is surely one of the most fascinating books of poetry to be published this year, with its meld of fervent enthusiasm and meticulous wordsmithery. It is never less than engaging and the interplay of factual and apocalyptic can be impressive, as in the sonnet on page 48 drawn from an account of the siege of Leningrad, which begins

> at last it has come to this: bread, dust, the artillery
>
> stretched through that crystal waterway
>
> our brains which reach the ice of silver burns...

and dramatically ends with a line recalling an earlier encounter with Hourvich's book on Russian village communism:

> the wheel of the field which exceeds the city

As a non-Jew I sometimes feel excluded, but this is perhaps inevitable when a writer espouses a specifically Jewish vision at the same time as the contemporary poetical insistence that nothing must be explained. I end by quoting an entire and untypical sonnet in rhymed couplets concerning the Yiddish theatre in New York, very little distressed as far as I can see, and causing no division among its readers, as an example of the author's skill:

> *bay mire bistu sheyn*, to me are you
> so beautiful; on Second Avenue
> the curtain rises, enter the greenhorn
> *yidishe meydel*, object of our scorn
> & mirth, our lust for the shtetl-born,
> she brings fresh air in songs
> love inconstancy and wrongs
> that struck her cynical swain
> father or severe again
> we participate in laughter, happy tears
> peel off to leave behind our plight & fear
> haunts our night & day since we were here
> teeters boundaries between chutzpah & pity
> this fear of drowning in a foreign city

The drift of this poem within the maintenance of the song structure is surely very fine.

The author speaks of possibly producing a prose work from this material. I suspect that this admirable project may not be entirely complete until that appears, and perhaps also the 56 more-or-less regular sonnets, if they are extant. I feel that the story deserves to be released from the maskings of modern poetry, without losing them.

§

Paul Brown's *A Cabin in the Mountains* consists of six poem sequences in two divisions, in which there is a strong suggestion of narrative, but narrative of what? This is impossible to say. There is narrative but no plot, tension without location, statements obscured by deviation. There is a frequent sense of intimate event but the language is so displaced and the elements and persons so concealed that there is no knowing whether the story hinted at is factual or derived from film or book or non-existent. Any possibility of an evident account is normally translated instantly into an abstracted and dramatic body language, frequently of the damaged body:

> Almost believed in
> the seduction of the sun
> behind hands bled to the bone
> each pore sweats a retina, skin
> so full of greasy images I
> could rub myself blind.
> This body permits no such modesty but
> a temporary thrust of blood
> flushes out the game
> to the perimeters of pain.

A certain amount of clarity surfaces from time to time but basically the writing is submerged, it is an under-text to perception, and as such it participates in a whole 20th Century art/psychology ethos, a prioritisation of subconscious event with Surrealism at its roots, though Brown's language is rarely surrealist.

The book is prefaced by a quotation from Beckett's *The End*, a particularly bitter paragraph where the speaker enters the disgusting and derelict "cabin in the mountains" that has been allotted him. Set in this position at the portal of the book it announces the enterprise as entry to a decayed or soiled world which is the normal term of our existence, rather than any natural or political disaster. One of the sequences has an epitaph from Freud, on games that are the most likely origins of future neuroses, and that sequence, 'The Games that Are', is particularly heavy in psychological theatre. A hinted narrative which seems to inhabit a personal zone translated into half-theory and half-confession is cut into by imagery of violent wounding and murder.

Occasionally the author rather defiantly states his position in a way which confirms his dedicated belief in the subconscious — "Dreams / help you bleed / more easily" [...] "Truth is never distinct / ever vacant. The imperative necessity / to incomplete itself." And his proposal "...to read these lines / between the lies / unlike / a listening machine pre-/ programmed to empathise...". The discourse is thus the very contrary to all the poetry which is put out these days to persuade you to empathise with the authorial self; if the author shows his face at all here, he appears as something like a probing surgeon or a psycho-invalid on the operating table. If this seems grim, well so it is because the rejection of surface validity is insistent, so that nothing is ever fully evident, but the ethos opens the poetry to a great variety of crises in many half-formed scenes, with episodes of bitter irony and an expert use of the spacing of lines, mainly the "floating" kind. And occasionally, as I said, there is a quite open little poem which while it drops the insistent tone nevertheless usually concludes with a sense of emptiness or Beckettian squalor or a trivialised version of ultimate extinction—

Hammer to Reflex

why a white carton

totters across the street

in mid-morning? There's

no breeze to speak of

maybe the heat

playing havoc with its particles

who knows?

The red bus with a hiss

of hydraulics

puts an end to it.

Paul Brown's poetry is at least as strong as many another in the tribes of the unconventional and although I probably disagree with the ethos which motivates it (truth, or the truth we seek, is in my book entirely distinct) I find his manner intriguing in its deployment of wit and the determination which extends the poetical impulses into sequential episodes. I'm also always glad to promote those the pundits forgot (or never knew about in the first place), for Brown has been but sparsely noticed among the hierarchies of the avant-garde, and Ken Edwards' Reality Street Editions showed enterprise and generosity in producing this book.

§

Catherine Hales' *feasible stratagems* has just arrived and it struck me immediately as a collection of substantial poems in a quite boldly modern idiom which maintains a sense of obligation to speak to the point of the time/place nexus in which the author finds herself, bearing the reader with her in pursuing an impulsion or a thought to a conclusion. These are not common qualities in a context where it is often considered enough simply to break the sentence. There is no punctuation (in some quarters punctuations seems to be becoming a thing of the past) but the use of extended spacing between words or phrases provides a substitute choreography, and a fine balance is maintained between continuity and disconnection, in the unfolding of a scene as in the pursuit of an argument, and particularly in the movement between perception and message.

The central issue might be put again as the despoliation of the city, the story or causality of which is assumed as a given and therefore not narrated either openly or occultly. This is particularly so in the opening sequence of fourteen sonnet-like poems entitled "City State" which is very much concerned with hostile forces in a city at war with itself and the conflicted and reduced state the mind is thereby put into. The blurb speaks of "the extreme depletion of space and sense in the contemporary city by agents of capital" but I think the scope is wider than that, the enemy less doctrinally defined, and the theatre more specific. It begins, "there's beauty in this dereliction..." and there is a constant unwillingness to relinquish the stately poetical line or the resonant scene for ideological reasons or in favour of totalised complaint. What distinguishes her poetry is its acts of *escape* from the vision of ruin, rather than let itself become an apocalyptic doom scenario. There is thus a great deal more hope than you would expect from a straight alienist reading. The issue remains a question, of whether there is or isn't an inhabitable space left, and the poetical disposition of the language itself, especially its confident verse movement, speaks of the existence of such a place whatever it says, by constantly returning to an ancestral elegance among the waste, and to authentic feeling. As she says: "the erasure of the lines   the tenderness"

These innocent personal interventions are able to construct a valid first-person plural by figuration of the largely resistant or brutalist scenarios that confront it, with a notable lightness of touch. "We" are not monodic victims, but multiple entities tangled in all the harm and healing. The ending of 'in the wash room'—-

> ...yet here we are, mon semblable, our
>
> hegelian lines unravelling, caught in a trip-
>
> le trick of utility mirrors. one spins

one measures one cuts & in between

we stitch momentous events

our history is here and now —

here else in time in tact (the sym-

pathetic harmonies on taut

wires, hear that?) attenuated

by circumstance to a rather damaged

version of ourselves germ-free environment indeed

wishing we could be better than we are

§

1   The exceptions and corrections to this fairly outrageous statement are too many to enumerate. They would include "versions" of Homer, Beowulf, Aeschylus, Dante and others done by Ted Hughes, Seamus Heaney, Tony Harrison and younger poets, where I have generally found that the need for "modern relevance" is understood as necessarily reductive and for some reason the big dignified verse forms have to be ditched. The most recent of these, *Memorial* by Alice Oswald (Faber 2011) which is based on the *Iliad*, declares from the first words of the introduction that no attempt at narrative will be made at all: "This is a translation of the *Iliad*'s atmosphere, not its story". It seems to be agreed in the whole of this new tradition of translation that our poetry can now only comprehend the small-scale. *Memorial* is an engaging book consisting of short poems made from all the accounts of death in battle in the *Iliad* — but without the battles. All these men are killed from nowhere and for no reason, perhaps like the victims of a drone strike. The book would be more engaging if so much of the text didn't occur twice.

2   There is a detailed biographical note at http://findingaids.cjh.org/?pID=1358888 Among other noteworthy acts Hourvich was the first to propose uncontrolled immigration as beneficial to the economy. Isaac, you should be here at this hour.

3   The Polish name Oświęcim is used instead of Auschwitz, which perhaps adds some hint of alienation from the dictum.

4   blog.saltpublishing.com/2011/02/14/crashawprize-the-shortlist-in-profile-aidan-semmens

MARTIN HARRISON: AUSTRALIAN PASTORAL

Martin Harrison, *Wild Bees: new and selected poems*.
Shearsman Books 2008.168pp paperback
Martin Harrison, *Living Things: five poems*.
Sydney: Vagabond Press 2013. 16pp booklet, edition of 100

The work of the Australian poet Martin Harrison is roughly characterised as "descriptive", which it is, though that is the merest beginning of the matter. To say it is "descriptive of rural scenes" is true of a majority of the poems but so inadequate a comment as to be closer to false. He does accept poetry's ability to convey a location, which he does with precision, and is much concerned with natural detail—

> I've given up talking
>
> save through the world as it is.

but adds—

> But the leaf is no philosopher.
>
> It's just an edge, a flare-mark,
>
> and not a thing in itself.

('On the Traditional Way of Painting')

The phenomena of earth are invoked in the writing and focused on in order to bring perception to a liminal position between the local and the total. The word "pastoral" thus suits him whether the experience notated is actually rural or, in many cases, not. My use of the word here is to indicate nothing about shrubs and milking-pails, but rather a particular power of language that only poetry has, to set before us a proposition which is fictive whether or not it coincides with the actual. Or to make it sound more attractive, a possibility is offered, a theatre in a detail of the world and time, which becomes a site for action (adventure, understanding, love, etc.) by being on the edge of presence in, and absence from, the world. The basic pastoral condition is that poetical writing sets itself apart from prosaic usage by being part of a structure which only operates as a whole, or gains resonance by becoming part of a specifically poetical history. There is a simple exposition of this at the beginning of Veronica Forrest-Thomson's book *Poetic Artifice* (1978, page x) where she points out that the sentence "Pipit sat upright in her chair some distance from where I was sitting" could be used to convey particular information in the external world for whatever reason it was needed, but when it becomes the first two lines of T.S. Eliot's poem 'A Cooking Egg', "The statement is altered by its insertion into a poetical context" such that it no longer necessarily indicates a particular event in a real or fiction-ally represented world. We must wait to see what its import finally is. [1] Poetical language is apart from but beholden to the external world, and elicits a particular kind of attention by invoking the nature and history of poetry. The speaker then becomes a voice rather than an author. In Martin Harrison's words,

> This, then is translation
>
> out of ordinary space—
>
>
> not word for word,
>
> but as someone might feel

sitting outside, in dusklight,
hearing bells and traffic...

('An Ordinary Communication')

The name for this transformation is pastoral, which is in essence
nothing to do with rurality but is a mode of representation peculiar
to poetry. Its literary use descends from classical Arcadian poetry
which set up a site of innocence in a remote elsewhere as a contrasting and reflective mirror of society and produced the traditional association with (actually) sheep-rearing, perhaps last used
creatively by William Blake. I'd add that Forrest-Thomson's definition does not necessarily hold in, for instance, narrative poetry,
and the textual condition for it is necessarily lyrical, which she
calls "formal".

This cautionary preamble allows me without fear of alienat-
ing the aficionados of advanced poetry to say that Martin Harrison's poems are brilliant and remarkable meditations on moments
of perception (or clusters of such moments) most of which take
place in the Australian countryside, presumably the "orchard and
vine-growing area" in which an earlier blurb says he lives for half
the year. The poems have starting-points which are experiences
rather than scenes — being somewhere and looking at something,
often in a stillness such as dawn, often with a sense of solitude.
Birds, snakes, leeches, wallabies, a dog barking, a lake, clouds,
paddocks, "fine rain at night", "a patch of grass" are the foci of
his kind of poetry. There are other, more urban, starting-points
but generally with the same contemplative atmosphere. He starts
from one of these points and unfolds the poem from it quite inde-
fatigably. Not for him the haiku-like brevity which is happy to
identify a feature, name it, put it through a minimal process and
stop — these are mostly substantial poems, enacting a continuing attention to the initial experience and extension from it. 50

lines later we can still be at the same place, its description still in progress, indeed sometimes we do not reach the announced subject until the end of the poem. The poem 'Wallabies' for instance (in *Living Things*) meditates for over 70 lines on a rural landscape before the wallabies appear in it ten lines before the end, like a reward. And these subjects are essentially simple things which do not themselves demand any explanation or reconciliation. But Harrison treats them as entities waiting to reveal their meaning and the important thing is to press on with the poetical description, and remain explicit and remain truthful, therefore without any of the recourse some poets have to rhetorical structures (or symbolical or metonymic), focused not on language nor on ideology but on the event itself, and the self that witnesses it. It is an act of concentration to the point where the subject yields something greater than itself, an understanding, say, or an interconnection between phenomenon and idea. It is "the glimpse opening up in you". All the energy and tension of the poem is built up between the object and the self as witness, carefully explicated in a poetically rich but direct manner. It is also a demonstration of the adequacy of an explicit tongue as a meditational vehicle. By this I do not mean plain language: the poems are thick with metaphor, though it is significant that he uses simile rather more than most modern poets would. If there is, and there often is, the phrase "it is as if..." he is immediately off on further reaches of the experience, possibly for quite a long time.

Although there is a sense of staying exactly where we are, however much reminded of something else or noticing something else on the edge of the field, the discourse itself gets involved in terms of surprising distance from the poem's subject and setting, and there are figurations which are beyond rational connection without becoming distractions or obstructions. You could not say the writing is verbally-centred but it is deeply verbally involved, seeking "the integration of meaning and sound which is essential to each poem". A full, sometimes perhaps "Modernistic", poetical resource is brought to bear on the task in hand, which is to coax a value out of the subject and so to complete the experience of the poem. [2]

I found it difficult to work out exactly how Harrison proceeds so fulsomely through the poem, what the mechanisms are which carry the discourse forward without departing from the principal focus, especially as there is little or no sense of declaration, no message which was not already there, no scenario except what the eyes see in stasis. When there is a human document involved it is treated in the same way as a conifer, by calmly saying how it appears to be, how the self seeks to cope with it or learn from it. To cope with this difficulty I thought of writing a précis of one of the poems but this proved impossible; the tightness of the writing could not be improved upon — a précis would mean copying out the poem. So I undertook instead a kind of description, inevitably longer than the poem, of one of the poems, one which does not have a rural setting — 'Summer', 70 lines in 5-line sections, which I've numbered.

(1) 'Summer' begins with a swimming pool on the roof of a hotel at dawn, perhaps in Thailand — its littered stillness (dead bugs etc. — "little shipwrecks") — which participates in the dawn because the stillness is represented in active terms — "...coolness... greyness and limpidity ... shimmering across its transparence, its daybreak light.".

(2) Its utilitarian features as a "rooftop machine" (caulk, paint, pump, chlorine etc.) forming this "ad-world image of a dream" "for (it says) hotel guests only." Continuing rational and plain description with a touch of the ominous, as if a critique is pending.

(3) Used by "exhausted travellers" (at the end we find that the speaker is an exhausted traveller) who will plunge into it with a sense of protected purity — "Water (they think) cares for them as it lets them through". To "think" is here redefined as a figure for

the implied meaning of an act, unlikely to be actually "thought" by the agent. This irrational idea is extended to the proposition that "someone jumping in won't worry" about the disturbance he makes, which is represented as a scene of violent and massive water action (peaks, valleys, hills, parabolas, "sprayed-out grunge"). This is what the swimmer is protected from, a kind of contra-world invoked in the disturbance of the meniscus. This stanza is surprising but too fanciful to disrupt the initial perception of stillness, to which the poem returns immediately

(4) with a kind of summary of where we are up to. The "mirror surface no more than a mirror deep" that "reflects a city's post-dawn sounds" (in stanza 1 it was, more rationally, the early light that was reflected) with a passing thought about how a lap-swimmer would navigate the pool, turning from underwater like a shark. Again a sense of the pool as a guarded protection from an oceanic elsewhere of which it is a miniaturisation.

(5) Attention is directed to a closer elsewhere as the speaker notices a Thai family waking up on the balcony of a neighbour-ing building. They paradoxically haven't slept but will have been operating some stall of "knick-knacks" all night. Here as time passes from pre-dawn to dawn and the city starts moving the stanza structure, in which most lines have been end-stopped and each stanza represented a distinct phase of thought, is transgressed, and from now on there is a lot of enjambement, even across stanzas, new paragraphs starting mid-stanza and mid-sentence, etc., returning to something more regular at the end of the poem. But the action represented is never other than that of pensive contem-plation; the speaker is never anywhere but motionless on a hotel roof in the early morning.

(6-8) Observation of the Thai family, speculation that they moved into the town from an up-country village. Both the village and their city habitat are felt to be exposed to touristic voyeurism, "Americans, heifer-garlanded with cameras" walking through the village, or "any bastard foreigner" with a camera for whom there's a "wealth of angles" available from up here. The complaint here is coined so as to indicate an appropriation of the terms of the particular and the different by foreign wealth. The interruptive anger, like the earlier imagery of turbulence, returns quickly to "this wind-free, cool lozenge of water". There is an alternation of still pool and turbid thoughts, both inhabiting the one mind, with a sense of accumulation and intensification. But the discourse remains rational; the move to new matter is made by noticing something different, and the focus returns again to the pool, now seen differently, as an artifice, "...arranged behind concrete tubs in a fake garden-effect."

(9-10) Stanza 9 begins after the hyphen of "garden-effect", an extreme disruption of the appearance of regularity. There are six white plastic recliners, which "articulate ... imaginary bodies, sipping martinis through straws". But immediately the chairs "are really signs of death". This is the major turning-point of the poem, marked not so much by the matter of it, as by the forms of figu-ration. The chairs firstly "articulate" bodies lying on them, as if the image is collaborative between poet and object, as if it as an inevitable result of the sight of the chairs. The next step in thought, which is what he calls it, is more radical:

> Those chairs—
>
> the thought's a shock rising over clear, bare seas—
>
> [Stanza 10]
>
> are really signs of death, sculptures signalling 'absence of body'
>
> while quiet water, I suddenly remember, is stagnancy and grief.
>
> (It's water with a texture that seems to look right past you.)"

We are still in a movement of thought and remembering, but as if involuntarily, and the connective grammar is neither simile nor metaphor, but identity. The chairs "are", the water "is"... The presence of the word "really" pushes the thought-process into a parallel world in which things stand as their evident meanings, a world more real than the one we inhabit, reached by a meditative thought process. Nothing exotic or mystical about this — the parallel world is more poetical than visionary. It is where you arrive by concentrated thinking within a necessarily poetical process, because only poetry offers the free resource of language you need, and the very act of writing leads you forward into the discovery. The stark realisation is grounded in an appeal to the reader's recognition of the justness of the figures, the way still water seems to ignore you, as something at once accepted but which you had never thought of. Neither is it definitive. It is the goal of this one moment of perception, this one act of writing. The same object, plastic recliner or whatever, might elicit a quite different identity in another poem. So this climax cannot be the end, this epiphany at the centre of the poem has to be retracted from.

(10-11) "There's always this desire simply to stop" but he drags one of the chairs over and sits on it to remove his runners. Remarks follow on the clothes travellers wear, like walking advertisements for a New York gym.

(12) What happens in the rest of the poem is a serious consideration of the momentary entity, explored in a richer and rather more difficult language than heretofore, which summates the experience of the poem. Thinking at first in terms of photography he asks what is it that "lines up a world famous shot" when so much is already visualised — "What is the accident that drags you to the shore?" ... What draws you to the focus? He is, in no hurry, drawing together the threads of the poem as glosses on the initial moment of perception, traversing its phases of imagery, and not without ambiguity — does the "accident" rescue you from the ocean or bring you towards it? In either case we are brought to an edge experience, a threshold.

(13) The moment is focused "not on that family, / but the one which flashes through its web of neurones / signifying the merest fact of being here, snapped / in this age of debris, smoke, and fire." The advocation of the revelatory moment is becoming almost homiletic, as it is represented as a "shot" through a dispersion, a dissolving "glittering electronic dust" in the mind, the attaining of a focus which reveals no more than presence, that you are here now, "indicative as a lawn's pink flamingo"

(14) "only the dead, their remembered messengers, walk in and out of it" — I take this to mean that only the dead in our memories of them traverse the clouded and obscured terms of human memory, in our acknowledgement of death as fact or absolute conditional. The scenario is now classical, the dead drifting ghostlike on the banks of Lethe (the water image again), where Odysseus no longer goes "with his flasks of blood" — a particularly difficult phrase which might intend that no epic (enhanced political) power with its participation in large-scale slaughter is now relevant to the process of comprehending the mortal condition. And the poem ends with a moral gesture drawn from the moment of the poem — "This split second — this jet-lagged moment" and what is won from it "...fixes my mind on home: a humane life that's rootless, mindless as summer is." So this intense extended focus on a particular place comes to the assertion that humanity is merely represented by the earth's surface, not constituted of it. "Human" gains its final E from "elsewhere" in the process of returning "home", and whatever else "home" is it is also the title-word, mentioned here for the first time.

The discourse at the end of this poem takes quite a lot of concentration and imagination on the reader's part, which is not always the case. It helps that closely related formulations can be found in other poems, such as the ending of 'Late Western Thought' which is concerned with the impress on memory of a scene of trees, birds, crickets, a slow-moving horse —

Of course, it remains no more than a story
About seeing and forgetting, its narrative is the
root of compassion,
Not least because, afterwards, you must still
capture it at one go —

yes, in a single, sharp flame of light—

setting and slanting,
raking deep fire behind the trees (they're black silhouettes on the ridge),
invisibly burning you, invisibly burning itself.

Or again, the ending of 'Suddenly, Trees' on the effect of night rain on trees seen in the early morning—

suddenly thinking what it would be like
to have seen this just at the point of having died,
to have had this moment of insight,
of thought—
then to have gone away—
glancing each thing in its passage,
as the light, the water, the bare trees
themselves glance out to me

Many of Harrison's poems go through a process similar to that of 'Summer' which is a form of intervention in the world, disturbing an initial adequacy and wholeness ("how we divide the world with thoughts") and then following the meditation round to a conclusion which closes the divide and returns the wholeness. This conclusion may be a moral perception, a chastening, or it may be simply a last glimpse of the scene in a singular feature. Senses of the stillness, extent, wonder, or beauty, of an experience initiate the process as if they hold a question in themselves which needs to be asked (while we know they don't), about what is the nature of the experience, why was it arresting, what does it "mean" to the agent who recognises it? This question is fed through the poem to reach an epiphanic point, where the experience yields recognition far beyond its initial silence — a telling of the human condition or a moral intent.[3] That may be the end of the poem but more often the poem subsides from this moment of revelation to reach a quiet and more localised conclusion at which the lesson can be more calmly, sometimes casually, indicated. But many poems, unlike 'Summer', end only with a brief farewell notation of the poem's focus, a close detail which returns us to the earth. He is in fact very adept at that kind of signing-off gesture in which a detail of the observed reality is felt as both confirmation and departure ("two swallows, scissoring, vanish across the sun").

In his Preface Harrison considers himself lucky "...to have so far escaped from being classified in a movement or a generation — new or old, innovative or formal." But neither, I think, can he be classified as a maverick operating in complete independence from and ignorance of his contemporaries. In some ways his procedures are those accepted in what I might call "standard" modern poetry, especially among poets first active in the 1950s, and their legacy. Sylvia Plath, for instance, in a poem such as 'Berck-Plage' and other late poems which do not lapse into authorial anger, grasps the principle perfectly. Even in Seamus Heaney's later work there are sometimes metaphors whose accuracy can be recognised without tracing a rational trajectory. In a way the usage is common, of more or less audacious extrapolation from a given experience, but the resolution is normally given in terms of human interaction and an empathetic appeal from the self, in both cases ultimately comforting. It is important to distinguish Harrison's art from this subjective mode. The poems, he says in 'The Particularity of Poetry', "...refer to situations which are collective and objective". The figure of the author is always there and dictates the progression through the poem, but nowhere are the earthly percepts claimed as a property of the self, any more than they are directed towards the public in a hortatory or accusatory sense. He could be said to turn aside from the human world and therefore from love, but I don't think he does. Its values are implied and interrogated in the entire process of constructing a parallel experience, and sometimes become explicit, as in the significantly titled 'Double Movement' which is about wave movement in nature—

> In the human world too, a dry force is introduced, one which requires everyone to acknowledge a separateness in the relations between living things, in how one person values another. Shadow is evaporated.

Harrison was born in UK and before he moved to Sydney in 1978 he was associated with some radical tendencies there (the "Cambridge" group) and had a book, entitled *1975*, published by Andrew Crozier's Ferry Press in 1980. Without wanting to cast him as the puppet of various movements I like to think his escape from popular subjectivism might have been aided by this association. That particular grouping was itself divided, between abstract and symbolised versions of poetical representation. His own poetry at that time was one of personal and vocal direct address in unpunctuated common English, avoiding both strong figuration and conservative formalities and thus aligning himself with the Americanising force of those poets, indeed sometimes slightly New York. Although he has reprinted none of it, there is in it a sense of driving forwards towards the consummation of an experience which recognisably leads forward to his later work. But the point is that Harrison knows what is going on in English-language poetry and uses what he needs of its attributes. For all the rural pastoral there is a freshness, a freedom to transgress accepted procedural norms and to formulate disarming connective figurations which might set him with the innovative poets, though not the experimental, but this quality is mainly his own claimed liberty. In an Australian connection too, where there has been a great deal of rural pastoral, he stands apart, for he is manifestly not saying that the rural is our site of basic earthly realities, its inhabitants sources of rural wisdom[4], and his narrative is not anecdotal, thus well apart from the interests of Les Murray or John Kinsella (or Seamus Heaney for that matter) though there is a shared ecological awareness. In the one poem I can find, 'A Breath of Wind on a Summer Night', which pays more than passing attention to an inhabitant, an old woman living in a remote place, there is no story to tell, indeed she is hardly identified, and her speech is valued not for its pro-verbial weight but for its accuracy in describing a natural event — precisely an aim of the poetry itself. All she says is, describing the appearance of a dangerous snake on her threshold which she had not seen, that she felt it "like a breath of wind when you don't expect it", and "that plain, deathless phrase", that hearing of the virtually inaudible, that sensing of the real, stands as his motto at beginning and end of the poem. Among Australians only Robert Adamson occurs to me as close to Harrison, especially with his poems of entranced extrapolation from the appearance of a bird.

I reckon Harrison had established what he wanted to do by the mid-1990s, before the book *The Kangaroo Farm* appeared in 1997, which is well represented in *Wild Bees*. But there are signs of a restless wish to progress, especially in his more recent work. The final section of *Wild Bees,* a dozen poems under the heading 'Music', has as much prose as poetry in it and seems to show a wish for expansiveness, to state himself as fully as possible with or without the concentration demanded by verse. He sometimes here seems to be on the track of an existential anxiety, and focuses on more disturbing experience, as of personal loss and accidental death. He is also free, at times, to seek out the terms he needs more widely, indeed across the world. The poem 'Winter Solstice' begins nowhere in particular—

> A vague mood, a sadness, a feeling as when recovering from illness, a
> kind of "whatever it is which is going on at the time" mode—

but this is immediately represented in earthly terms:

> a defile bulldozed between trees where the powerlines go through on a ridge top,
> their suspended wires as out of place as a street's tramwires would be...

and goes on to examine and enlarge upon this emotional correlation at length, passing through Miró, Calder, and the Berlin Wall in search of what is damaged and what can be recovered, before returning to that first scene.

The five poems of *Living Things* are named after singular entities: four creatures and a cloud, though in two cases they don't manifest themselves until the last words of the poem. They are very much in Harrison's established mode but enhanced both in detail and in scope, moving freely among more daring figuration and more freely abstract discourse, while continuing to tangle with serious notations of loss and destruction. There is less firm a sense that the ending of a poem resolves anything but the construct it terminates, and a self-questioning about his whole enterprise ("And how will it end? this half-traced ecstasy at merely being here."). I think that this tremulous uncertainty as it works its way through his impressive techniques of resource and continuity, produces some of the finest things he has done.

Martin Harrison's poetry is described in a blurb by Nigel Wheale as creating "utterly convincing places where ordinary happiness might reside". Though written before the more recent work which admits of a negative epiphany, of "details too terrible to bring to mind", I think this is true. His modernity allows him to deploy exploratory figuration without that unkindness to the reader which is almost ubiquitous in British and American "innovative" poetry. However abstruse he gets he is always explicit, which means there is none of that double-bind on the reader, that yes-with-no, give-and-take-back, now-you-see-it-now-you-don't as practised (and encouraged and taught) in advanced circles, but also to be found among conventionalist poets, courting and absorbing the reader in a world reduced to language.

> For, as I drove, earth was paradox
>
> flat for miles yet curving into clouds —
>
> sensed like a rear-view mirror's glimpse
>
> yet always opening up, leading onwards

('Clouds Near Waddi')

Paradox but not contradiction, thus an opening for a richer perception and not a door closed in your face. An important statement in his Preface says: "...the limits of our experience and understanding of the world are the limits of time and of our senses, and not just of language. The provisional nature of our selves, our own temporary glimpse of the world's tragedy and loveliness, is at the heart of the matter." [5] This, as it is manifested in the tentative and studious nature of the poetry, and the ordinariness of the perceptive encounter, is a gauntlet thrown down before a vast (and growing) industry of artistic and literary production and the institutionalisation and theorising that props it up.

The last poem of *Living Things*, labelled as a coda and shorter than usual, is entitled 'Frog'. It is untypical in its smiling light-heartedness, and more so in being actually spoken by the creature itself—

I'm a member of the kingdom of happiness

and I live under a dream-stone. Yes, you're right:

I'm a frog, it's obvious.

This friendly frog speaks of its song for a few lines, defining it as "the source of metaphor", apparently through its double, or paradoxical nature. But then the frog is suddenly allegorised into a member of the general public speaking out against the assumptive elitism of modern poetry (and modern other things) by which he is normally and automatically cast as idiotic and in need of (our) enlightenment. Against this the *lumpenproletariat*, the sack of potatoes, the frog, actually speaks—-

I'm the source

of metaphor. My sung trills and rising clacks,

back and forth, up and down, here and there,

on and on — and on — into the rainy murk,

give me time for thoughtful immediacy.

It's far too much. You think I eat chips, drink beer,

waste my time on crap TV — I'm thinking, see —

my movements lithe, smart, enviably athletic.

---

1   *Poetic Artifice* is sadly long out of print and the web book-sharks want £150 for it. There are useful selections from it in *Poets on Writing* edited by Denise Riley (1992) introduced by Martin Harrison.

2   *Poets on Writing* also contains two more essays by Harrison, one of them from 1973. The other, more recent one, which my quotation comes from, is 'The Particularity of Poetry' in which he gives in his own terms a version of the textual condition under discussion, how it rests on "the tonality of individual perception" and the question of "what kind of 'is' a poem brings into being". "This", he says, "is a lyrical task." and "Poetic ideas are emblematic sensations".

3   "...poetry is epiphanic, anticipatory — and no matter how external, how painfully cumbersome one's means for making it are forced to be, it is essential to remember what this self-announcing quality of each new poem is." —'The Particularity of Poetry'.

4   He neither finds nor claims wisdom: "The prerogatives of superior wisdom can become another trap" because they do not start from ignorance and wordlessness. —'The Particularity of Poetry'.

5   And in 'The Particularity of Poetry' he speaks of the need to accept both the largeness and
     the limits of feeling and perception "in order to locate, live in or possibly emigrate from
     them." ... "There is no other way through to copiousness".

WORRYING AROUND ENGLAND

Peter Robinson, *The Returning Sky.*
Shearsman Books 2012. 108pp paperback
Peter Robinson, *Like the Living End.*
Tworple Press 2013. 36pp paperback; £7.00
John Welch, *Visiting Exile.*
Shearsman Books 2009. 84pp paperback.
John Welch, *Its Halting Measure.*
Shearsman Books 2012. 90pp paperback.

I'm sure that the fact that both poets under review are the sons of clergymen has no significant bearing on their poems, and I shall try not to mention it again.

Peter Robinson writes normal poems, or appears to. What this mainly means is that we know where we are, and where we are is where Peter Robinson is. The poems follow him through the streets and rooms of Reading, where he now lives, and join him in excursions to Liverpool, where he grew up, and to other places, picking out significant, poignant or typical moments in his day-to-day life, usually in connection with memory. The windows we look out of are his windows, and the eyes by which we see the world are his eyes. The voice too is his, but who it is addressed to is more difficult to say, often seeming to be an interior amalgam of himself and another, the reader or a specific person alive or dead. When he begins a poem "So there we are.." (p.30)[1] , where we are and who "we" are remain questions to be answered in the unfolding of the poem, but we can usually be sure that they will both be identified, if not by name, and indeed they eventually are: "So there we are, a married couple...". Although this poem is then clearly addressed to his wife, there is a sense of interior monologue in which she serves as a fictional auditor, as indeed there is a sense of solitude in the most familial or social of his poems. He habitually addresses a "you" which is no more than himself, using "you" as the impersonal pronoun, — "this is what I did" is rendered as "this is what you do", thereby claiming himself as typical, an everyman in a recurrent situation shared with all others. This feels like an unusual usage in contemporary poetry, especially any such as his with its careful attention to perceptual detail, but its purpose remains a normal trope of typicality or empathy. Indeed all this is "normal", including a running appeal to the reader to validate the author's percepts, and an equally constant affirmation of a sense of the normal, everyday world as the poem's field of action, from which he will not be tempted by the faintest trace of surrealism or disjunctive verbalism. Nor will he be tempted from the town into the countryside if he can help it. The tone is quite familiar, as a steady, meticulous address, a sorting through of detail in an unhurried quest for a result. These are, more or less, the normal procedures of many poets, especially those who place themselves in a 20th Century Anglo-American continuum of explicative self declaration in straight language in an urban scenario such as Robinson likes to praise and blame in his books of criticism. But all this normality leaves features unaccounted for. He appears to write normal poems, but there is more to it; there are abnormalities or aberrations, many of which could easily escape attention in a casual reading.

So we are led through these streets, rooms, houses, towns, waste lots, and cemeteries (which, like John Welsh, he seems drawn to), as well as occasions such as viewing a family album, meeting or losing old friends, a bird crashing into a window, etc. — subjects English poets have been choosing for about a century. They are chosen as sites of emotive impulsion, sometimes overtly (an old friend's funeral, revisiting his childhood home etc.), sometimes teasing out the emotive force in the course of the poem. The unity of descriptive and lyrical effect frequently bespeaks a poet of considerable experience—

> Today the sky has a period flavour,
>
> distances whipped in by cumulus piles
>
> covering ranges of blue
>
> from a near turquoise through to deep azure.

> ("Period Sky" p.81)

Such dexterity (the half-rhyme of "flavour" and "azure" across the semantic fulcrum of "blue") is as likely to speak of bulldozers or a row of portaloos, and only a certain amount of time is anyway spent on contextual details, for Robinson always wants to push the poem on towards a larger scale or more intense utterance. The second stanza of the same poem shows him making such a transition—

> Enough to make weak eyes water, the sky
>
> bares a memory of pain
>
> to which your heart goes out...
>
> Sharp on the tongue, and getting keener,
>
> it's tickled by a kitchen garden's
>
> fennel, thyme, rosemary, lemon verbena.

The process is thus an elaboration of a subjective and irrational sense he has of the "antiquity" of the sky in its setting (he seems to be among old buildings and gardens) claimed as so intense that "your heart" (i.e. my heart) "goes out"... oddly "tickled" by four old English herbs, perhaps with their emblematic overtones. In the third stanza he almost hears the shrieks caused by 16th Century torturers and the sky is one moment "gory", twinned with its "glory", and finally empty and indifferent. He cannot claim any necessity for this sequence. It is simply cast at us that "the sky bears a memory of pain", which a different experience of the same place could legitimately deny and refuse to feel. Although the arbitrary progression is stark here, I think it is always more-or-less the case in his poems and his skill is in persuading us to accept it as a true event of the world by authenticity of expression and poetical interplay. There are often transitions like this in his poems, by which the intensification or inauguration of an emotive response is suddenly made to open the poem to greater issue. Here's another, with the same you/I merge and a quite disturbing shift of tense:

> Above the bridge, an easyJet
>
> plane descends to the renamed airport,
>
> and in its higher sky's
>
> releases, burdens being lifted
>
> from you into an uneventful air
>
> were shaming re-stirred memories...
> *Like the Living End* p.16

The poet's strategies for gaining authenticity include those aberrations I mentioned which delicately separate his work from the absolutely normal while allowing him to stand in its light in opposition to obscurantism. While it remains "talking poetry" it can rarely for more than a few lines be recognised as identical to the statement-centred, faultlessly normal talking English, smoothly flowing and ever self-explaining, telling us unproblematically what it wants us to hear, which dominates most successful (and all very successful) English poetry now. The tone of this 'normality' is readily ingratiating, seeking to befriend the reader and assuring him/her of the poet's human qualities. Robinson's tone is not thus, though neither does it offer the pitfalls and jolts that some poets rejoice in — great gaps in the syntax or disconnected words, acts of the poet as enemy. Rather there are slight jerks in a flow of speech. Here are a few such lines, out of context, to which I've appended what I think would be a more normal wording (these are not corrections) —

> "and farther are the ancestors..." (farther *off* / *away* are the ancestors...)
> "I come out of my reverie and find a pair of splashing coots feud like rival poets." (*feuding*)
> "Muntjac deer surviving by carved angels..." (It's a cemetery scene and he means surviving *beside* or *among* carved angels)
> "and hall's revealed rafters..." (*rafters revealed* or at least *the* hall)
> "Usage and tones of the local fauna can't help unsettling, their behaviour like to get you hence..." (can't help *unsettling you* or *being unsettling*, their behaviour *likely to* or *as if to*...)

The point here is the slightness of these shifts, a few inches to the side of the settled normal mode of talk: little contractions, clipped speech, a rather archaic subjunctive... moments of awkwardness or stiffness which don't halt the flow but which I nevertheless think are decisive. Some of them may be shifts of meaning or emphasis which are called for, but they still disturb the somnolence of the normal. Their effect is to remove the text from a spoken to a written status. Many more normalising poets do this by stressing the poetical tone in balanced phrases and formal regularity of various kinds but I find Robinson's little peculiarities more disturbing, especially in their similarity sometimes to careless writing, which I don't think they ever are. They are joined by other ways of drawing you towards a "written" reading — that is, a reading which does not expect simply to be fed a continuum of language but is prepared to contemplate the textual surface in the awareness of a poetical tension. These include subsumed quotations, rather difficult metaphors, metrical patterning which seems half there, and degrees of rhyme, about which he is rather casual, allowing it to happen from time to time usually at three or four lines' distance, except for some fully crafted sonnets.

All this careful crafting of the lines into a texture which may be somewhat stiff, or poised, or not as yielding as they at first seemed, draws attention to the process of the poem rather than any conclusion. In fact there is a tendency to the inconclusive and to not quite disclosing situations referred to, especially occluded personal histories. There is a melancholy attached to conclusions which do not solve. He makes no claim to insight, repudiating the value in "lived historical situations" of "moral or political correctness" in the poem. [2] Rather he offers to delineate accurately on a poetical stage processes of self perception which are indirectly educative of emotion and understanding.

So the transitions in the poems, which can be quite dramatic, lead not to gems of wisdom but to prolongations or intensifications of the coverage already under way, further consideration of the situation. The poems go in a series of steps marked by these transitions which as well as intensifying the discourse can also stretch the rationality of the language and of the progression to the uttermost. A short poem called 'World Enough' (p.42) introduces each of its three stanzas with the deprecating phrase "Such as it is..." beginning with a sunset and old brickwork (such scenes seem to attract him) and a sense of long time passing independently of humanity. Then—

> Such as it is, reality
>
> slips past on a warehouse
>
> without the slightest emphasis,
>
> thrives if it fail to become
>
> yet one more news item—-
>
> hoarfrost, a whisper, or kiss.

The word "on" is arresting, even if the sense is not difficult. The old brickwork which gives him this sensation of a departing hold on reality is presumably that of the warehouse walls, and the strong sense of ephemerality could indeed therefore be "on" the brickwork, rather than, say, "in" anything. But the construct "reality slips past on a warehouse" remains bizarre with its suggestion of a warehouse on wheels. Actually I think it is perfectly accurate as a delineation of a subjective percept attached to a particular site, a sense of loss, including loss of control, in the passage of time, which is a common motivation to a poem for him. But short of writing an extended paragraph I leave it to other readers to say exactly what is happening in the next three lines. A fragile sense of loss has itself become an actor in the drama, which leaps from metaphors to instances over big conceptual gaps. And continues to in the final stanza, happily resolving on a stroke of ironic wit—

> Such as it is, and everywhere,
>
> it comes at us sideways
>
> from bits of grey sky
>
> as when a bureaucrat asked me
>
> where did I plan to be buried?

I wasn't planning to die.

The option to rhyme third and sixth lines, which is not taken in the first stanza, creeps in unobtrusively (off-accent) in the second, and finishes the third with a resounding clang. There is a sense of final resolution in the patterning here while ironically the conclusion is entirely irresolute as regards the poem's subject.

A hint dropped by Roy Fisher identifies exactly the force of the steps into disorientation which Robinson's poems so often take, and which do seem to be the point of the exercise, whether resolved at the end or not — "It is as if he carries a listening device for the moments when the tectonic plates of mental experience slide quietly one beneath another to create paradoxes and complexities that call for poems to be made." [3] The poems exploit a paradox: the sense of meticulously careful writing which places the poet in complete control, reinforced by his access to formalities of metre and rhyme when he needs them, work to undermine his self-security, his sense of standing firmly on the ground. And the language as it gets progressively more highly wrought through the poem participates in the same process, without ever being entirely released into fantasia (though there are some close moments).

When a poet has produced several volumes of criticism of modern poetry, as Peter Robinson has,[4] it can be helpful to refer the version there of how a poem works, to the poet's own practice, though it should never be allowed to become definitive. Looking quite cursorily through some of Robinson's poetry criticism for useful hints, I was struck by his pervasive anxiety about the performance of poetry on the page. With the exception of poets, such as Pound, whose moral failures are glaring, whoever he is writing about and however much he admires, he seems constantly worried as he nervously follows the writing, that the poet will at any moment lapse into some kind of betrayal, and may do it by very slight linguistic acts — a misplaced comma, an unbalanced epithet, an unwise adjective... And the qualities betrayed are those of the selfhood, especially by an imbalance amounting to self-absorption or a lack of "self-awareness"; they are qualities of character rather than belief, in lives lived through the challenges of guilt and reparation, always in danger of a failure to balance the self-referential and the abstract. He uses biographical information freely and chooses poets who thrive on it. Thus with Hardy's late work he is much concerned about the quality of the poet's relationship to his dead wife as subtly enhanced or betrayed in details of diction, rhyme, rhythm, etc. I could not possibly apply to his poetry the kind of strictures he does to Hardy's; it would seem harsh and assumptive, and anyway I do not know half as much about Robinson's relationship with his wife as he seems to about Hardy's with his. There is no chance in Robinson's discourse of a Hardy poem lifting off the page and flying into an independent existence, in spite of all the lyrical wings Hardy has supplied it with. The poets he deals with are seen primarily as self-declaring subjects, rather than anonymous craftspeople. It is a policing of the poem by an ideal of personal integrity. He is not alone in this but belongs to a succession of empiricist critics (Bernard Williams, Donald Davie et al.) who pick at lines of poetry in similar ways, and like all of them he is repelled by any display of sonorous effects, thus the outright rejection of Dylan Thomas, whose work he sees as an infantile subjection to verbal music, though occasionally he commits resounding sonic fanfares himself — "...and streams flowing forwards to Seaforth", which sounds half way between Thomas and Housman. And there is in this critical lineage a steady dislike of any purveyor of high or "prophetic" tone, such as Ginsberg. Behind a lot of his strictures, and quite far away in his past, I suspect the presence of the art critic Adrian Stokes, who had a considerable influence on Pound, and on the Cambridge group of Donald Davie, J.H. Prynne, and R.F. Langley in his categorical rejection of the "moulded" (plastic, rhythmic, fluid, etc.) in favour of the "carved" (static, balanced, etc.) —- a judgement which I doubt was ever rationally validated either by Stokes or his poetical progeny, but which could be one of the forces lying behind the entire cultivation of disjunction in modernism. Things, ultimately words, are meant to stand before each other distinctly, rather than merge into a discourse. Robinson was in his student days involved with the Cambridge circle of Prynne but is generally looked upon as having deserted that camp, and he has himself questioned the Stokesian pronouncements.[5] But in him they seem to have been to some extent interiorised into features of his taste, and possibly enforced the refusal of effusion and generalisation in his own poetry. Even the particular interest taken by some of those poets in economics is echoed in such poems as 'Ode to Debt' (p.28) in which a sense of economic justice as an act of balance is, as he himself declares,[6] interiorised as a guilt, but this does not prevent him from outright complaint on grounds of insubstantial foundation which remind me of Pound on the gold standard:

> Hordes are pouring along the gauntlet
> of arcade emporia filled
> with promise to be bought with promises—
> and this is the rock on which we build.
> Banks and building societies
> have queues outside their doors.

Wanting to identify some quite elusive features of Robinson's style which I think distinguish him, I have ignored a lot of other things, including the way he can build up a substantial sequence by pressing ever onwards in pursuit of the inflatable ramifications of his percepts (e.g. 'Epigrams of Summer' pp.92-97, and the title sequence of *Like the Living End*).

Robinson says in the interview that it is impossible for him to write the kind of lyric poem he needs to without seeming self-absorbed, "because nothing else returns an echo". Why nothing else returns an echo I don't know since the world open to modern poetry seems such an immensely rich and variegated platform. But it is an honest declaration, and "seeming" shows the hope and belief he has for and in his own work. He has defied the panics of the polemical avant-garde without succumbing to quiescence. I think his course, if limited in scope, has been a courageous sticking to guns.

§

Clergyman fathers aside, I think Peter Robinson and John Welsh have quite a lot in common, but handle it differently. Again the reader more-or-less inhabits the poet, and within that persona is led through a lot of streets, rooms, hospitals and cemeteries, always with a problem in mind, a melancholy or a lingering dissatisfaction, a need for resolution, suffering from an "enormous pointlessness". But we are led further, into different places: an art gallery, the inside of a book, a performance of *Hamlet* aboard a ship off Sierra Leone in 1607, an Asian estate in East London... and sometimes nowhere in particular. So we do not always know where we are, and do not always need to because some poems are securely based in a conceptual focus, and sometimes we do know, except that bits of the poem escape from time to time into some unknown language laboratory, but this happens less and less these days.

There is also a greater range of manner. There are coherently worded poems of thought and situation, and there are poems which take up a double or multiple discourse asking us to be simultaneously in several locations, or several persons, or the same person (the poet) at different times. The paradox of his work, when set beside Robinson's, is that it is indeed enclosed in a selfhood, taken up with inner anxieties about guilt and the failure of language, but at the same time, as if defying this inwardness, it shoots its attention here there and everywhere and will risk itself into very strong figurations, reaching out from the introspection to senses of distance and resistance. In the comparison Welsh confronts the world more directly, and is eager to attach politics and aesthetics and any other issue he meets, but is drawn back from actual declaration by his modest inwardness, and this tension results in unyielding determinations, moving towards avant-gardery. It is as if this is the price to be paid (by the reader too) for the openness of his engagement.

His two latest books follow a *Collected Poems* of 2008 [7] and each is a single project with a sense of focus and purpose which is not new to him, but is newly intensified, especially *Visiting Exile.* which is about the Asian immigrant communities of London. The later book, *Its Halting Measure*, is more of a collection of poems but in a four-part structure which I'm not able to interpret — possibly a progression towards a more sophisticated consideration of writing and artistic process and purpose ("our words like scented gardens for the blind" as the blurb quotes). On page 29 is a short poem of a more personal kind which reads as an account of his experience of the poetical process, in no straightforward manner but without disruption. I quote it entire.

Meditate

Space under chest a seed of growth
Mind crosses the paper—

Ink-trace, the flying white—
Sleeps briefly, to wake on the minute.

Cross-legged on the fire cushion,
Active in watchful sitting

Mind so close to itself
So close it lies

On its way to those bones
Buried in a distant range.

The departures throughout, specially obvious in the first two lines, from normally articulated language don't of course have anything like the effect of Robinson's stylistic quirks. They don't disturb anything, but are simply the chosen poetical language of this poem, a quite familiar one, a discourse of substantives and active verbs, without specifying articles and pronouns, the whole cast of the language agreeing with the (imperative?) title — *Meditate*. The subject of "sleeps" is of course the poet — while Robinson tends to elide "I" and "you", Welch tends to elide "I" and "he", indicating a more objective frame of mind, an observational distancing from the self rather than an engagement with it, but here all specifying personal terms are omitted to arrive at the abstract "mind", the one truly active thing at beginning and end. This little poem is not a manifesto, but an account of an experience. He briefly falls asleep while writing a poem and awakens in a state of active suspension... I defy anyone to attempt to paraphrase the last four lines, except to say that they are very fine and affective lyrical lines, and in them the creative process is consummated as a kind of mental self-embrace in touch with earthly extent, and the whole structure closes as it suddenly vanishes into a distance which abolishes poet, mind and everything. But the poem does demonstrate the characteristic simultaneous engagement with personal and impersonal matter. It is all himself, but its images and effects, including the mind, are as it were pushed away from the self to stand independently of his volition and to act as and be read as objects. Something similar happens in his habitual walking poems (John Welch is said to be an early riser who goes walking in the streets of London every morning) in which anything can occur — sights, thoughts, encounters, trees, shops, slogans, loneliness, beer cans... but they will occur distinctly, not moulded into mutual articulation except in the final accumulation of the whole poem, an accumulation of a distinct nature rather than a theme. Things are to stand by and for themselves — and yes, there is a poem with an epigram from Adrian Stokes, though it is on one of his few completely undisjointed poems.

I don't want to imply by over-stressing these verbal features that Welch never tackles a subject of concern head-on — in these new books he does it more than he has ever done. He has spent his working life teaching English language to Asians in London and there have been many poems referring to this experience and to his involvement with Asians in general. More characteristically there are pieces which seem to derive from such concerns but treat the matter in a more abstracted way, such as a dialogue-like poem in *Its Halting Measure*, 'In Camera', which seems very much to be addressed to an immigrant or some other person under duress, but without depictions or declarations—

> Our actions are proportionate
>
> ...
>
> Being made entirely of such words:
> 'Proportionate' 'Governance'
> Recording 'for training purposes'
> The anxious tremor in your voice
>
> ...
>
> And this vetting procedure
> That harbours our darkest desires,
> Its wavering attention,
> Its careful perplexity—
>
> ...
>
> And another justice secretary's
> 'Non-conviction disposals',

Each one a licence then

To break into your past...

(I have omitted an italicised counter-text between the quatrains.) Here we are not fully told, it is not spelled out, and identification of the voice as an alien authority is somewhat wavering as it also suggests the poet's voice. But does anything need to be spelled out any further than it is?

Visiting Exile is more purposefully structured and is focussed on Asians in London as immigrants, refugees, victims, and artists. All John Welch's concerns come to be involved in this focus: his introspective psychological self-concern, his contemplation of artistic structures, his walking, his knowledge of classical Asian history and poetry... and increasingly the characteristic emotions of his poetry are *shared* with the immigrant, his sense of alienation twinned with the experience of aliens. The poetical craft assures us that this process is not appropriatory; the immigrant's experience is not absorbed but understood. Two sculptures/installations by the London-based Lebanese artist Souheil Sleiman. are referred to again and again, and the substantial texts which start and end the book are extended involvements with them. The text moves towards edges. In the "prologue" he describes, interprets and extrapolates from one of Sleiman's sculptures, which involves a large heap of sand on the top floor of a former warehouse, and mainly his attention is drawn to its edges where they meet the edge of the floor hovering over the scene below, and from there through to the entire marginality of the immigrant experience — "Marginal existence, flyblown hot light where the street is an edge." (We are in a derelict cemetery again, presumably the one in the next poem which borders a housing estate in East London) and this form of attention extends to the poetical process itself: "The poem a site of lost meanings. Archaeology of a once-self, it hovers, a work that disappears and then re-appears...". We approach "the edge of what we almost know". A poem such as the following comes right out with it—

Refugee

They'll come, from there to here.
No, it is not a pilgrimage, this
Distance from you to I.
Relentless caravan,
The always being forced
To choose a different sky—
'I' wants to know where 'you' is from,
It wants your story
But you were so carefully folded
Into your own silences.

Once over here you're doing the dance of shadows
Hanging about the courts
Waiting for judgement,
Something to be 'handed down',
Ambiguous inheritance.

This is the poem of someone who not only sympathises, but has known the refugee world for most of his life and lived alongside its results. It is a kind of stripping-down of the refugee situation and a direct confrontation with it, "you to I". There is of course no "problem" and no "solution" — The Daily Express would not be impressed.[8] There are only personal fates, which are acknowledged between visitor and native.

There are many poems in the book as direct as this (which is in fact one item of a sequence) but the other side of his poetical writing is shown by the impressive last item in the book, a seven-page poem entitled "yearn glass" (there is an explanatory note on the title, the name of a defunct mirror factory). So you get that hint which reinforces propositions from earlier in the book (poetry as mirror of lost meaning) and then you get the epigram which is from Sleiman himself: "cut a long story", which is a phrase he wrote across a fragment of broken mirror. So before we start the poem we seem to have two significant pointers: the broken self-image cast back to the poet as to the immigrant artist whose life "story" has been cut short by displacement. The poem itself allows no limitation to its field. It begins like this (with the lines spaced further apart than normal):

> cracked glaze song
>
> I constructed a journey
>
> soothed the inner chaos
>
> slanting afternoon sun
>
> eased the ice and it started again
>
> a mouthful of cheap wine
>
> defunct maleness
>
> made out of dust and sunlight
>
> we thought it might be art
>
> reborn in another air
>
> imaginary return such being
>
> the distances we live

There is no authorised sense of the function of the pronouns here and thus of the entire address-structure. The experience of the "economic refugee" (which Sleiman calls himself) might claim priority, and so might that of the poet, but especially when the pronouns are pluralised, the question remains open, and we have a developing series of senses and actualities in all their abstract nakedness. Note that with "a mouthful of cheap wine" we are probably back at the "private view" a description of which opened the book, but images of the second Sleiman sculpture are especially dominant here. This, "All Dressed Up and Nowhere To Go", is described as "hundreds of fragments of mirror attached to a framework of chicken wire" (It is depicted on the cover of the book). The white Londoner poet and son of a vicar sees his identity cast back to him fragmented and broken in the Asian art-work of mirror-fragments; the damage done to poverty-stricken populations, the disintegration of identity, is reciprocal. But the terms of the text reach beyond this duality and none of us can escape them as the mirror turns from us and returns as a civic threat which divides the person —

> here's a mirror that turns you away
>
> the anti-narcissus machine
>
> it drinks up the ground
>
> disappears into distant dry hills
>
> an insubstantial tower's
>
> glass wall will remember
>
> and afterwards here in Mirror City
>
> mirror will drink you and drink you
>
> return you the stranger you are to yourself

---

1   "Double Portrait". All page references are to *The Returning Sky* unless *Like the Living End* is specified.

2   See, in the interview by Nate Dorward in *Talk About Poetry* (2007), his account of his conflict with a senior representative of the school which sees poetry as dispensation of the poet's specially gifted insight and moral superiority through linguistic damage.

3   In the Preface to *The Salt Companion to Peter Robinson*, Salt Publishing 2007.

4   *In the Circumstances*, 1992. *Poetry, Poets, Reader: making things happen*, 2002. *Twentieth*

Century Poetry: selves and situations, (note the symptomatic sub-title) 2005. *Talk About Poetry,* 2007. He has also produced two books of aphorisms and recently a book of short stories: *Foreigners Drunks and Babies,* Two Rivers Press 2013, some of which go over experiences which lie behind the recent poems, and the protagonist is sometimes himself thinly disguised if at all.

5   In the interview cited in note 2. Robinson himself edited Stokes' collected poems in 1981. He tells me *(2014)* that he is now more receptive to both Ginsberg and Thomas than he was in the books I consulted.

6   In an interview by John Kerrigan on *The Returning Sky,* which covers many aspects of the book which I have not pursued. Issue 9 of *Black Box Manifold.* http://www.manifold.group. shef.ac.uk/issue9/JohnKerriganPR9.html

7   Reviewed by me along with an autobiographical volume in *The Use of English* volume 60 no2, 2009.

8   As of yesterday, 5th November 2013, the newspaper The Daily Express claims to be conducting a campaign in favour of stopping *all* immigration to UK from anywhere, for which it claims 98% popular support. Even the Confederation of British Industry is alarmed.

LYRIC AND ANTI-LYRIC

Simon Perril, *Nitrate.*
Salt Publishing 2010. 90pp
Simon Perril, *Archilochus on the Moon.*
Shearsman Books 2013. 96pp.
Anthony Mellors, *The Lewknor Turn.*
Shearsman Books 2013. 108pp
John Mateer, *Unbelievers, or 'The Moor'.*
Shearsman Books 2013. 174pp
Andrew McMillan, *protest of the physical.*
Red Squirrel Press. 28pp. £5.00

Archilochus, whose works survive only in fragments, is known as the first Greek "lyric" poet in a comparatively modern and vague sense, for the term in context means mainly poetry sung to a musical instrument (i.e., all poetry). But at least if the instrument is the lyre we have a probable distinction from epic poetry, and perhaps his best label is "iambic" meaning "satirical". He is known anyway as "the first poet to set aside the stock figures of literary [epic] tradition and build whole poems round his day-to-day experience of the world." [1] It is this experience, as given in the surviving texts and in ancient commentaries, rather than the actual substance of the poetry, which Simon Perril's set of 80 numbered short poems takes up. There is no translation and only occasional sightings of images or motifs from the poetry. Archilochus was a warrior (and so perhaps also the first occidental "amateur" poet) involved in several major expeditions of colonisation, and can be represented as a lover from what bits of his biography may (perhaps!) be inferred from the poetry. In Perril's book he has, at the end of his career, been sent to the moon to found a colony there. The lover is thus defeated by age and circumstance, and the warrior, with his army, is lost in a wilderness.

This fiction enables Perril to use Archilochus' voice (though not every poem seems to be spoken by him) for a collection of modern lyrics mingling seriousness and wit and dominantly bitter in tone. The moon is a barrenness and a reversal, a nowhere, a dead land, a hopelessness and a futility, a sense of approaching death; it is both a mental state and a punishment, and it is inescapable. Archilochus remembers and yearns in vain for his lost mistress, notes dryly the reduction of his body to basic functions and his language to crudity. The poet finds no victims for his satire except himself and the commander has adversities but no battles to fight, no reward ("house of holes / land of collisions, / you rain rocks / like a battle-field / yet deal no victory, / heap no spoils.") (No.12). No.59 is a good example of how a poem can realise these possibilities and range out from them, then end cynically—

> and what of our words
>
> when the weight
>
> has come off them
>
>
> and Earth's a sapphire
>
> set upon black;
>
> this space

that comes between all

folk and things,

yet strings us along

beads at market

among the stars

and other gaseous bodies

As in a lot of the poems, there is a chiming lyrical texture in tone, sound values and rhythm (words-weight/ sapphire-space/ things-strings / market-stars) only to be denied at the last moment. Similarly Perril has a rich command of metaphorical resource, generally deployed negatively in the end. And sometimes there is more than metaphor, and the lyric is more than a theatre. No.40:

you can hide

the Earth

under your thumb

like casualties vanish

in a puff

of statecraft

exfoliate

like the bad skin

of the moon

This is less staged, even if the earth is reduced because it is as seen in the sky. The syntax is uncertain (I would read the first "like" as a conjunction, and "exfoliate" as either an adjective describing "casualties" or a verb in apposition to "vanish") and the implications of the last three lines are left to the reader. The reach of the poem is extended beyond the fictive security of the plot. A lot of the poems seem to move towards this condition and even to approach a real poetical afflatus (glimpsed at "the earth's a sapphire / set upon black") but finally sink back in bathos.

For we know, do we not, that this scenario is our condition here and now, if not totally then in terms of the literary negative hyperbole associated with Samuel Beckett. We are irredeemably sunk into a failed society which allies with our mortality as a double victimisation. I get a sense that the poet feels obliged to follow this course, that his skill and inclination might be towards a more outright singing; his fondness for close internal/external rhyme is noticeable in many of the pieces, where it pushes the poem forward quite light-heartedly but towards a hole in the ground. This ambiguity is expressed too in Archilochus' reluctant refusal of the Dionysian mode, the dithyramb (No.26: "Would that I could / accept Dionysus' counsel / let his words / grease my speech-parts..." but the poem ends with desiccated testicles). So it is, I think, that the forward-moving emphatic writing which seems natural to Perril, manipulating ingenious and thoughtful metaphors and at its best achieving poems like Nos.40 and 56, is not only constantly pulled down to a bathetic conclusion but is also inter-mittently peppered with the awkwardness of "advanced poetry" — grammatical omissions and confusions, clashes of singular and plural, items which cannot be connected... not everywhere, but liable to cause hiccups from time to time.

A helpful prose apologia at the end of the book suggests that Archilochus is a "rhetorical garment", his song "an artefact, not a vehicle for personal rage", and if that is so Archilochus is the "garment" that Simon Perril wears, and we are encouraged to read the entire scenario allegorically, the moon's emptiness and barren-ness a figure for the state of society. That is not to say that Perril represents himself as a terminal wreck, nor indulges "rage", but that the voice is the author's, its lunar complaints his disguised or garmented version of the real. The very lyric mode which Perril obviously relishes is denigrated as it is said to be in conjunction, at its foundation, with colonialism: "Lyric is territorial, it stakes claims; it desires to occupy, it forms an erotics of coercion." So it is that so many of these well crafted poems seek to negate themselves, and become anti-lyrics. Why is perhaps more apparent in the other book.

§

Nitrate is more difficult. It too is a unified set of poems, concerned with the birth of cinema and its earliest manifestations. The poems dwell on the facts and circumstances, mainly concerning E.J.Marey, and in the second part early cinema is cast against the Situationism of Raoul Vaneigem in connection with "the discontinuity of continuity itself", because in it "the human form is an exaggerated irritant spasm ticking across frames." These are strong (again Beckettian) accusations not easily proven or disproven in their implications for the current reality. But there is no story line, no central protagonist or voice, no situation rich in possibilities of comic irony. The poems come out of information and theory; from moments of the cinematic history they spin out semi-lyrical accounts formed into poems by their movement towards a telling conclusion. But the tone derives from the theory.

I can indicate this best by reference to the prose "Afterward" [sic] which closes the book and the verse Preface which opens it. For we are here under the cloud of central European mid-century aesthetic philosophy, and even if Adorno is not mentioned, Walter Benjamin and Ernst Bloch are. We are among talk of "the ideological vacuum of a time that corrodes salvation" [Bloch]; the emergence of cinema is referred to 19th Century "increasing rationalization and standardization of time in capitalist modernity". I've never paid much attention to all this and in principle have nothing against it; I just wish it would leave poetry alone. I do attribute partly to this current and partly to English academic study and teaching of poetry more recently, the sinisterisation which goes on in Perril's account, the insistent entailment whereby quite harmless terms are made to reveal an unpleasant underside. Nitrate itself, the notoriously inflammable material of early film, was derived from a substitute for gunpowder and a substance proposed as a dressing for wounds, "So the origins of Nitrate have destruction and healing all bound together." Indeed they do, if you work it that way, if you refuse to countenance the innocence of sheer accident. The terms "gun" and "shot" in Marey's terminology "opened a wound that leaked contingency", and his study of human loco-motion contributed "more ominously" to "the industrial manage-ment of work" and "the pursuit of efficiency". It is typical of this poetical climate that even "efficiency" becomes a shadowy figure of harm, though nobody explains how. Film (like lyric) is said to be "a holding, a claim". We are constantly under threat, or we are constantly threatening the other.

It is not surprising then that instead of the lyrics teetering between sublime and grotesque of *Archilochus* we have this kind of textuality—

> Wake up. Wake up now. Take
> again piped wind squeezed off at the knot
>
> securing a swing above ground
> to touch you felt blistered brain
>
> contaminant black. Reject
> 'Consciousness as Doom'. X-ray analytics
>
> bores a world-sized hole here
> removes all prospect, burrows

out a hollow; an anti-keep.

From the fortifications the disenchanted forest

lies. At the edge some kind of ex-reef
since the sea died

boiled beyond doubt...   [p.70]

It's difficult to know what to do about this sort of thing. Vocabulary, syntax, figuration and reference conspire to block the road and to mystify what is evidently a passionate address of complaint, possibly quite optimistic if you could reach it. Actions and events fall over each other in such a throng that there is nowhere to stand. This is not a problem to those, and there are many (mostly professionals), who relish this kind of writing, which already has an established tradition, for it inhabits the legacy of J.H. Prynne and its way with images and concepts resembles what he was doing in the 1980s (flinging them at you like cricket balls from a bowling machine).

Not all the poems are like this but they are generally a good deal spikier than in the later book, especially in an almost constant refusal of any ready figural recognition, combined with a tone of definitive impersonal address, among a lot of wobbly syntax. Twice a main section of *Nitrate* begins with the question, "What wraps the present so tight?". I don't think the question gets answered, but the accumulation of poems seems to spin more and more webs which will either release the present from the constrictions of singularity, or bind it all the tighter in unreachable secrecy. There is, however, no doubting the seriousness of the enterprise in both books, nor the invitation to a verbal circus enacted with skill.[2]

§

Anthony Mellors inhabits in many ways the same poetical climate as Simon Perril, one which was largely made possible by the work of J.H.Prynne. Mellor's commitment to this is the stronger of the two, and is in evidence most of the time, whether in verbal habits, or the fields of reference, or the general drift of the poetry, which is marked by an almost constant sense of identifying wrongs, especially those of a commercialist reading of the world. Even the verbal rhythm can be Prynnian and sometimes we are faced with a glaring example —

> The manner of subsistence is
>
> chaos as vatic order, drifting on
>
> a reed, *stridenti*, hard-wired to DNA
>
> on multiple platforms. (p.78)

This is exactly Prynne's voice, exactly his kind of syntactical manoeuvring, and his tone of disdainful reprimand. But normally the allegiance is more thematic than stylistic. None of this dismisses the writing as derivative, for Mellors has his own poetical identity too.

Being influenced responsibly by Prynne means at least two things, and the principal one is that you are made to think seriously and critically about the cultural condition you inhabit, which you probably reject as entirely corrupt and derelict. Mellors sometimes takes on even the lesser details of the polemic, such as the idea that to seek to get anything at a bargain price is reprehensible, which has always baffled me, perhaps because I do it all the time. You are also encouraged to make the reading process as problematic as you possibly can by all sorts of linguistic abnormalities and to throw in all technical terms and abbreviations without a murmur of explanation. Mellors is well able to take on these burdens — he did after all write a book on the subject. [3] I nowhere feel that he is making the Prynnian gesture nor acceding to the tone of this whole tendency without having done the homework. But neither is he exempt from complaints about the problems this way of writing constantly throws up. [4]

This is not the whole story, though it is a dominant one. Mellor's poetical inclination is on the one hand towards the joker, the professional Fool satirising all the holy cows of our cultural farm in archly elaborate and erudite terms, on the other a wish for plain self-declaration, to state his personal or public complaints quite directly. There are five sections in the book of which the second is "Homage to Rod McKuen", a set of 16 poems in which he abandons the intellectuality of the rest of the book and, as the title suggests, speaks openly and plainly, the poems addressed to a "you" who is clearly a big love problem. Sometimes the writing is just too bald, but his skill in handling characteristically wry figures shows up clearly ("The curling sandwich / of my misplaced love for you") and with an effectively pathetic ending, saying that hope is never abandoned—

> ...I maintain my exile
>
> cooing over dogs and Christmas cards
>
> my absent family rosy in firelight
>
> and a station-wagon purring in the yard.
>
> (p.52)

Here and in the following "Epigrams" section there is an alternation of what I can only call the ups and downs of his discourse. One moment "the quality is the beauty .. the music of birds or fall of waters", next "All a poet can do today is annoy", which I think he means, but as always in this department there is no "why" offered. We are expected to recognise our alienation instantly, and to expect to be annoyed.

The meat of this volume is in the first and last sections. The first, "bent out of shape" is a set of twenty-four 24-line poems which start from a location in Greece: a trip to the southern tip of the Mani peninsula in the Peloponnese to visit a cave which was a legendary entrance to Hades.[5] As the set moves on from there the sense of this or any place is more and more submerged as the text moves away from any setting, and we lose our whereabouts in a stampede of pronouncements which are themselves increasingly elusive. It is possible that the narrative of the journey to the entrance to Hades is allegorised, though if so it remains hard to trace; there is though a tendency for poems to begin quite brightly or serenely and end in bitter recrimination, a self-chosen Hades.

The everlasting problem in this currency is the precise identification of the enemy. IX, for instance, goes through an extended quotation of a visit to an ancient healing site of wells and springs, eloquently lineated, switches to "a dull urban waste" and suddenly ends with a fierce but unspecific literary attack (the first two words do not connect to anything graspable) —

> as in silly poems
> dedicated to the well being of *rus in urbe* charlatans
> always lifting up their hope in the hope that metaphor
> will relieve them of the adequate symbol.
> (p.19)

Who are these charlatans, and who are the authors of the silly poems? What is wrong with "the rural within the urban" (such as allotments? I find the use of glass and trees in new architecture of the City of London a very satisfying thing), what is wrong with metaphor? The claim to have avoided metaphor in American poets and their admirers remains (like Pound's claim to have avoided symbolism) unproven, especially if this avoidance can only produce entirely untransferable tropes (such as the title of the book). I think this is an Olsonian insistence, and Olson does raise his head now and then in this sequence, notably at the phrase "the causal mythology of the 9/11 premodern" in XIII, which raises immense historical and cultural questions which I'm not prepared to accept or deny, and would need them spelled out at length in prose. But it does propose something entirely serious.

If I have complaints about this very serious and ambitious sequence it is not to deny Mellors a strong sense of commitment and a sharply critical mind deployed over a vast cultural range. It is just that the poetical stance keeps throwing up completely inert formulations and unknown names which yet seem to challenge the reader's perceptual abilities. So you Google them or pass them by, and eventually find yourself, in this case, among attractive descriptive lines of a classical feel concerning landscape.

I must emphasise, though, that for those who accept the foundational thesis there is no problem with any of this. The thesis is apocalyptic, and requires basically two commitments: first to what amounts to the total damnation, corruption, and despoliation of the entire western world (or in Prynne's own version, the planet); secondly a belief that language is the governing mechanism of this disaster, and to use it in any way serviceable to humanity at large is to be complicit in the harm. Given these premises all the ups and downs of Mellors' lively and richly inhabited poetry will be accepted with relish, as a kind of vengeance.

The book ends with a set of 25 sonnets called "The Gordon Brown Sonnets" (though sonnets only in having fourteen lines and a roughly pentameter line length). What I have said about "bent out of shape" serves well for this sequence too, save that the brevity of the form makes the quest through it seem more approachable. And again there tends to be a calm in opening lines which is shattered by the time you get to line 12. The very first sonnet opens: "In the softening gloom of mid-November / fill the bin with gold...". This obviously could be the overture to a very different performance from what we get, which by line 4 has turned the tables on itself: "the feeble sonnet of supine content / from a mound of rubbish". The poet seems to want to destroy his first line and all it might have promised, its Pre-Raphaelite richness. At the end: "I can't begin to tell / how the rot set in..." We could ask "what rot?" but we don't, because we know that this poetry constantly seeks totalisation, and the rot is all round us, represented in the under-mining of the poem by itself. And the justification, of course, lies in the implications of "gold" in the second line, where "supine" happiness at natural bounty is already wrecked by the appropria-tions of the finance industry, all our "gold" passing out of circula-tion into their (rubbish) bins.

There's no need for me to enumerate further instances, with which this sequence is crowded, many more acute than this, as it gallops along in a dominantly homiletic mode, but a homily which seems to seek to evade our grasp in its constant leaps from figure to unprepared figure. But sometimes the homily is entirely pointed and clear:

> The man who walks away from his bonus
>
> without remorse is no toga-party
>
> emperor amazed by plastic laurels.   (XXI)

There are also 11 pages of notes on this sequence (but on nothing else) some of which are actually helpful, others prolix and entertaining tongue-in-cheek dissertations, including a lot of fas-cinating information well beyond any required by the poems, and some acute and highly challengeable literary judgements.

The main question I am left with is Gordon Brown himself. I have no idea why the sequence bears his name, or what it "says" about him ("say" is a verb you have to be careful with in these regions) or indeed whether it is for or against him. The word "Brown" appears once in the 25 poems, as does the expression "a fur of Brownian noise". There are a few references to an unnamed blamed voice (a deep one), and four possible references in the notes, only one of which is certain, in which Brown is paired with his enemy Blair. If we have to take into account citation of Sir Thomas Browne and Elizabeth Barrett Browning things have got out of hand. The poems don't tell us, and yet I think I know full well — if you're committed to the group beliefs it is axiomatic: mention the name of any living politician, British or American, of any persuasion, and you have before you a contemptible figure, whose speech is lies and whose acts exist on a scale from ineffectual to harmful. It seems more than likely to me that the "Gordon Brown Sonnets" are titled as an act of mock homage, because it would be absurd to dedicate any poetical work to a nonentity and a figure of fun. I don't think that anything about Brown's career or beliefs is involved.

I shall always be glad to have *The Lewknor Turn* in the house because you never know what you might come across when you open it, what points of stabbing critique will be made by links and undertexts which you hadn't noticed or thought of. In this respect the writing seems inexhaustible.

§

John Mateer comes from somewhere quite different. After an immersion in Anglo-American modernity his poems stand on the page as bejewelled things, bright, exotic, calm and sometimes cryptic utterances in perfectly poised language, free of literary hostility or gesturing, but entirely contemporary. The first-person, the "I" in it, is far too taken up in experience and discovery to start claiming a position anywhere. But exactly where he comes from is difficult to say. Geographically, in *Unbelievers*, he comes from South Africa (where he was born), Australia (where he lives), Portugal, Al'Andalus, Egypt, Istanbul and other places. Culturally he comes from everywhere and nowhere, he comes from where places and languages leak into each other.

His concern, explicated in a very helpful Afterword, is with overlapping margins, with perception of linguistic, cultural, poetical and political currents which are concealed by our normal mapping, but are "influential although invisible", "histories that appear and disappear" and he traces these, often as a kind of slippage, in both personal and public areas of experience. He pays homage to the book *Echolalias* by Daniel Heller-Roazen ("Echolalia" is the title of his Afterword), a thesis on just such submerged currents as seen by a linguistic scholar, which begins from the fact that the babbling baby, not yet able to speak, has at his/her command all the sounds of which the human organism is capable globally, and can only progress into speech by forgetting almost all of them. Remembering and forgetting become, in poetry, simultaneous acts of creation and understanding. As Heller-Roazen says of a renowned 8th Century poet:

> It is as if for him [Abu Nuwas] the sole place of poetry were in an indistinct region of speech in which memory and oblivion, writing and its effacement, could not clearly be told apart.[6]

and Mateer on page 39:

> (*to be translated into Farsi*)

> I will learn what the world is,
> not from the beginning, that's
> the impossibility of meaning,
> but from that place where
> shiny thoughts are twilight
> and everything, like a child's first NO,
> furthers the sun.
> (p.39)

The poems seek out moments, and narratives, of realisation that the western "either/or" position is eroded by incursions arriving across time and distance which are "not really there" but are recognised. These are moments of translation, possession, even vision, but importantly not obtrusive or violent or proclaimed. Possibly they do not fully register until embodied and clarified in a poem. And the self of the poems, usually identified as "the poet", remains a written entity serving as the agent of the process, not necessarily identified as "John Mateer", though a sense of the authentic event is everywhere.

The political dimension of this, which does not take up a great deal of the poetry directly but is implied in many more intimate scenes, perhaps makes the process clearer, especially that these echoes are not a product of *agreement*, not a harmony, but of a deeper sense of lost identity across conflict or a forgotten refuge in no man's land. (Farsi is the Persian language as spoken in Iran, and indeed some of Mateer's poems have been translated into it and published in Tehran, officially the enemy zone). Here he turns to another scholar, Maria Rosa Menocal, who proposes, rather surprisingly, "that Provençal poetry, the source of much of the poetics of the Romance languages, and the ideal of Romance itself with its notion of unrequited love, has its origins in a repression of the syncretism that is to be found in the poetries of Iberia under the Moors."[7] This would then be a Christian fundamentalist repression which carried with it into its own poetry much of the lyricism of Al'Andalus, but shorn of what the French call *jouissance*. The lyrical side of Mateer's poetry seeks to get behind that division and connect across opposition rather than across emptiness. He follows the story to the expulsion of the Moors from Iberia, and later the Jews, as the beginning of the take-over of the world by Spain and Portugal, in which these powers initially trod in the Moors' footprints and followed their example, as also in their entry into the slave trade. "I saw the War Against Terror as something akin to this expansionism." ... "I felt then, as I do now, that the conflicts and political structures of the Middle Ages have more to teach us about what is going on today than the ideas of the Modern Era." Rather than a simple historicism, this is a question of the hidden presence of Islamic and Arabic structures (and possibly tones, acts, understandings... *surfacings* as he calls them) in the ideologies of a West that has remade their bearers into enemies.

And the purpose of all this in the poetry?—- "...wanting to rid my language of violence" which these intimations do because they induce peace; they merge the enemy into our history, they identify war-lords both here and there, and they do this in the poet's diurnal experience as much as in the News. "a voice, calming, calling / across centuries of noise."

This says "All poetry is political" in a, to me, completely new way, where the impulsion is not towards alienation, rebellious-ness, hoisting the banner of opposition, the substitution of noise for music, but a much broader and less driven sense of capturing forgotten historical forces cloaked in modern politics, and the same processes at work in the most small-scale and intimate areas — memories of submergence. He also makes it clear that there is an ideological presence in the very *tone* of the poetry, which works against "a fear of the emotional and the personal, a fear of the honesty that is required to pay attention that is typical of our kind of Western capitalist logic. With this book I am hoping, in one way at least, to introduce this idea that we need to imagine tones we can't quite hear, that we should acknowledge, too, how partial our sense of reality is." (p.169)

This results in a variety of poems, many of which are very short, like memos, marginalia, asides, notes made in passing when a cultural junction is noticed. They are superficially reminiscent of parts of *Personae* but with none of Pound's disdain. There are nine sections in the book and some of them, such as "(Twelve Poems)" (of which there are ten), consist of such tiny pieces that we are persuaded to read them as verses of one poem, especially as they seem to use the same vocabulary in concurrent progressions. However short the poems, they connect to larger concepts, even two lines—

> Am I hearing a mbira warmed up by twenty thumbs?

> No, it's the flock of sheep down there in the misty valley.
> (p.106)

which is not merely an impression, but the surfacing of a submerged sub-Saharan presence in Portugal. It is from the section "Monsanto", written from his residence in a Portuguese village, a particularly endearing picture of the poet as stranger embedded in the local, and transcending the singularities, as too in the section "Azanians", set in south-east Africa, the homeland where the poet particularly acknowledges "my half-heartedly foreign soul". The thematic sectioning is never rigid. In the middle of one locality is a poem from another, and this locational flexibility is important. The poet seeks to be a stranger in his presence, his language, and his poetry, all the better to see through the dichotomies imposed by power. But again, it is not a campaign; it is more a hoping and an urging. There is, in spite of everything, never too much seriousness and there is room for fleet-footed prancing across ponderous zones—

> *Question for António Damásio*
> Doesn't all European thought
> disappear into the void
> between Spinoza and Pessoa,
> that cornucopia
> of nerves and that Tibetan
> skull-cup? [8]

and there are poems of outright sensuality, but in which the quest is never set aside—

> With me she sleeps
> as though the world were intimate and curious.
>
> Like a small animal, her tongue walks
> around my face.
>
> And when her tongue is over my eyes,
> I remember the visionary,
>
> and how he kissed his girlfriend:
> her eyelids were translucent, stainless,
>
> a flickering name...
> (p.46)

and the emphasis is not on the Romance of unrequited love.

Mateer's poetry is passionately wide-ranging because every notation he makes is offered as a personal experience, and is entered into a passionately inscribed theatre. He is aware that "in the poem the poetic form and the language are always at issue" and however slight or attenuated the text there is always a tension between singular and extended awareness which brings every word into line. He refers to poetry as double voiced, "half way between one culture and another" and "a kind of ghost writing". The poetry is also incomplete ("Poesia Incompleta", the name of a bookshop in Lisbon, is one of his titles) — as if space must be left in it and around it, not for the reader's intervention (an Anglo-

American avant-garde superstition) but for the proposed distances to be felt.

A lot of the writing might seem "Modernist" but if that implies an oppositional stance it is beside the point. He defines Rimbaud as a poet at war — his "Je est un autre" makes everyone into an enemy, and the (adolescent) self defies the totality (so "Maybe that's why it wasn't strange for Rimbaud to become an arms dealer and slaver?"). The conclusion of a later poem is at first glance the same proposition but in fact contrary: "We are all someone else". We are then talking about common experience, and not any kind of divisive self election. A multiple presence underlies our acts, which the poems identify in moments of realisation, sexual, political, and literary, in places and in people, in which the self is (however silently and momentarily) felt to become someone else and which poetical translation and heteronomy reveal. It is the domain not of Rimbaud, but of Pessoa, "that proliferating ghost".

Mateer is thus able to use his culturally and linguistically multiple experience as a white South African without claiming any special dispensation. His eye is always on the horizon. The section "Os Elifantes Brancos" consists of two narrative poems spoken to and by two such "white elephants" (which also seems to be the name of a bar or brothel) and it is here that the fullest exposition is to be found of the pasts that linger beneath us.

This awareness is both a loss and a gain, and encounters with it are realisations at the same time as glimpses of a kind of worrying depth under our senses, or of cosmic spaces into which our memories disappear. At times it is as if they pursue him. He cannot cross Galata Bridge in Istanbul without meeting the Slovenian translator of Chaucer and Milton. They greet each other, *"As if on the snowy peak of Mount Sumeru, we're the axis of memories whirling away."* Mount Sumero is the central world-mountain of Buddhist cosmology.

I hope I haven't given the impression that this book is a collection of instances illustrating a thesis. It is a collection of experiences expertly crafted into poems of various kinds and dimensions (from one-word to six pages), poems which echo and abrade each other, mutually confirming or questioning. The reach of the poems is broad but quite distinct from the encyclopaedic impulse, while benefitting from the poet's wide knowledge of cultural history, especially of the near-eastern border lands where most of the trouble is. But trouble is not necessary for his purposes and neither are claims of enhanced vision. In the poem "Ode" the image is of a tallness which sees further — a palm-tree in the desert over a gated community, but this image is eroded as the poem passes it through the minaret calling to prayer, the "mobile phone tower" and any such claim is finally a mingled broadcasting of "falsity and truth / new tower / of Babel."

The events of these fascinating poems normally occur in a calmer tone and the seriousness has to share its bed with verbal congeniality. The multiplication of self involved is clearly and unemphatically shown in the ending of his poem on a visit to the house of Camilo Pessanha, a Portuguese "symbolist" poet who influenced Pessoa, again a much voyaged and a multilingual figure who spent most of his life in Macau, where he died in 1926. After the house the poem returns to a bar where his friend Carlos is waiting; he has been listing all the cities of Africa and Asia with which he is familiar. Mateer's response is immediately cosmic and casual:

> Carlos may be
> right: there are the starry conurbations
> of the departing world, and then,
> always, the kindly void of the Mother.
> Like this bar, that, he says, he's
> frequented over the decades,

each time under a different name.

(p.69)

This is the second time recently (see my review of Martin Harrison) that I have been able to turn to an Australian (etcetera) poet who offers some kind of alternative to the deep divisions and resultingly aggressive writing (so expertly and aspiringly performed but under constant threat of narrowness) of the English poetry scene. I think he is a real discovery and it would be interesting to know how his poetry developed to where it is, but an earlier selection, *Elsewhere* (Salt Publishing 2007?) seems to have disappeared without trace. His Australian publisher is Fremantle Arts Centre Press.

§

But you don't have to go to the antipodes. Andrew MacMillan gave a reading locally not long ago and I was interested enough to get what appeared to be his one booklet (actually his fifth). There is a tendency to assume that what we have before us is an "aspiring young poet". I don't think there are any of them around any more. At the age of 25 McMillan is well advanced in his career, teaching creative writing at a college (ça va sans dire these days) constantly in demand for appearances and residencies, has been invited to read at the prestigious Aldburgh Poetry Festival and was commissioned for the Cultural Olympiad 2012 and broadcast on Radio 4. Makes me feel like an aspiring old poet.

This is all entirely beside the point, of course. *protest of the physical* is one poem, a lively, even perky, version of the solo self in the city, except that the city is a town and he described the work as "like *Howl* set in Barnsley" which is a former coal-mining town in Yorkshire.[9] I think what attracted me to it, and was confirmed on reading, is that you think you know exactly where you are — a lively chatty self-presentation, a vaunting of youthful zest — but in fact there's a lot more going on. It's a broken monologue which progresses steadily without a lot of worries about relevance, picking things up as it passes by, constantly leaping to new and unexpected matter — apostrophes to the town, personal declarations concerning homosexual encounters (some not too happy), lists of pub names... But it never becomes facile or obvious, it always avoids clichéd perception, and nothing is done for mere effect. The town is taken seriously in the imagery of bodily failure ("town that sunk from its centre / like a man winded by a punch / town that bent double   carried // young men and women and younger men and women / as long as it could but spine broken / had to let them go...") and never runs out of energy, each question immediately passing to the next as the verse gallops on. Some sections enter into quite opaque matter of personal desire, then suddenly words copied from walls — "pits close / we still sink / into them" which links back two pages to "people were shoulder to shoulder / as in a cage waiting to descend" which is part of the section on the broken-down town. Here as elsewhere the poem repeats images or structures from time to time as a felt gesture to coherence, and references to coalmining are unselfconsciously run into the discourse, as the personal and the civic struggle to keep apart.

About half way through the poet Thom Gunn[10] appears and is addressed in such a way as to suggest the poet and he were lovers, but what he is doing is quoting small phrases from Gunn's diaries and letters which he researched at Berkeley University. The intensity here blurs the generational distance, and in the middle of this comes the list of Barnsley pub names, which suspiciously includes "The Closed Since Smoking Ban", "The Soviet", "The Keep Drinking" and "The We're Still Here." This joke section is actually, I think, a representation of northern working-class persistence and resilience. And then on into further explorations with a certain mounting intensity towards the end as the personal narrative goes through a crisis. There is always a pressing-forward movement, not so much that the eye is kept steady for a goal in sight, but more that the movement and variety of the text are valued as such, as cohering and challenging things which must not be let go of.

town as a face with one eye closed

twn as a mspelt txt town without its eyes

contraction

theory there is beauty in the ordinary

the row of shops on Shambles Street

the day chasing its own shadow

behind twentythousand windows   threethousand

sexual advances   not all pleasant   not all denied

silent christenings renaming of each other

What he is doing is playing personal and impersonal sexual experience and its failure against the dereliction of the town, but also attaching senses of earthly distance and temporal urgency into a kind of dispersed plea on behalf of both self and place. It isn't very like *Howl* because it hasn't the rhetoric of public address, and I find the title reductive, but it's a fine performance.

---

1   Sherod Santos, *Greek Lyric Poetry*, New York 2005. See especially the Introduction and the notes on Archilochus.

2   The author's website www.simonperril.com contains collages associated with the poems of *Nitrate*, and a 20-minute audio-visual "trailer" for the book.

3   Probably the best book in this field, *Late Modernist Poetics, from Pound to Prynne*, 2005. Paperback edition 2011. This is not available to me at present but as I remember it is quite severe on Prynne's later work which abandons articulation itself. In *The Lewknor Turn*

Mellors inserts a footnote denying that Prynne is in any way difficult, but quotes only from the very early work, which is more-or-less where he sites himself as a poet.

4   I was about to indicate one such problem with the lines I have just quoted, which was that *stridenti*, which is the Italian for "strident" in the plural, seems to gain nothing over the English word but constitutes only an unnecessary jolt. However, a note reveals that the word is nothing of the sort, but a Latin coinage derived from Virgil via Milton, meaning a rural reed flute (Milton's "scrannel"). Well and good, though a problem requiring such far-travelled solutions might be said to persist. At least we can be grateful that there is no reference to Stridentism (Estridentismo), a Mexican artistic movement of the 1920s.

5   Due to the generosity of the poet Kelvin Corcoran and his partner in allowing people to use a small house they have in this area, I have now read three poetical accounts of this trip and written one myself, and am convinced that when it comes to the cave we were all in completely different places.

6   Daniel Heller-Roazen, *Echolalias: on the forgetting of language* (New York 2005) p.193.

7   *The Unbelievers* p.161, summarising from Maria Rosa Menocal, *Shards of Love: exile and the origins of the lyric,* Duke University Press 1993.

8   The addressee here is surely António Damásio, professor of neuroscience at the University of Southern California and author of *Descartes' Error* and *Looking for Spinoza.* His theories about the biological and interactive origin of thought would seem to fit with Mateer's (or most modern poets') work.

9   Barnsley has never been a very happy place. It was known in the 19th Century for the miserable pay and living conditions of the miners, things which Orwell found unchanged when he stayed there for a few days for the writing of *The Road to Wigan Pier* in the 1920s. It's name is now something which would fetch a mild laugh if a stage comedian merely spoke it. I think it's to Andrew McMillan's credit that he doesn't take advantage of this mock-northern snobbery; his humour about Barnsley, when it occurs, is situated and gritty.

10   I don't know whether Thom Gunn (1929-2004) needs a footnote these days. An English poet whose repute was at one time equal to that of Ted Hughes, who moved to the States and there embraced extremes of style, from "Movement" thinness to "Beat" freedom. For present purposes the point is that he was openly gay, and declared himself as such in his poetry.

ROBERT DUNCAN: OCCULT POETRY

The Collected Early Poems and Plays,
edited by Peter Quartermain. University of California
Press 2012. 870pp hardback, £34.95
The Collected Later Poems and Plays,
edited by Peter Quartermain. University of California
Press 2014. 922pp hardback, £34.95
The H.D. Book,
edited by Michael Broughn and Victor Coleman. University of California Press 2012. 692pp paperback, £25.95.

I find myself looking back, across forty years, at an episode of American poetry which at one time seemed to be the answer to everything, and in which three poets in particular conceived works of immense and unprecedented ambition, whose purpose was to transform human consciousness completely, to re-form and re-think the human world from top to bottom: history, society, culture, politics, perception, language, religion... everything was cast into the cauldron to undergo total change. The world was to be set right at last, and through poetry. They were, of course, Ezra Pound (in *The Cantos*), Charles Olson (in *The Maximus Poems*) and Robert Duncan. They were not the only ones and it was not an exclusively American ambition; indeed it remains for some the ultimate purpose of poetry here and now, while to others it transgresses entirely the legitimate bounds of poetry by making it a religion substitute which also happens to be full of politically unacceptable habits of mind. Nothing like the global scope of address would be attempted now except in coded and cryptic forms, and the grandiloquence of manner is unthinkable. The knowledge and learning then seen as integral to the role of the poet have been largely eradicated — what would a creative writing class teach you about economics and Egyptology? Compared with these pseudo-epic performances most contemporary British and American poetry remains small-scale, concerned with the symptoms and paradoxes of existence, including the contradictions and hypocrisies of power.

Another view of these global exercises is that they were the late work of poets who, having written a lot of at least interesting poetry, decided in their seniority that they had a mission to transmit messages and visions of the greatest importance to humanity, at which the interestingness evaporated in a mass of pulpit rhetoric and obfuscation. I don't necessarily espouse this view but like to bear it in mind. This was certainly a fate which overtook the career of one of their principal precursors, William Blake. The important common factor here is obfuscation, the act of obscuring your own message, because in all cases the new dispensation had to divorce itself from all "official" discourses of revelation, and could not use any of their recognised vocabulary without becoming tainted with their falsity, but must necessarily enunciate an unknown tongue, under the licence of "poetry".

Robert Duncan's way into this kind of Modernism was the occult. He was raised in a theosophical family and cultivated every possible occult, mystical or mythological channel open to him for ever after. This is not actually saying very much, for reading Duncan makes you realise how important occultism was to the whole of Modernist poetical writing, and a lot of other writing from the 1880s onwards, and how its structures have invaded just-about the whole of modern and contemporary poetry, whether declared or, more normally nowadays, subsumed in habits of thought and language. From dedicated devotees and practitioners like Yeats, Duncan, Merrill, Plath-Hughes[1], etc., through whatever grades of believers and dabblers: Pound, Eliot, Lawrence, H.D., Olson, etc., etc., while the whole of Modernist London was rushing to G.R.S.Mead's theosophical lectures, and then all the continental occultist authors — Strindberg, Hugo, de Nerval, Sur-realism — and Rilke's exploitation of "mystery".... Modernism was soaked in it, and long after the days of spirit mediums, poetry still maintains the attitudes and verbal processes of mysticism, which are essentially compounds of hiding and revealing, access to "hidden wisdom", and the speaking of tongues. Most of the assumed habits and devices of contemporary poetry are involved with both mysticism and the aestheticism brought down from the 1890s, whether experimental word-salad or conventional-ist subjectivism — in these matters they are equal. The belief in the reader's subliminal absorption of poetical quality, or that the power structure is challenged by deformed language in poetry (a kind of spell-casting), the belief that silence and blank space on the page carry significance in themselves, as do irrational meta-phorical leaps and homonyms, these and other fond beliefs take on ex-mystical authority and the resulting stew gets tangled with poetry's legitimate involvement in the verbal notation of shifts in perception, the revitalisation of fixed metaphor, and the "natural obscurity of song", and anyone who suspects that reality might in fact be at least to some degree *evident* and that it could be both grasped and registered in the mother tongue is likely to be thought of as pedantic, shallow, conservative or complicit in harm, though in fact such realism is possible in an experimental mode as readily as in any other.

Duncan was familiar with all the species of occultism involved in this, and a lot more. He left no stone unturned. Theosophy, Hermeticism, astrology, Kabala, Platonic mysteries, Rosicrucianism, Pythagorean numbers, gnosticism, Tarot, spirit mediums, the Cambridge ritualists, alchemy, ... he was constantly involved with all of these and many more, not to mention the incorporation of *Oz* and the *Alice* books, and he rightly attached the "discoveries" of Freudianism as another esoteric cult, another lifting of the veil to reveal the secret substrata, knowable only by codes. It is from this glorious treasury, or this glorious mess, as you like it, that his poetry emerged, but it did emerge, irregularly and obsessively perhaps, but we are left with a true body of it. He differed from Pound and Olson in producing no single, bible-like, work like *Maximus* or *The Cantos* (unless it be the prose *H.D. Book* [2]); rather a missionary purpose extends though his entire career among various kinds of poetical writing as well as prose and other genres, emerging finally as governing impetus to the otherwise scattered and haphazard ordering of his last books. He called himself a "heretic" rather than a "revolutionary".

But there is also a paradox, which could be his saving grace. Through the early work, and intermittently later, there is a sense that poetry itself is a priority, sometimes explicitly in prose statements, and whatever is understood by "poetry" here it involves recognisable human experience and the poem as an artistic construct thereof. This is particularly confirmed by two important disclaimers in *The H.D. Book* which come as quite a surprise, for that work is the heaviest in the exposition of mystery and magic:

> "There is something else about looking behind
> things. There is the fact that I am not an occultist
> or a mystic but a poet, a maker-up of things"
> (p.278)

"I do not believe, for I am a poet; I imagine as I
make it up." (p.500).

This echoes Eliot on Dante, but shortly before the first of these
he had been saying that Eliot by rejecting the occult (specifically
ritualism and the Tarot) becomes merely "literary", because in the
Four Quartets "even religious matters are literary in character,
having the proper artistic distance". Similarly in a biased attack
on Robert McAlmon he equates "mysticism" and "imagination":
if you reject one you reject the other. So in this synthesis the occult
itself serves to free poetry from detachment and convention. This
is not, however, always the reader's experience, since the commitment to the occult as it is manifested in the writing is doctrinal
more than motivational, whatever he says. But if this is a problem
it lies with the prose more than the poetry.

§

Now that we have all Duncan's published poetry before us[3]
we can follow its long and involved development, which I see as
reaching its apogee in mid-career in the late 1950s. It is a quite
monumental record of a continual devotion to poetry as such, as
he understood it, which was as a universal power. Although his
allegiances were at first with the reticence of Imagism his own
early work was situated in "Romantic" poetry, a word which he
accepted as self-description throughout his career. For he was
in no way willing to accept what became a standard American
Modernist dismissal of English Literature, but declared his foundation ("seeking a rhetoric" he called it) to stand on the two
pillars of Milton and Pound. I think this served him in the long
run; the early verse is fairly overwhelmed in a sense of poetical or
dramatic echo from Elizabethan to Swinburnian, in a symbolism
which makes the world devolve basically upon the first person. He
is normally very much the hero of his own poems. It is a work of
unification in which symbolic scenarios enunciate a strongly felt

thematic content, a self-drama dressed in the world you might say, with constant acts of attachment or appropriation, casting through mostly literary resources for parallel or identical instances. 'Towards an African Elegy' (1942) for instance, inhabits an Africa of the printed page, resolutely read as a property of the self and thereby all the more removed from the actual:

> Negroes, negroes, all those princes
>
> holding cups of rhinoceros bone, make
>
> magic with my blood.
>
> [...]
>
> I know no other continent of Africa
>
> more dark than this
>
> dark continent of my breast.   *Early*, pp. 43-4

The atmosphere can be very different from this: occasionally realist, pastoral, or even surreal-jocular, but there is no doubt about the basic purpose of the poetry, which I think remained with him for ever. It is to bring the known or imaginable world down onto the self, to represent all the self's passages and experiences whether crises or victories as participating in a limited repertoire of cosmic event through the "eternal" substance of poetry, endlessly repeated in the whole of human history.

Some version of this could be said to be present in all poetry (or all "Romantic" poetry), but in Duncan's case it is primary. It lacks calm but it is spacious, meaning it has "breadth of vision" (which is an interior space), but lacks engagement with the exterior, earthly and circumstantial world. There is a continuous development of the craft, and already before 1950 he achieves an abstract-poetical discourse which will make extended passages of serious exposition possible, especially in the long poem *Heavenly City, Earthly City*.

This process of assimilation is of course the result of the occultist beliefs, for one thing they all seem to agree about is that all is one, but specific occult or religious gestures only arise occasionally, with a sentence like "What against chaos then my Christ avail?" but this kind of pastiche soon becomes rare in such a stark manifestation. This is not of course the historical Christ but the mystic one, and indeed as you grow accustomed to the interweaving of mysticism into Duncan's writing you begin to recognise that any of the many named persons are likely to be their own mystical emanations, their presence in mind and poem, rather than the physical human being, or represent a point of convergence. The intrusions become less obtrusive, woven into poetical textures which advance from Victoriana towards London 1920:

> Great Venus came into the room,
>
> Ishtar, the full-blown rose.
>
> The room became a shell of pearl,
>
> the petals of the shell flung back,
>
> it was so likened to Beauty's tomb.
>
> 'The Homecoming', *Early*, p.152

There is an increasing desire in the earlier poems to achieve a larger structure, sequences especially, which meant setting up thematic or locational foci — theatres for the poems to act in, notably *Medieval Scenes* (1947) which has been much admired, though I find the set-up serves to obscure the poet's individual utterance. It is a coterie work, speaking as we, "the poets", of Duncan's circle. It is also a set of ten poems written in ten nightly sessions, and supposed never to be changed after the first inspiration. This was an insistence of Jack Spicer, a friend of Duncan at the time, whose belief in inspiration (which he called "dictation") and magic seems to have been less inclusive but more severe than Duncan's, who did not finally obey the rules.

I find, in fact, that in this large body of writing which still only brings us to the early 1950s, the most engaging pieces are mainly among the "uncollected poems" tucked between the books. Some of these show a relaxation from his mission which engages a bright, realist, virtuosic texture and can be quite casual about all the mythologising. The books are more concerned to fulfil a purpose, fuller of importance, whether of utterance or of visiting deities. One of these uncollected sets is 'Domestic Scenes' (1947), ten poems which are exactly what the label says, from 'Breakfast' onwards, forming a companion piece to the ten *Medieval Scenes.* Both begin with a poem of awakening, the latter has—

> The magic in convolutions of our company
>
> winks its lights. Its touch is slight
>
> but vital. But we are bearish magickers,
>
> makers of lightnings in half-sleep of furry storm.

'Domestic Scenes' has—

> I shall awake to the ennui of breakfast foods,
>
> to teach morning's bright of commonplace,
>
> redundancies of tasty goodness.
>
> [...]
>
> Disorder of dishes, the wisdom of soild spoons,
>
> of discarded forks and knives, exciting litter
>
> excites the domestic dreaming mind
>
> to that brief of wisdom called disgust.

The difference here is not so much the domestic clutter and its bright(ness) [4] as the first person, the reduction from plural to singular, bearing the weight of the discourse much more lightly and reaching less elevated conclusions. The contrast is not great and the two sequences make a good pair, but I feel that that lyrical notation of the ordinary and of earthly, gravity-bound perception is what is missing from much of the earlier work.

Another sequence excluded from the books is 'Poetic Disturbances' which handles lunar imagery adroitly (with Lorca behind it) and is concerned with the poet as creator of the real, an ambitious theme but the paradoxes are calmly negotiated—

> Let us organise a dream
> along Freudian lines.
>
> But my moon is a real moon
> produced out of myself.
>
> The great moon in his grief
> emitting howls of light
> that ran from tree branches,
> a laughter that mockt him.   [*Early* p.302

'The Venice Poem' (1948) is another substantial sequence which has been singled out, by the author and others, as a major step forward. It is indeed impressive in its ability to sustain an extended discourse. For me it is too much the world wrapped round the self, personal and intimate events projected out into a vast theatre, made wilfully into "myth" as Venice itself is, which he knew only from pictures and art history lectures. There is also some curious allegorisation of the plot of *Othello*, in which Iago is "The Doge" and Othello is (I think) the poet.[5]

§

The Opening of the Field (1960) was Duncan's first book from a commercial publisher and I well remember its first arrival in Britain at about the same time as Olson's *The Distances*, O'Hara's *Meditations in an Emergency* and the anthology *The New American Poetry,* all four Grove Press paperbacks. They were revelations, Duncan's in a particularly attractive way, and I still think it is his finest work. Perhaps it was that for all the unknown quantities by way of mythic lore, we also encountered a sustained discourse in lines of recognisable weight and balance, a dignified and authoritative verse continuum which didn't project verbal objects at us whole or broken, but declared its purpose openly, even if the nature of that purpose was strange to the uninitiated. It was, and is, clear that much of the time the individual, represented by the author, is being conducted into experiences far beyond the ordinary or mundane, but that it is done by enhancing rather than transcending or negating, the singular and local.

For Duncan was not doing anything very new or different here. He had continued through the 1950s to work at consolidating and extending his religio-symbolic vision, and had particularly tried to renew his attention to language, its hypnotic power by repetition, through about a hundred imitations of Gertrude Stein. There and through Pound he cultivated a greater awareness of syllabic weight and what Pound called "leading", the way line endings produce movement and disturbance, and so forth. In *The Opening of the Field* he is still chasing archetypes all over the place, still uniting personal accounts with ancient stories, indeed still calling all of history and myth onto himself, and still sermonising on the sacred force of poetry through beauty, and the poet as elect. There is no escaping the mysticism, the Platonic transcendence and occulted presence of deity even in the unforgettable first poem 'Often I Am Permitted to Return to a Meadow'—

> as if it were a scene made up by the mind,
>
> that is not mine, but is a made place,

that is mine, it is so near to the heart,

an eternal pasture folded in all thought

so that there is a hall therein

that is a made place, created by light

wherefrom the shadows that are forms fall.

[*Later* p.3

But the account here is not of certitude but of longing, and of working through revealed contradictions — mine/ not-mine, made by the mind/ made by light... This meadow clearly contains no earwigs, but the passion of the account and its classic verse dignity sustain our donation of belief in it as a state of mind, at least. And the craft of the poem is now highly developed, more so later in the book than here; the moving, rhythmic and experiential course of the writing is steadily sustained but also liable to take us by surprise as it twists round corners, back-tracks on itself, leaps over connectives, lurches into the unexpected, and subtly absorbs references, such as the quiet incorporation above of a reminiscence of what I know as the Corpus Christi Carol ("Down in yon forest there stands a hall..."). The central theme itself, about poetry (all poetry has for some time been *ars poetica*) seems to overspill its bounds, so that while the "meadow" may well stand for poetry further possibilities lie open to the reader's experience.

In several commentaries he wrote (given in the notes) Duncan made clear his intention that this was meant as a whole work, a poem made up of poems, which he likened to sewing a tapestry or carpet, thread by thread and syllable by syllable, with more in mind than any one motif. Jack Spicer said that it was Duncan's one true serial poem. But in view of what happened later it is important here that the poems are the completed thing, rather than fragments or atmosphere of the poetic. Studying Jack Spicer's "serial poems" as he called his dictated sequences, I found that one poem leads on to another poem not because it ends prematurely or with unanswered questions, but by its very completion, and the lesson or closure of the poem forms a new basis, a passionate arrival which is the start of new venturing. It is something like this with *The Opening of the Field* though in a secular reading one is mainly aware of certain recurrent terms or motifs which succeed each other and return in new light: meadow, dance, children, Law, Lady... So the first poem is followed by 'The Dance', because something needs to happen in the meadow, but both dance and meadow recur through the book as properties not to be let go of, while the elliptical course suggested by those images is avoided.

Duncan began *The H.D. Book*, his immense prose commentary on Hilda Doolittle which is also a poetical autobiography and compendium of his occult and literary learning, towards the end of writing *The Opening of the Field* and it runs concurrently with his poetry from then on. But the next two books, *Roots and Branches* (1964) and *Bending the Bow* (1968) certainly participate in the pitch of writing he had achieved in *The Opening of the Field,* making the 1960s the optimum decade for Duncan's poetry, though I cannot escape the feeling of a very slow sunset. Even in the first of these there is an increase in prosaic writing in the poems, recounting now not only image visions but also accounts of mediumistic returns from the dead by his mother (p.162), with an increasing amount of self commentary, and a mounting sense of poetry as something that attracts study rather than surrender, though there is plenty of that too. Sometimes we are clearly being lectured: "Theosophists teach that primeval man is a vast dispersed being..." (p.130). None of these things are new to the poetry, but the previous book seemed on the whole to be more subtle and circumspect in handling them, and even modest, though modesty was never his forte. There is also increasing reference to Charles Olson, on whom he leans for the insistence that the self is the only "sign" the poet can erect, the central pivot of the whole cosmic structure. Among such vertigo it is good to see the meticulously calm script of a true poet suddenly emerging, every syllable held in the hand—

> the boat of bone
>
> so light it turns as if earth
>
> were wind and water.
>
> ['A New Poem (for Jack Spicer)' *Later* p.*205*

The two bits of alliteration here are not the point so much as the complete lyric integration of sense in the whole sonic and rhythmic ensemble. And perhaps this fragment is, for a moment, not "about poetry", though the poem in which it occurs absolutely is. And some poems, such as 'The Continent', are very satisfying wholes built of impassioned speech, however much they leap around restlessly from one god to another. One thing that never lapses is writerly confidence and competence.

I feel that it is after this book that there is increasing cause for concern, through *Bending the Bow* and the immense and continuous *Ground Work* which occupied the rest of his career, though I'm happy to leave it to other readers to investigate in detail. There was always a tension in the writing between the indolence of the occult (all your thinking done for you because all is one anyway) and the urge to write *the poem*, the singular created thing, beginning middle and end, with its own *raison d'être* and its own distinction. Increasingly now it is, among the proliferating wizardry, an urge to write *poetry*, that is, a poetical substance, a continuum, an atmosphere, an environment inhabited by the imagination, to which every passing thought or experience contributes, so instead of concentrating and shaping, you accumulate. There is also a sense that the reader is free to enter or leave this edifice at any point.

It is said that Duncan viewed the later 'Passages'[6] as scriptural, therefore sacred texts to stand for ever. But there is no consistency. 'Envoy / Passages 7' (*Later* p.316) is a brief prayer, (represented here whole without the complex lineation. The lines are double the normal distance apart and variously indented) — "Good Night, at last / the light of the sun is gone / under the earth's rim /and we / can see the dark interstices / Day's lord erases." 'Spelling / Passages 15' (*Later* p.338) has lines like this—

Christos, Chronos, chord are spelld with *chi*, **X**, not **K** *(kappa)*

Xristos, Xronos, Xord

chi: "the first letter of κίλιοι,αι,ι = 1000

—Later

"X was used either simply or with points ...

What these are is notes, and when we reach *Ground Work* (this is from *Bending the Bow*) the writing frequently has the character of a commonplace book, in which whatever Duncan happens to be reading at the time, periodical articles or a Seventeenth Century poem or an occult treatise, is likely to be copied in, among a mass of original writing of many kinds. The nature of Duncan's interest in text in 'Spelling' would seem to have shifted into unreachable corners, such as one where any word beginning *ch* may invoke Christ, and yet shortly before this there is that old disclaimer again—

Only passages of a poetry, no more. No matter how many times the cards are handled and laid out to lay out their plan of the future — a fortune — only passages of what is happening. Passages of moonlight upon a floor.

['Structure of Rime XXIII', *Later* p.317

and on the next page after 'Spellings' begins 'My Mother Would be a Falconress'—

> My mother would be a falconress,
>
> And I, her gay falcon treading her wrist,
>
> would fly to bring back
>
> from the blue of the sky to her, bleeding, a prize,
>
> where I dream in my little hood with many bells
>
> jangling when I'd turn my head. [*Later* p.341

Here we are back in the territory of 'Often I am Permitted...' not only in the clarity of image and classic interplay of stress and lineation, but also in the tenuous, wonder-struck, quality which comes from the fact that the poem retails a dream (actually the opening sentence coming to him in the night) which he is trying to understand. But to say that poetry wins out in the end in *Ground Work* (or *Maximus* or *The Cantos* for that matter) is not easy. But it does have the advantage in this respect that many of the pieces in it are still conceived as poems rather than notes towards a world-scheme, even if they turn out to be yet again poems about angelology or the writing of poetry as epiphany, which not all of them do. In the diary-like construction of the work (as of *Maximus*) so that things are recorded as they happen, dream is one of his most effective ways into a distinctive poem and produces the most arresting moments. There is moreover a constant sense of the poet in the grip of an excitement which never relaxes, registered in text through the Romantic afflatus of the heroic self. Whether this is enough to keep everyone happy I don't know.

§

And then there is *The H.D. Book*, and if ever a poet dumped a greater load of headache on the world before departing I don't know who it was. Deciding about value or making almost any statement true to the whole of this work is virtually impossible.

By following H.D.'s work and biography, with immense digressions, at the same time as his own autobiography and all the mysteries, he made this the principal encyclopaedia of his beliefs and practices, held into some kind of order at least, by the constant return to H.D.'s texts and the stories attached to them, in chronological order.

This is the first complete book publication of the work, which previously saw print as nineteen excerpts, one to each chapter, in a variety of American magazines, some of them small-scale. Most interested persons in Britain, such as myself, only saw a few of these, but they nevertheless had a great impact and turned many people's attention towards what were perceived as large new apertures in thought and experience, avenues towards a new version of the world, and towards the "new American poetry". But the story told is principally that of the development of Duncan's own understanding and practice of poetry through his fixation on certain older poets (now thought of as founder Modernists or something), and his detailed narration forms one of the best histories of that so-called movement you are likely to get, mainly because the account is always of direct experience and doesn't transgress into subsuming theoretics. Duncan's rather fierce dislike of academic literature is here an asset.

Early in the book there are two accounts of Duncan's first realisations of the power of poetry. Both were mediated by women, and this became a quite obsessive pattern — however much he worshiped a male poet such as Pound his extended engagements with poetry in study or discussion were mostly through women (H.D., Stein, Denise Levertov). When he was sixteen a young woman teacher in his home town read to a class the poem 'Heat' by H.D. which transfixed him, and this seems to have launched his entire career. His account of this and his consequent attachment to what Pound labelled Imagism is comprehensive and intelligent. We see from the start the appeal of a dynamic quality in a verse not shaped by traditional devices, as in H.D.'s lines (addressed to the wind) "Cut the heat / plough through it, / turn it on either side / of your path." — that it is not passively descriptive but actively evocative, and was also valued for the absence of rhetorical generalities: the moment is all and enough and in it "the reader finds his own life". Equally important is the conjunction of "soft" (feeling) with hard and cutting imagery, later "poetry as sculpture", which also by uniting disparate qualities projects the experience into the reader's perceptive field.[7] A similar episode is recounted from when he was a student, reading Joyce's poems to two young women, whose attention to them is pursued through to their personal and ethnic identities. They find their own lives in the little poems, as Duncan said he found his own thought in Dante's thought. All this is a coherent and helpful account of a rebirth into poetry which is pursued intermittently through the book in his entire attachment to Modernism, including the later history of it, especially the comings together and driftings apart of the various poets, which is an authoritative history in passionately involved terms. He has repeatedly to wrestle with aberrations or even betrayals which damage his sense of a unified and unifying poetical force.

One thing he insisted on in this narrative was that the contribution of female writers to modernism has been as if deliberately suppressed. Here he was a pioneer of explorations which are still taking place, and he was probably right, though to say so involves value judgements which can be difficult. He included at least some account of Mary Butts, Dorothy Richardson, Edith Sitwell, Laura Riding, Marianne Moore and Virginia Woolf in this respect.[8]

From this history Duncan formed his personal constellation of modern poets, basically H.D., Williams, and Pound, with secondary attention to Lawrence and Joyce, to which he remained faithful, skilfully steering himself among their lapses and antagonisms. (Some, such as Eliot, Stevens and Marianne Moore, figure at first but deviate and join the enemy). H.D. was of course the principal figure here; she could do no wrong and her entire output is followed through to the end, sharing, of course, in all or most of the occultist issues. Pound was his guide to culture, obviously a very risky commitment, but even at the earliest stage he was not willing to accept such things as the arrogant dismissal of Milton, although he was willing to engage in the dismissal of Dryden and the 18th Century. Of Pound's opinions he said, significantly, "We are lost if we take his uses as having an authority other than the truth of how the world is felt and seen by the poet if he keeps alive in him the defects inherent in a record of struggle" (p.55). This sentimental regard for personal authenticity over and above objective truth is even used, on p.510, in what comes close to being an exoneration of Pound's anti-semitism: "Pound does not pretend to the urbane anti-semitism of Eliot but breaks into the true voice of his feeling — not only what he feels but exactly as he feels it. Because of this we see, as we are never quite sure in Eliot, the nature of Pound's hatred of the Jews." Authentic feelings must therefore be considered sacrosanct, whatever feelings they are and whatever harm they may cause. The same idea is used occasionally when Duncan speaks of his focus on the self and especially poems built on his emotional condition at the time. Some might consider this a flaw in the entire structure, which reduces the transfer of substance to the reader to an emotional empathy, and all the vast cosmologies end up as "feelings". The great enterprise begins to look rather small.

His pursuit of his course was obsessive, as is obvious in *The H.D.Book* from his identification of the enemy. Just as the same three or four poets are deferred to again and again through the 500 pages of the book, so the same enemies are invoked again and again with the same quotations attached, especially those who participated in the 1930s attacks on H.D. — John Crowe Ransom (dismissed as "small town"), Randell Jarrell (his dismissal of

HD's war trilogy as "more than a little silly" repeatedly quoted, in variant wordings), Louise Bogan, Richard Wilbur and others, which resulted in the dropping of H.D. from a new edition of a major anthology. In general terms the enemy is the literary academy, the "makers of curricula" (but who was a more eager maker of curricula than Ezra Pound, whose curriculum for British poetry swept almost all of it out of existence?), "Roman" rather than "Greek" (he even seemed uncomfortable with Virgil) and terms such as "orthodoxy", "institutional" and of course "reason", to which he preferred "madness" as authenticated by Artaud. But the attack on these critics is as empty of content as their own attacks on H.D. were — they "hooted" at her (and at Freud), "industrious literary businessmen", "the mercantile skeptic voice"... Duncan was personally hurt and angered by these attacks on H.D. There is no discussion. Olson and other influential American poets shared strongly in this anti-establishment resentment which enforced a sharp division in poetry and culture, loaded with a strong but unargued attack on commerce or commercialism, an elitist claim of independence from the social structure they inhabited. This remains strongly in operation in America, chiefly in the academies it once despised.[9]

§

In the end it is impossible to know what to do with these mountains of writing of many different kinds all heaped up together and especially with the invasion of poetry by the occult. How should I, or Duncan, or anyone, know whether all of creation is one act, or whether Osiris "is" Christ or Christ "is" H.D.? I think it has to be recognised that Duncan was carving out a quite narrow path for himself, but doing it with such ambition and fervour that it took on the trappings of an entire world catalogue, while periodically insisting himself that they *were* trappings and that the heart of the matter was the poet "making things up". It is possible to read a lot of it within that narrowness, and a lot can be gained from this, but the way his assimilative insistences operate with both occult and poetical histories is difficult, I find, to tolerate. The trouble lies principally with the verb To Be. Of the work undertaken here, he says on p.79, "It is" the work of creation; "It is" Poetry; "It is" also the *opus alchymicum* of Hermetic and Rosicrucian alchemy, and further down the page, palaeolithic cave painting and Aristotle are drawn in. The love he felt for that first schoolteacher is immediately identified with Dante's love of Beatrice. All these entities are typically attached, as many others are throughout, *as if they are all the same thing.* A suspicion that some of them may be very different things from each other not only threatens the whole structure but arouses the possibility that all these entities, from Orpheus to Troubadors, are understood by Duncan in digest versions. It is a willed and declared insistence: "The drama of our time is the coming of all men into one fate". "The dream of everyone, everywhere", "there is no isolate experience of anything", and more cosmically, "To evoke an image is to receive a sign, to bring into human language a word or phrase [...] of the great language in which the universe itself is written." (p.314). The trouble with this being that it is irreversible because we can't identify the "great language" except as defined by the proposition itself, or why, of all the things with which artists of any kind work, only "image" bears this inflation. A similar impasse arises when he focuses (following Olson) on the syllable as the minimal item which is the basis of articulation and that its handling in poetry is pivotal: "In this minim, in our articulation of vowels, lies the crucial evolutionary fact underlying the word" (p.332), forgetting that the syllable is itself constituted.

Does he not by this insistence on absolute unity falsify the actual nature of the transfer effected in, say, Dante, on whom so much of his thought rests, as if not the slightest trace of irrelevance or period demand could possibly arise? A set of hero-poets so full of poetical wisdom as to entirely transcend history is quite an alarming thought, especially if they are all one. The pandemic dream is surely marred by claims of elitist qualities peculiar to some poets and the rejection of consideration of a massive working population which is deaf to everything and simply irrelevant, <u>unless</u> the poet is a Christ-like figure bringing salvation to humanity at large. And so she is.

1   Sylvia Plath and Ted Hughes regularly made attempts to contact the dead, and their beliefs entered their poetry, but the anti-British attitude of the American Modernists was so strong that no cognizance of them was taken at all, nor of any other British poets from the 1940s onwards. Dylan Thomas was in fact one of the early influences on Duncan, later mentioned in passing as a kind of sport permitted by powerful academic critics in an otherwise wrecked poetry scene. (*The H.D. Book* p.522)

2   "H.D." was the monogram by which the American poet Hilda Doolittle (1886-1961) was known, and still is, to whose work and person Duncan was singularly devoted and who is the principal subject of the enormous *H.D. Book*.

3   These volumes are part of an unannounced complete works, of which there is a fourth volume, of essays, which I chickened out of, and two future volumes, presumably of previously unpublished writings. All are or will be published by University of California Press. Peter Quartermain's editing of the poetry is expertly professional and includes all necessary textual accessories, save for page references in the notes of the first volume. The editing of *The H.D. Book* is appropriately uncluttered but very helpful in supplying a bibliography and subject index.

4   The use of noun as adjective occurs occasionally throughout the early work. It is difficult to know why unless as a simple gesture of defiant modernity.

5   Shakespeare is referred to as "Saint William Shakespeare", also as "Beloved", and (twice) as "simple-minded". He is said to have written *Othello* because he was "plagued by flies of jealousy and rage", as by curious coincidence Duncan was at the time. Am I alone, I wonder, in being irritated by the assumption that Shakespeare's gift was to be so "inspired" and governed by emotion, that it was not necessary for him to think? Anyone in doubt could look at the book *Shakespeare the Thinker* by A.D. Nuttall (2007).

6   Since about 1960 Duncan had used two serial titles for supposedly more expository texts interspersed among the poems, 'The Structure of Rime' for poetics, 'Passages' for texts or citations of a more religious nature, though it is often difficult to tell the difference or to distinguish in either of these a writing greatly different from many of the poems.

7   This became a critical polemical issue, in Britain as much as anywhere else, which set up demands on writing, painting and architecture to reject the "rhythmic" and "moulded" in favour of the "carved", a matter of distinct planes and edges. Pound tried to read this into music but was so ignorant of musical history that he could only pontificate. The same idea is certainly present in Duncan's praise of Pound's "clean mindedness" and "healthy mindedness" producing "the clean line" (p.306).

8   I don't mention in this review that Duncan was homosexual, because I can't think of any reason to. But academic studies of him, especially in U.S.A., have of course raised this as the central issue of his poetry, making all of it a specifically gay issue not fully open to the understanding of the heterosexual mind. I think he would have abhorred this.

9   This is an unfairly crude account. The idea was to set up alternative places of learning, divorced from the influence of state and commerce. To some extent this happened, pipe-dream as it was. If there was a single reason for its failure it was that the *en bloc* denial of one perceived culture fell foul of the *en bloc* acceptance of another culture, one of alienation, escape, and indulgence. We should remember that Duncan was of California, home of libertarian and alienated "hippie" communities marketed as gentle and benign but some of which became murderous.

PETER RILEY

Peter Riley is a former co-editor of *The English Intelligencer*, the former editor of *Collection*, the current poetry editor of *The Fortnightly Review*, and the author of fifteen books of poetry – and some of prose. A recipient of a 2012 Cholmondeley Award for poetry, his latest book is Due North (Shearsman Books 2015), which was shortlisted for the Forward Prize for Best Collection 2015. After many years in Cambridge, he now lives in Yorkshire. His webpage is aprileye.co.uk.

www.ingramcontent.com/pod-product-compliance
Lightning Source LLC
Chambersburg PA
CBHW072134090426
42739CB00013B/3192